CW00686110

The Management Shift

How to Harness the Power of People and Transform Your Organization for Sustainable Success

The Management Shift

By Vlatka Hlupic

First published 2014 by
PALGRAVE MACMILLAN

Palgrave Macmillan in the UK is an imprint of Macmillan Publishers Limited, registered in England, company number 785998, of Houndmills, Basingstoke, Hampshire RG21 6XS.

Palgrave Macmillan in the US is a division of St Martin's Press LLC, 175 Fifth Avenue, New York, NY 10010.

Palgrave Macmillan is the global academic imprint of the above companies and has companies and representatives throughout the world.

Palgrave® and Macmillan® are registered trademarks in the United States, the United Kingdom, Europe and other countries.

ISBN 978–1–137–35294–1

This book is printed on paper suitable for recycling and made from fully managed and sustained forest sources. Logging, pulping and manufacturing processes are expected to conform to the environmental regulations of the country of origin.

A catalogue record for this book is available from the British Library.

A catalog record for this book is available from the Library of Congress.

Typeset by MPS Limited, Chennai, India.

In loving memory of my parents Helena and Vladimir Hlupic, with gratitude for all love, support and wonderful past moments

and

To my inspiration, my children Ana Helena and Tomislav Vidjak, with gratitude for all love, patience and wonderful present moments.

Praise for *The Management Shift*

"Dr Hlupic's insights are truly groundbreaking. What makes her ideas, which are brilliantly described in *The Management Shift*, even more meaningful is how she has integrated them into her 6 Box Leadership tool. The result is that executives and consultants can now easily implement 6 Box Leadership principles in practice, so that organizations can benefit from tomorrow's management today."

Jack Bergstrand, CEO of Brand Velocity Inc., former Chief Information Officer
for The Coca-Cola Co., author of *Reinvent Your Enterprise*

"The 6 Box Leadership diagnostic and management methods will give your organization everything it needs to unleash its creative power and win in today's fast-paced, hypercompetitive world. Without this new way of management, firms will be stuck in the past and hopelessly left behind by competitors who adopt the 6 Box approach."

Richard A. D'Aveni, Bakala Professor of Strategy, Tuck School of Business
at Dartmouth College, www.radstrat.com; listed by Thinkers50 as one of
the most influential management thinkers in the world in 2007, 2009 and 2011;
author of *Strategic Capitalism*

"I have had the pleasure of working with Dr Hlupic including co-authoring several whitepapers as part of the Management Information eXchange (MIX). I am thrilled at her success in capturing a powerful and much needed corporate transformation model wonderfully described in *The Management Shift*."

Michael Grove, CEO of CollabWorks, Inc., serial entrepreneur, and founder of
the WWW+W thought leadership community of the New World of Work

"Vlatka's insights on how to put innovative theory into practice is a true step change in management. She shows many cases where it is actually possible to transform organizations to become more profitable while at the same time to become more engaging for all employees. She provides clear guidance on how to successfully create the future and sets the new management standards for the digital information age."

Carsten Hentrich, Director Digital Transformation, PwC Germany

"Vlatka Hlupic has enjoyed an impressive career in the world of leadership studies. I strongly endorse the ideas which she has developed and presented in *The Management Shift.*"

William Hopper, former Member of the European Parliament, investment banker and co-author of *The Puritan Gift – Triumph, Collapse and Revival of an American Dream*

"A great book for the challenges of our time. I hope aspiring managers and entrepreneurs will read it!"

Sajda Qureshi, Professor of Information Systems, University of Nebraska at Omaha

"Dr Vlatka Hlupic's work is a significant contribution to transforming management thinking and organizational life that we need for today's and the future world. *The Management Shift* shows the big picture and, at the same time, offers a proven method related to how to tackle the route to unfold human potential in organizations for sustained prosperity."

Franz Röösli, Professor for Organizational Behavior, Zurich University of Applied Sciences, Director of Beyond Budgeting Round Table

"In the aftermath of the financial crisis managers had to confront harsh criticism and blame. It has become clear that a renewal of management is required for regaining the credibility and legitimacy to address the huge challenges we face in our economies and our societies. The good news: management doesn't need wholesale reinvention; it just needs to rediscover its true vocation and priorities. Vlatka Hlupic provides a timely and important contribution in this field by combining the Drucker-inspired systematic approach to the discipline of management with latest thinking and relevant tools for practitioners."

Richard Straub, President of the Drucker Society Europe, Senior Advisor IBM Global Education Industry

"Vlatka Hupic's *The Management Shift* is a rich exploration of the way in which the corporate landscape is increasingly emphasizing people and purpose — and not just profit. As such, it's not only useful; it's quite hopeful."

Rick Wartzman, Executive Director of the Drucker Institute and columnist for Time.com

"For many of us writing about the principles of enlightened leadership over the years, the rate of progress has been frustratingly slow. Vlatka Hlupic in *The Management Shift* has achieved a potentially significant breakthrough by linking theory to practice on how to transform workplaces. She takes management teams through the levels of progress that leaders and their teams experience as they move towards higher levels of engagement, in an approach where people are rightly viewed as the source of all value."

Philip Whiteley, co-author *New Normal Radical Shift*

"For any business leader looking to get more from their people, this book is a must-read."

Rob Wirszycz, Chairman and Advisor to major IT companies and former Director General of techUK

"Vlatka Hlupic's wonderful book provides the methodology to implement Management 2.0 using her 6 Box Leadership system. The key is putting people first. Improving your organization's performance has never been so easy."

Paul J. Zak, Professor of Economics and the founding Director of the Center for Neuroeconomics Studies at Claremont Graduate University; author of *The Moral Molecule,* a finalist for the Wellcome Trust Book Prize

Contents

List of Figures

List of Tables

Foreword

The stock market is booming. Corporations are reporting record levels of profit. House prices are recovering. There are signs of a manufacturing expansion. Multiple indicators at the aggregate level point to positive economic outcomes for the time being.

Yet behind the scenes, many big organizations today are teetering on the brink of chaos. As markets change faster and faster, and exponential improvements in technology lead to exponential innovation, evidence is steadily accumulating that organizations with legacy mindsets, structures and management practices are not keeping up.

Businesses today are in fact facing a fundamental paradox. On the one hand, new technology is indeed creating vast possibilities for doing things better, faster, cheaper, smaller, lighter, more conveniently and more personalized. Per capita labor productivity is steadily improving. There are massive opportunities for big-win investments with huge upside potential.

Yet most big organizations are failing to capture value from these new possibilities. Core performance has been deteriorating for decades: the return on assets for US companies has steadily fallen to around one-quarter of 1965 levels. The "topple rate" of industry leaders is accelerating. Only one in five employees is fully engaged in his or her work, and even fewer are passionate about their work – a critical problem at a time when innovation is a key to success. The conclusion is inescapable: big hierarchical bureaucracies with short-term mindsets have not yet found a way to flourish in this changing world.

The Management Shift shows that there is another way. It describes a "Management Shift" that focuses on managing people, fostering collaboration and creating a sense of purpose. Based on many years of research, the book outlines a new approach to creating more value, innovation, employee engagement and sustainable success. It explains why the changes are needed, what needs to be done, and particularly how to go about it.

The Management Shift is part of the consensus emerging among leading thinkers of the need for new management approaches and new mindsets. There is increasing recognition that traditional management approaches do not work anymore and that the time has come for a major change in the way organizations are run that will lead to a different future and more prosperity for everyone.

This book contributes new elements to the discussion to enable that to happen. In particular, it explains the 6 Box Leadership diagnostic tool, which is based on more than 20 years of interdisciplinary research and consulting experience. The book shows how to apply it to spark the changes that are needed.

As the book says, the implications of the changes needed are enormous. They imply not just new processes and practices, but radically different mindsets, attitudes and values, managerial behaviors and approaches to organizational governance and development. *The Management Shift* is a comprehensive guide to what is involved and how to achieve all these changes.

Stephen Denning

Author of *The Leader's Guide to Radical Management*

Preface

In business management, there is a problem. There is also an historic opportunity. The problem is that our conventional hierarchical approach, with a senior management operating "command and control", is no longer a credible option for a rapidly changing, unpredictable, global business environment. The opportunity comes from the wealth of evidence and thinking behind an enlightened alternative. In this book I shall describe what I call The Management Shift, which focuses on people, their collaboration and sense of purpose.

My research and consulting experience over the years enables me to demonstrate that companies that embrace this new approach go through a transformation and create more value, innovation, employee engagement and achieve sustainable success. Many leading management thinkers have recognized the need for such a shift, and I cite the work of others as well as presenting my own work. The implications are immense, because they imply not just new practices, but radically different mindsets, managerial behaviors and approaches to organizational governance and development. My intention with this book is to bring all dimensions together: the *why*, the *what* and the *how*, as many books focus on the first two, but leave the practical manager with little insight into *how* to run things differently from the next working day. My ambition is that what you will read in this book will have a profound impact on your organization's ability to innovate, engage employees and adapt to a rapidly changing world.

In Chapter 1, I describe the *why* dimension: detailing the reasons behind an organization's need to adopt new management practices to survive, thrive and have purposeful existence. This chapter describes how some of the mechanistic, dehumanizing theories about organizations are conceptually flawed and no longer fit for purpose. In Chapters 2, 3 and 4 we move on to the *what*: showing what needs to be done in organizations to adopt new management practices for organizational transformation, better innovation, engagement and value creation. Finally, in Chapters 5 and 6, I address the *how* dimension, demonstrating how this Management Shift can be achieved in practice. I describe a proven method called the 6 Box Leadership Model, based on more than 20 years of my interdisciplinary research and consulting experience. I have used it successfully in more than 20 organizations worldwide, large, medium and small, in private and public sectors, to help them transform and create more value. At the end of the book, I reflect on the implications of The Management Shift in terms of creating better social conditions as well as more effective companies, and describe existing initiatives that are helping to bring about this radical change.

This book is the culmination of many years of my academic and practical work, diverse consulting experience and, most of all, my huge passion and desire to make a positive difference, facilitate a shift in corporate consciousness and make this world a better place. I strongly believe that the purpose of life is to help others, to work on something far greater than ourselves, and my research shows that such an approach creates organizations that are more dynamic and resilient as well as socially responsible. It is the difference between building a cathedral and just carving the stones, to borrow the vivid metaphor of management thinker Peter Drucker in his book *The Practice of Management*.[1]

This book is about turning knowledge into action to achieve a transformation. This is not a lofty ambition: I describe how it has been done. It is about igniting changes of individual mindsets and organizational culture that create The Management Shift, creating many positive ripples that will go far beyond individuals and their organizations, positively impacting societies on a large scale. The power of creating positive ripples is beautifully illustrated in this quote from Robert F. Kennedy: "Each time a man stands up for an ideal or acts to improve the lot of others, or strikes out against injustice, he sends forth a tiny ripple of hope, and crossing each other from a million different centers of energy and daring, those ripples build a current that can sweep down the mightiest walls of oppression and resistance." This book also shows what organizations should aspire to be like, what some of the progressive ones are already like and what the majority of organizations will be like in the future.

A summary of research presented in this book was submitted as written evidence to the All-Party Parliamentary Group on Management, and it was included in the report "Management 2020"[2] produced by the Commission on the Future of Management and Leadership and Chartered Management Institute. The key findings of this report emphasize the importance of focusing on People, Purpose and Potential – this book provides research evidence on why this is so important and how it can be achieved in practice. With the cost of time wasted by poor management estimated at £19.3 billion per year for the UK, the improvement in management practices is essential!

For years, I have felt that this work is my life purpose and that, as part of this, it was essential to find a sympathetic publisher to distribute this book internationally. I was therefore delighted to receive an offer for a book contract from Palgrave Macmillan, not just because they cover the global market but also because they specialize in bringing high-quality academic work to a practitioner market. My aim is to bridge the gap between academia and practice, to put ideas and theory into action and make an impact on the real world of business.

I endeavor to inspire many leaders to adopt more people-centric management practices, to demonstrate ways of uplifting and engaging employees whilst creating value and innovation. The book is also written for academics at business schools and their students (at MBA and Business Studies courses), the future leaders – to educate and prepare them for the type of leadership that will fulfil them and inspire those they will lead.

Last but not least, I wanted this book to show my children what their future working places should be like and not to settle for working for an uninspiring boss.

Patton Boyle, in his book *Screaming Hawk*,[3] says "The truth comes in the silence between the words. It is grasped and experienced with the heart." As you are reading this book, I hope that you will attempt to do just that – listen with your heart to the silence between the words and observe the echoes the words evoke in you.

The academic aspects of this book would appeal to scientific, left-brain focused individuals. The practical, consulting aspects would appeal to more pragmatic, action-oriented professionals. But, most of all, I hope that the humanistic, compassion and purpose-driven perspective of this book will create a powerful impact on the silence between the words that any reader will experience.

A final note on the cover. The graphics represent growth, transformation and success. The butterfly is the most well-known symbol of transformation and is also related to the notion of chaos and complexity theory, where small changes in initial conditions can lead to significant outcomes, both of which are foundations of my work presented in this book. The origami theme shows a holistic blend of Eastern and Western philosophies which are also incorporated in my work. Western cultures tend to be more individually focused; Eastern cultures are focused more on the whole system. Finally, the three white origami ribbons represent ascension and growth, and, most importantly, they represent the wealth, health and happiness that this book aims to bring its readers!

I also sincerely hope that reading this book will inspire you to take an action that will set you and others around you on the path to embrace and harness the power of people. A sincere desire to make a positive change that comes from the heart has the power to transform, restore and elevate individuals and organizations to the new level of thinking, acting and achieving. If you are yearning to play a part in producing more purposeful, fulfilling and happier workplaces, you will indeed make this world a better place and leave an extraordinary legacy. The choice is yours!

Acknowledgements

Any insight and research is often the product of interactions and reflections of many people. A great deal of people helped with the creation of this book, in many different ways over many years, and I am very grateful to all. First of all, I would like to thank my children Ana Helena and Tomislav for their understanding and patience with my often preoccupied mind and their forgiveness for evenings and weekends disrupted by this work. I would also like to thank my late parents Helena and Vladimir for being wonderful role models and instilling courage, integrity and persistence in me. I am very grateful to many other special people who have touched my life in different ways and helped me to keep going on my path. A special gratitude goes to: Adeeb, Ahlya, Annetta, Arci, Bobi, Boris, Bozhena, Cathy, Chris, David, Duska, Fran, Eileen, Gordana, Iman, Jack, Jasna, Jo, Katarina, Karen, Kristina, Marianne, Mario, Mladen, Mirna, Neil, Paul, Roy, Sajda, Sally, Sasa, Shirley, Snjezana, Sue, Susan, Susannah, Suzana, Vanda and Zrinka.

Many friends and colleagues have provided insights, encouragements and inspiration on the journey of writing this book and I thank them all from the bottom of my heart. With apologies to anyone omitted from the list, a special thank you goes to: Eleanor Davey-Corrigan for commissioning this book; my book editor Tamsine O'Riordan for helping me to improve my book draft; Stephen Partridge for his help as book editor in the last phase of this project; Philip Whiteley for helping with editing the final draft, providing an endorsement and for managing the book launch project; Josephine O'Neill for managing the production of this book; Jamie Forrest for helping with the marketing of this book; Josephine Taylor for her editorial assistance; Jack Bergstrand for helping with positioning and fine tuning the 6 Box Leadership diagnostic, and providing an endorsement as well as feedback on an earlier draft of this book; John Adair for inspiring me to write this book and providing an endorsement; Lynda Gratton for encouraging me to write this book; Julian Birkinshaw, Richard D'Aveni, Marshall Goldsmith, Michael Grove, Jules Goddard, Sunil Gupta, Carsten Hentrich, Sajda Qureshi, Franz Röösli, Richard Straub, Fons Trompenaars and Paul Zak for providing endorsements of this book; Rick Wartzman for providing an endorsement and feedback; Steve Denning for writing the Foreword and sharing his wisdom and passion to achieve the management paradigm shift; William Hopper for inspiring me to set up the Drucker Society London and for providing an endorsement and feedback on my book draft; Arie de Geus for sharing his wisdom and for all the inspirational conversations on management innovation we shared and for writing an endorsement for this book; Bruce Lewin for helping with an earlier version of the organizational diagnostic tool, Performance Ecosystem; Chris Walton and Karen Welch for providing feedback on an early version of the 5 Level Emergent Leadership Model; Mark Hawkswell for introducing me to some amazing books that shaped the development of the 5 Level Emergent Leadership Model; Peter Blue for his help with developing the 6 Box Leadership software platform; Phil Shepherd for providing an innovative software to help me structure my ideas for the book; Cliff Findlay for advising me on how to improve the content of this book and position it on the market; Jo Brightwell and her team for producing graphic designs for this book and branding; Rob Wirszycz for his advice on business aspects of this work and for providing an endorsement; Gordan Bosnjak and Alec Saiko for helping with website development; Fiona Leslie, Michele Horaney, Cory Torrella and Jan Schapira for help with book promotion; Andrea Rumenjak for helping with quantitative data analysis; Barbara Allan and other colleagues from Westminster Business School for their support for my work over the years; Dan Cable and other staff from the London Business School for enabling me to share my models and ideas with hundreds of MBA and MSc students; Fran Kruc, David Chan, Peter Starbuck, Mary Wu, Alex Ritson, Pablo Lloyd and other volunteers from the Drucker Society London for spreading the positive ripples I started; Gary Hamel and Michele Zanini for providing me with an opportunity to lead four teams for the Management 2.0 Hackathon and talk about this experience at a TEDx event in Oslo; David Lennon for introducing me to getAbstract facilities; Neil Ashby for providing advice and feedback on my ideas in the last phase of this project; Shazia Sheikh and Oliver Baxter at Herman Miller; Ahlya Fateh and her team at Amanda Wakeley for sponsoring the book launch event; Rehman Chishti, a Member of Parliament for Gillingham and Rainham, for hosting my talk about research published in the book at the House of Commons and his Excellency Ivan Grdešić, the Croatian Ambassador in the UK for hosting the book promotion event at the Croatian Embassy in London. Thank you all!

About the Author

Vlatka Hlupic is a Professor of Business and Management at the University of Westminster, a former Adjunct Faculty at London Business School and founder and Chief Executive Officer of the Drucker Society, London. She is a renowned event speaker, presenting regularly at major conferences worldwide and has published more than 160 academic articles, including the award-winning *Harvard Business Review* article. "To be a Better Leader, Give up Authority". Professor Hlupic is a respected leadership and management consultant and has advised major international organizations including the House of Commons, GlaxoSmithKline, BP, Learndirect, Brand Velocity USA, the Drucker Institute USA, the Croatian government and the Hungarian National Bank. A sought-after thought leader, she has a growing media platform and her expert commentaries and interviews have appeared in the national press, including *The Times*, *Sunday Telegraph*, *Independent* and *Guardian*, as well as leading industry publications such as *Edge Magazine*, *Marketing* magazine, *Business Executive*, *HR* magazine, *Strategy Magazine*, *New Europe* and the *Training Journal*. She has led the development of four Management 2.0 "hacks" within Gary Hamel's Management Innovation eXchange Management 2.0 Hackathon, and as a result of this was invited to give a TEDx talk in Oslo in 2012.

Why it is Time Now for The Management Shift

This chapter provides answers to the following key questions:

- What are the key challenges that organizations and societies are facing today?
- What are the main causes of the problems we are facing today?
- What is the solution to these problems?
- Why do traditional management approaches not work anymore?
- Why do individuals and organizations need The Management Shift to survive, thrive and have a purposeful existence?
- What are the key characteristics of the emerging management approaches?
- How can Peter Drucker's timeless wisdom be applied to organizations today?
- What are the financial benefits of adopting new management practices focused on collaboration and higher purpose?
- What are the examples of companies that have implemented inspiring management practices?

Organizations Today Face Unprecedented Challenges

Organizations today are surfing on the edge of chaos. Markets change faster and faster, unforeseen influences require quick adaptation, and organizations constantly need to be one step ahead and to reinvent themselves. Many businesses, including small and medium-sized businesses, are becoming global, helped by advances in connectivity and digitalization. This means that competitor profiles are constantly shifting and there is an increasing emphasis on innovation, cooperation and collaboration. Other challenges include an accelerating pace of change, complexity, uncertainty and the fast transition towards a creativity economy. The management dogmas of the past do not serve their purpose anymore; it is time to adopt new thinking, take a different type of action in organizations worldwide and make these organizations more human and fit for purpose. Organizations and societies are better able to adapt by taking a path based on values, integrity, purpose, compassion, continuous innovation and the commitment to make a positive difference and safeguard the future for subsequent generations.

Continuous learning and innovation are becoming progressively more important for sustainable performance. Engaged employees who feel passionate about their work create innovative cultures but can be held back by outdated management practices. Managers need to create the conditions for unleashing the power of human passion, wisdom and ingenuity. It is becoming apparent to CEOs, management thinkers and practitioners that we cannot use old solutions for new problems, as we have never experienced such a magnitude of changes before. There is a dramatic need for a shift to a new mindset and new management practices, what I call The Management Shift. The need for the shift in mindset and actions in turbulent times can be illustrated by this quote from Abraham Lincoln: "The dogmas of the quiet past are inadequate to the stormy present. The occasion is piled high with difficulty, and we must rise – with the occasion. As our case is new, so we must think anew and act anew."[1]

Many organizations, both in the public and private sectors, need to make profound systemic changes, not just to management practices but to organizational cultures, business processes, regulatory frameworks, work arrangements and work ethics. Traditionally managed organizations resemble supertankers, finding it difficult to respond to any sudden changes in their environment and to change their course. Modern organizations should be managed and led as sailing boats – a general direction is to be determined but the journey towards the destination should be flexible depending on the environmental conditions.

Management thinking has been traditionally influenced by scientific discoveries. Conventional management approaches have been based on the Newtonian machine model that focuses on hierarchical linearity, a culture based on rules, command and control and formal relationships. It is no more than a metaphor, and while such an approach might have worked well in predictable and stable environments when the objective was efficiency in the production economy, there is ample research evidence that in dynamic and complex business environments this traditional approach inhibits creativity and innovation and decreases motivation and productivity. In traditionally managed organizations, structures distribute power and processes distribute tasks. Structures and process are about creating stability, repeatability and predictability, and this is happening in an unstable, chaotic world, which demands innovation. So we ask people to innovate in a system that is designed to produce the reverse. We cannot then be surprised that many organizations are not utilizing their potential for innovation.

Management innovation is a greater potential source of competitive advantage than traditional innovations of products, services or technology.[2] Einstein's insights into relativity influenced other disciplines such as art, music, religion and literature at the beginning of the last century. The main paradigm was that rational and analytical were inseparable from emotional and intuitive, but this has not affected management thinking until recently. The main reason was the "If it isn't broken, don't fix it" mantra. From the 1950s, the traditional management model flourished with the wealth creation for industrial nations based on increasing productivity. Then, with all the technological changes and the increasing importance of knowledge, new business models emerged (such as Amazon.com), where talent, collaboration and innovation enabled faster commercialization of ideas. However, embracing these new management approaches requires a shift in mindset, which is not easy to achieve, and the majority of organizations today are still managed using conventional, Newtonian management approaches.

As John Mackey, CEO of Whole Foods, and Professor Raj Sisodia state in their inspiring book *Conscious Capitalism*:[3]

> ...the world urgently needs a richer, more holistic, and more humanistic philosophy and narrative about business than the one we have encountered in economics textbooks, in business school teachings, and even from the mouths and pens of many prominent business leaders.

This new approach to business and value creation is now more important than ever, as we are facing unprecedented challenges, as outlined in the following section.

We have a problem!

Organizations, institutions and societies are going through a major crisis. Performance, whether measured through Return on Assets (ROA) or Return on Invested Capital (ROIC), continues to decline; US firm's ROA has progressively dropped 75 percent since 1965, despite rising labor productivity.[4] In the last 50 years, the average life expectancy of Fortune 500 companies has steadily decreased from 75 to 15 years. Furthermore, data shows that only 25 percent of the workforce is passionate about its work,[5] despite the plethora of techniques and resources spent on Learning and Development (L&D), and global figures for engagement show that 80 percent of employees are less than fully engaged at work.[6]

Only 25% of the workforce is passionate about its work

The report "Management 2020"[7] launched by the Commission on the Future of Management and Leadership and Chartered Management Institute in July 2014, reveals problems with management and leadership in the UK. For example, it is estimated that **the cost of poor management in the UK is over £19.3 billion per year in lost working hours;**[8] productivity output in the UK is 21 percent lower than the G7 average;[9]

43 percent of UK line managers rate their managers as ineffective;[10] only 34 percent of employees provide management training;[11] risk taking and innovation is appropriately encouraged in only 38 percent of UK companies.[12] All this data shows that there is a big problem with current management practices as well as an opportunity to address them.

A survey of the US workforce[13] indicates that employees who are passionate about their work are twice as likely to have a questing disposition, which gives them a desire to achieve new levels of performance, and a connecting disposition, which makes them connect to people who share their interests and can help them address new challenges, which are very important for success and value creation. This research also revealed that there is an inverse relationship between the level of passion in the workforce and the size of the company. The larger the company, the lower the level of passion among the workers, and the most passionate workers are those who are either self-employed or working as freelance contractors. These data show that executives need to pay close attention to engagement and level of passion amongst their employees on a sustainable, long-term basis, as they are crucial for innovation, value creation and the long-term success of their organization.

High levels of employee dissatisfaction are apparent in many surveys. For example, a 2011 Mercer survey of 30,000 workers worldwide[14] showed that between 28 percent and 56 percent of employees wanted to leave their jobs. Another source of job satisfaction data[15] shows that only 45 percent of US employees find their jobs satisfying, 60 percent intend to leave if the economy improves, only 20 percent feel very passionate about their job, fewer than 15 percent agree that they feel strongly energized by their work and only 31 percent believe that their employer inspires the best in them. A recent survey of 32,000 employees[16] shows that only 35 percent of the global workforce is highly engaged, stress and anxiety about the future are common and employees have doubts about the level of interest and support coming from senior leaders. According to a 2009 survey by the UK-based Chartered Institute of Personnel & Development (CIPD),[17] only 37 percent of employees are satisfied with their work.

Another problem is related to decreasing levels of trust. Only about 50 percent of the wider public in the Western world puts faith in the ability of business to do the right thing,[18] and governments are faring even worse. According to the 2013 Edelman Trust Barometer,[19] less than one-fifth of the general public believes business leaders and government officials will tell the truth when confronted with a difficult issue. The trust gap between institutions and their leaders is also growing – trust in businesses is 32 points higher than in their leaders. This research also confirms trends in democratization, where influence is redistributed from traditional authority figures such as CEOs or government ministers towards employees and peers, as well as to people with knowledge and credentials, including academics and technical experts. Another prominent trend is related to replacing hierarchies by horizontal networks.

According to the National Bureau of Economic Research[20] there is growing inequality between the rich and poor, with substantial disparities in the growth of price indexes and in life expectancy. Between 1980 and 2000 the life expectancy of the bottom 10 percent of earners in the US increased at only half the rate of that of the top 10 percent. Furthermore, the top 10 percent of earners saw their share of overall income rise from 27 percent in 1966 to 45 percent in 2001. A study of 1,500 firms found that the compensation earned by the top five corporate officers in 1993 to 1995 equalled 5 percent of their firms' total profits during that period; by 2000 to 2002, that ratio had more than doubled to 12.8 percent. In 2007, CEOs in the S&P 500 had an average compensation of US$10.5 million annually, 344 times the pay of an average American worker. In 2000, this ratio was even higher at 525 times the average pay.[21] Astonishingly, one of the recent S&P reports shows that the CEO of Walmart has been paid 1,034 times more than a median Walmart worker's salary.[22] Over-compensation of C-suite executives is leading to disastrous business consequences,[23] including a serious misallocation of capital and talent, rising income inequality, repeated governance crises, and a lack of international competitiveness.

Other problems include increasing unemployment,[24] especially among young people,[25] continuing failing of the banking system,[26] declining Consumer Confidence Index (CCI),[27] decreasing Life Satisfaction Index,[28] declining Purchasing Managers' Index (PMI),[29] declining house price affordability,[30,31] gender inequality,[32] career stagnation,[33] child poverty,[34] increasing debt,[35,36] declining retail outlets,[37] and growing dissatisfaction with services.[38]

Leading international accounting firm Deloitte's Center for the Edge has developed a Shift Index[39] designed to provide insights into long-term performance trends. The Shift Index in 2009 highlighted long-term performance challenges of companies. For example, the ROA for US firms has steadily fallen to almost one-quarter of 1965 levels despite improvements in labor productivity; the "topple rate" at which big companies lose their leadership positions has more than doubled, suggesting that "winners" have increasingly precarious positions; the US competitive intensity has more than doubled during the last 40 years, increasing rivalry and the pressures companies are facing; increasing customer disloyalty indicates that customers also seem to be gaining and using power, enforcing the need for companies to focus on customers rather than share price. Furthermore, the 2010 Shift Index reveals that, unsurprisingly, passion for work remains low and in some industries has declined, with less than a quarter of the workforce feeling passionate about their current work; capital movement slowed dramatically; and executive turnover reached a five-year low. One of the conclusions from this study is that all long-term trends point to a continued erosion of performance.

Another problem relates to too much focus on short-term share price at the expense of long-term sustainable performance. For example, 80 percent of respondents in a survey of more than 400 executives[40] indicated they would decrease spending on R&D and other similar expenditure to meet short-term earnings targets. According to a Harvard Business School study,[41] over a period of 18 years companies with long-term and sustainability focus outperformed matched companies in terms of shareholder returns by 4.8 percent annually. Similarly, Justin Fox and Jay Lorsch show in their *Harvard Business Review* article "What Good are Shareholders?"[42] that the companies that are most successful at maximizing shareholder value over time are those that pursue other goals instead of aiming to maximize shareholder value. The problems with shareholder maximization are well summarized by well-known author Dan Pink,[43] "CEOs and others often spend more time smoothing earnings to benefit themselves personally in the short term than they do building companies and benefiting shareholders in the long term".

In order to reverse these worrying trends, fundamental changes are needed in various areas, including restructuring firms' economics to generate maximum possible value from existing resources; development of new management practices to more effectively utilize growing knowledge flows; significant innovation in institutional arrangements to drive scalable participation in knowledge flows driven by rapid developments in digital infrastructure and utilize open innovation and process network initiatives.

An IBM global CEO survey conducted in 2012,[44] comprising more than 1,700 CEOs from 64 countries, revealed that leaders are recognizing that the new connected era is changing how people engage. The increasing convergence of the digital, social and mobile media connecting customers, employees and partners in new ways creates new opportunities for the organizations as well as the need to mobilize a collective brain power to innovate. High-performing organizations are creating more open and collaborative cultures, encouraging employees to connect, learn from each other and thrive in a rapidly changing world. Three essential imperatives emerged from this survey:

1. The need to empower employees through values, purpose and creating a collaborative environment
2. The need to engage customers as individuals, improve understanding of their needs and reduce time to respond to their needs
3. The need to amplify innovation with partnerships, where high-performing companies are working on challenging and disruptive types of innovation – that is, not just creating new products but also moving into other industries or creating new industries.

A similar survey conducted in 2010,[45] which canvassed over 1,500 CEOs, revealed that the key challenges faced by CEOs include: the ability to manage complexity; the ability to encourage experimentation and innovation; the ability to co-create products and services with customers, based on deep customer insights; and the ability to increase organizational dexterity, that is to change the way organizations work, connect, access resources and enter markets around the world. Yet a surprising number of CEOs reported that they felt ill-prepared for today's environment. Table 1.1 summarizes key problems, citing the studies that confirm these patterns.

Common themes emerging from these surveys and other studies show that the senior executives are aware that the current turbulent and complex business environments require new skills, new ways of working and leading, new strategies, new organizational cultures and processes to

TABLE 1.1   Key problems we are facing today

Problem	Examples of studies
Declining performance	ROA has progressively dropped 75% since 1965
Decreasing life expectancy of large companies	The average life expectancy of Fortune 500 companies has steadily decreased from 75 to 15 years in the last 50 years
Low levels of passion for work	Only 25% of the workforce is passionate about its work
Low levels of engagement	Global figures for engagement show that 80% of employees are less than fully engaged at work
Low levels of employee satisfaction	Only 45% of US employees find their jobs satisfying, 60% intend to leave if the economy improves, only 20% feel very passionate about their jobs, fewer than 15% agree that they feel strongly energized by their work and only 31% believe that their employer inspires the best in them. According to a CIPD survey[46] only 37% of employees are satisfied with their work
Career stagnation	A research sample of 2,000 employees in the UK revealed that 39% of them have no career progression plans, only one in ten employees feels they have opportunities for long-term development with their current employer
Focus on short-term share price at the expense of long-term sustainable performance	80% of respondents in a survey of more than 400 executives indicated they would decrease spending on R&D and other similar expenditure to meet short-term earnings targets. According to another study, over a period of 18 years, companies with long-term and sustainability focus outperformed matched companies in terms of shareholder returns by 4.8% annually
Decreasing levels of trust	Only about 50% of the wider public in the Western world puts faith in the ability of business to do the right thing,[47] less than one-fifth of the general public believes business leaders and government officials will tell the truth when confronted with a difficult issue

(*continued*)

TABLE 1.1   Continued

Problem	Examples of studies
Growing economic inequality	Between 1980 and 2000 the life expectancy of the bottom 10% of earners in the US increased at only half the rate of the top 10%, and the top 10% of earners had its share of overall income rise from 27% in 1966 to 45% in 2001
Gender inequality	Research conducted amongst a sample of almost 40,000 executives in the UK has shown that females will earn £400,000 less over their lifetime. They are also awarded less than half of the male bonus, and are far more likely to be made redundant
Over-compensation of C-suite executives	In 2007, CEOs in the S&P 500 had an average compensation of US$10.5 million annually, 344 times the pay of an average American worker
Increasing unemployment, especially among young people	In April 2013, 2.56 million people (7.9%) in the UK were unemployed
Continuing failure of the banking system	386 banks failed in the US alone in the period 2008–11
Declining Consumer Confidence Index (CCI)	In March 2013, the CCI was 59.7 (1985=100), down from 68.0 in February 2013
Decreasing Life Satisfaction Index	In the UK, the Life Satisfaction Index fell from 7.4 out of 10 (or 74%) in 2009 to 7.1 out of 10 (or 71%) in 2011
Declining Purchasing Managers' Index (PMI)	In April 2013, the PMI was 51.3%, a decrease of 2.9 percentage points from the February 2013 value of 54.2%
Declining house price affordability	First-time buyers in London face house prices six times higher than their annual income
Increasing debt	Research conducted on behalf of the Bank of England found that 62% of households reported reduced income. Research by Legal & General has found that as many as 2.64 million households (12%) across the UK are "overwhelmed" by rising fuel costs and other bills
Declining retail outlets	A report by PricewaterhouseCoopers shows more than a 1000% increase in high street store closures between 2011 and 2012 in the UK
Growing dissatisfaction with services	A survey of 75,000 rail users has discovered that over half of the UK's train companies score only 50% or lower in terms of customer satisfaction ratings. A nationwide survey of 46,000 patients who have been treated at A&Es in the UK, has revealed an increase in hospital emergency service waiting times
Increasing child poverty	A report released by the Save the Children charity reveals that 3.5 million children are living in poverty in the UK, and that this figure is expected to rise by 400,000 by 2015

survive, thrive and innovate, to engage employees and achieve sustainable performance and value creation. They realize that business as usual is no longer an option, but they are not quite sure how to respond.

There is a cause to the problem: outdated management paradigm and practices

One of the key causes of the many problems organizations and societies are facing today is outdated management (or Management 1.0) practices based on Newtonian mechanistic paradigm, bureaucratic organization, hierarchical command-and-control mindset, standardization and specialization.[48] Outdated management practices are also largely based on the principles of scientific management inaugurated by Frederic Taylor in his seminal book *The Principles of Scientific Management*.[49] The key premises of this approach include: a detailed instruction and supervision of each worker, defining the task and dividing the work nearly equally between managers and workers, so that the managers plan the work and the workers do the work, managers use command and control and ensure strict standards are achieved, there is a focus on quantity, the cost of workers for a task needs to be minimized.

The Management 1.0 Taylor-based approach worked well for driving productivity and efficiency in a production economy, but it is detrimental for the innovation, engagement and resilience required for knowledge-based organizations in the modern economy. Knowledge workers tend to ignore corporate hierarchy and need autonomy to be more innovative. Mechanistic management practices cause such people to become less engaged and to collaborate less. They cannot thrive and achieve their full potential.

There is a solution to the problem: the emerging management paradigm and practices – or The Management Shift

To address these problems, organizations will need to create more value and become more engaging, innovative and resilient.[50] This requires a fundamental change of both practices and mindset, based on Management 2.0 principles[51] such as collaboration, transparency, meritocracy, purpose, community and autonomy. Authority is distributed and decisions are made on the basis of knowledge rather than a formal position in organizational hierarchy[52] and organizations are managed holistically as complex adaptive systems.[53]

Many leading management thinkers have recognized the need for this shift. In addition to Peter Drucker,[54] examples include Charles Handy,[55] Henry Mintzberg[56] and Gary Hamel.[57] A synthesis of a large body of the literature on leading knowledge workers[58] also reveals that in order to foster innovation in knowledge-based organizations, a different leadership style is needed, based on horizontal rather than vertical leadership, where power and authority are distributed on the basis of knowledge.

The Management 2.0 Hackathon, conducted within the Management Innovation eXchange (MIX),[59] an online community of over 20,000 leading management thinkers and practitioners passionate about reinventing management, generated a set of principles that contributors recommended organizations should adopt:[60] Openness, Community, Meritocracy, Activism, Collaboration, Meaning, Autonomy, Serendipity, Decentralization, Experimentation, Speed and Trust.

Many of these principles are not new and have been advocated by prominent thinkers in management literature. For example, in their book *The Puritan Gift*,[61] Kenneth and William Hopper argue that the key management principles that include decentralization of decision-making were brought to the US by Puritans in the 17th century and were responsible for the economic prosperity of the US, as well as the prosperity of the Far East when these principles were in turn brought there by Americans in the 20th century.

Peter Drucker's timeless wisdom

Management based on Taylor's ideas is in contrast with ideas advocated by one of the most influential management thinkers, Peter Drucker. He has advocated that the task needs to be understood by those who are involved in executing it; that employees need to be given autonomy; that organizations should strive to achieve continuous innovation; that there should be a focus on quality; that there should be an emphasis on continuous learning and workers should be treated as an asset not a cost.[62]

In knowledge-based organizations in particular, Drucker-based management will lead to more value creation, innovation and engagement. Peter Drucker was always hostile to a reductionist perspective where organizational parts are viewed in isolation, making humans mere cogs in a money-making machine. Running organizations productively requires Taylor-based management for repeatability and predictability, but most organizations today have to deal with ever-changing processes and circumstances. Changing organizations productively requires Peter Drucker-based management. Running and changing organizations productively requires a holistic management and leadership approach; continually keeping key stakeholders on the same page, heading in the same direction, solving problems together, and finding breakthrough opportunities within and across stakeholder groups.

A closer investigation into the key ideas of Peter Drucker[63,64,65,66,67,68] reveals that his key ideas advocated for more than half a century in 39 management books are not dissimilar to the Management 2.0 principles that emerged from the 2012 crowd-sourcing Hackathon. Key ideas and areas of Peter Drucker's influence in management thinking can be summarized as follows:

- *Productive organization/Decentralization* – command-and-control management model should be replaced by decentralization for better productivity
- *Respect for the worker* – employees should be treated as an asset rather than a liability
- *Knowledge work productivity* – productivity of knowledge workers is essential for economic prosperity
- *Importance of community* – organizations should contribute to the wider community; voluntary work for non-profit organizations is vital for the health of the society
- *Focus on serving customers* – customers are the reason for a company to exist and there should be a focus of any activity on serving the customer

TABLE 1.2   The key ideas of Peter Drucker mapped to Management 2.0 principles

Key Drucker Ideas	Management 2.0 Principles											
	Openness	Community	Meritocracy	Activism	Collaboration	Meaning	Autonomy	Serendipity	Decentralization	Experimentation	Speed	Trust
Productive organization/ Decentralization	✓	✓	✓		✓		✓		✓			✓
Respect for the worker	✓	✓	✓	✓	✓		✓					✓
Knowledge work productivity	✓	✓	✓	✓	✓	✓	✓	✓	✓	✓	✓	✓
Importance of community	✓	✓	✓		✓		✓		✓			
Focus on serving customers	✓	✓	✓		✓	✓	✓					✓
Responsibility for the common good	✓	✓				✓						
Focusing on core competencies/ Proper executing of business processes		✓				✓						✓
Management by balancing a variety of needs and goals		✓		✓						✓	✓	

- *Responsibility for the common good* – organizations as one of humankind's most noble inventions should contribute to the common good of societies
- *Focusing on core competencies/Proper executing of business processes* – organizational strategies should be focused on core competencies
- *Management by balancing a variety of needs and goals* – organizations should be managed by taking into consideration needs of various stakeholders.

An analysis of Peter Drucker's key seminal ideas and Management 2.0 principles reveals a substantial overlap, as illustrated in Table 1.2. Peter Drucker's visionary thinking is still very applicable for modern organizations and can form the basis for other new management ideas emerging in the management literature and practice.

One common thread throughout all relevant seminal and emerging literature in management is that most authors focus on *what* organizations should do to address their challenges, create more value and improve innovation and engagement. However, research on *how* to do this in practice is rather rare.[69] In order to address this gap, the 6 Box Leadership Model, which will be examined in detail in Chapters 5 and 6, was developed.

Moving from Newton's Mechanistic to the Living Systems Management

From the old to the new management paradigm

A growing number of leading management thinkers and practitioners are advocating the need for change. In one of his *Forbes* blogs on a management paradigm shift,[70] award-winning author Steve Denning identifies some of the global thought leaders advocating a management paradigm shift: Alan W. Brown, John Seely Brown, Rod Collins, Bill George, Ranjay Gulati, John Hagel, Gary Hamel, Umair Haque, Vlatka Hlupic, John Mackey, Roger Martin, Lisa Earle McLeod, Vineet Nayar, Franz Roeoesli, Fred Reichheld, Raj Sisodia and Jeff Sutherland.

A *Harvard Business Review* report, "Competitiveness at the Crossroads",[71] based on a survey of nearly 7,000 Harvard Business School alumni and more than 1,000 members of the US general public, concluded that the US was losing the ability to compete in the international marketplace. The report identified the causes as: flaws in management practices that focus on share price and short-term performance, resulting in a decline in investment in shared resources; social problems, such as increased unemployment and inequality; and public sector decline, reflected in decline in the investment in research, education and information infrastructure.[72] The pattern is confirmed by Harvard Professor Clayton Christensen,[73] who explains how short-term pursuit of profits has been detrimental for innovation and competitiveness of the US economy.

In his book *Fixing the Game*, Roger Martin also critiques the excessive focus on the short term:

> We must shift the focus of companies back to the customer and away from shareholder value. The shift necessitates a fundamental change in our prevailing theory of the firm…The current theory holds that the singular goal of the corporation should be shareholder value maximization. Instead, companies should place customers at the center of the firm and focus on delighting them, while earning an acceptable return for shareholders.[74]

This view is echoed by John Mackey and Raj Sisodia, the authors of an inspirational book, *Conscious Capitalism*.[75] They argue that the myth claiming that the ultimate purpose of business is to maximize profits for investors originated from a narrow view of human nature and an inadequate explanation of the causes of business success. A simplistic view that humans are maximizers of economic self-interests and businesses are pure profit maximizers helped neoclassical economists to create simplified mathematical models to explain some of the economic phenomena. Whilst profits have been important for the progress of the society, the truth is that most entrepreneurs who start businesses are inspired to do something that they believe needs doing; they use their passion to improve lives and create value for customers, suppliers, community, employees, investors and other stakeholders. The authors concluded that "business is good because it creates value, it is ethical because it creates voluntary exchange, it is noble because it can elevate our existence, and it is heroic because it lifts people out of poverty and creates prosperity."[76]

Profit maximization and other elements of old management thinking and paradigms found their way to the management textbooks used on courses at business schools worldwide, and created generations of executives educated on the premises of outdated management thinking. Some of these courses and premises include:

1. Courses on corporate governance grounded in agency theory,[77] promoting the idea that managers cannot be trusted to do their job (maximizing shareholder value) so their interests must be aligned with shareholders' interests (hence they get stock options as part of their pay). There is overwhelming evidence that companies prosper when they pay attention to the interests of customers, employees, shareholders and communities in which they operate, all at the same time

2. Advocating shareholder value maximization assertion, which has many flaws. Shareholders do not own a company; they contribute financial capital, while employees, including managers, contribute human capital, and both are needed by a company to create value. The question becomes, if value is created by combining the resources of both employees and shareholders, why should a value distribution favor only shareholders?

3. Courses on organizational design grounded in transaction cost economics have advocated the need for tight monitoring and control of people to prevent opportunistic behavior;[78] this led to the use of a hierarchical authority to prevent opportunistic behavior, which causes employees to feel neither trusted nor trustworthy and their perception of a lack of autonomy decreases intrinsic motivation

4. Courses on strategy based on Michael Porter's "five forces"[79] (Threat of new entrants, Threat of substitute products or services, Bargaining power of customers, Bargaining power of suppliers and Intensity of competitive rivalry) preached the need for companies not only to compete with their competitors but also with their suppliers, customers, employees and regulators

5. Adopting a "scientific model" of research based on partialization of analysis, where a phenomenon is analyzed as an isolated part, excluding consideration of human choice and intentions (leading to a denial of ethical considerations), and use of strict assumptions and deductive reasoning. The use of a scientific method in the analysis of a social phenomenon has led not only to a loss of morality but also to a loss of a common sense[80]

6. Adopting a pessimistic "liberalism"-based ideology[81] focused on solving the negative problem of restricting the social costs arising from human imperfections, and theory in the social science tends to be self-fulfilling, so managers start behaving according to the theory, leading to pathologies in management behavior

7. Focusing on the scholarship of discovery (research), and marginalizing the scholarship of integration (synthesis), the scholarship of practice (application), and the scholarship of teaching (pedagogy)[82]

8. Predominantly adopting a "Newton-style" management based on the Newtonian machine metaphor where all parts of an organization are viewed (and managed) in isolation instead of more holistic approaches based on complexity theory and other related theories

9. Prioritizing neoclassical economics focused on the allocation of resources for profit maximization, neglecting the systemic view and context in which business operates.

Table 1.3 shows a summary of theories, concepts and terms used within traditional and new management paradigms.

A number of leading management thinkers have criticized the current state of management research and pedagogy, including Porter and McKibbin,[83] Leavitt,[84] Mintzberg and Gosling,[85] and Pfeffer and Fong.[86] They argue that there is a lack of impact of management research on management practice as well as a lack of effectiveness of management education for business performance of students. Even more importantly, Ghoshal[87] argues that outdated management paradigms and academic research related to the conduct of business and management have had some very negative influences on the practice of management, and by propagating ideologically inspired amoral theories, business schools have freed their students from any sense of moral responsibility.

TABLE 1.3   A comparison of the key concepts, terms and theories used in the traditional and new management paradigm

Traditional management paradigm	New management paradigm
Management 1.0	The Management Shift, Management 2.0, Management 3.0, radical management, agile management, conscious capitalism, customer capitalism, stakeholder capitalism, reorganizing for resilience, the power of pull, employees first, the net promoter system, Wiki-management, Scrum, etc.
Newton's theory	"New science"-based theories used/applied to management: complexity theory, chaos theory, systems level analysis, quantum theory, field theory, multilevel theory, connectionist theory, general systems theory, living systems theory, process theory, social evolution theory, theory of complex responsive processes, Wilber's theory of everything, etc.
Newtonian machine paradigm	Complex adaptive systems paradigm
Scientific or mechanistic management	Human-oriented management
Taylor-based management	Drucker-based management
Industrial/production economy	Knowledge/creativity economy
Vertical leadership	Horizontal leadership
Shareholder value maximization	Stakeholder value, shared value maximization
Non-actionable research	Actionable research.
Agency theory	Focus on customers and long-term growth
Transaction cost economics (leads to command-and-control based management)	Delegating responsibilities, distributing authority and decision-making
Porter's five forces	Forming partnerships with suppliers, customers, employees and regulators
"Scientific model" of research, deductive reasoning	Holistic, social science-based approach, inductive and iterative reasoning
"Liberalism"-based ideology; pessimistic view on human nature; focusing on weaknesses	Analyzing corporate behaviors in terms of the choices, actions and achievements of individuals; positive psychology; focusing on strengths; pluralism
Causal (based on statistical estimates of aggregate outcomes) and *functional* (based random process of evolution) explanations	*Intentional* explanations (mental phenomena focused on ethics)

(*continued*)

TABLE 1.3   Continued

Traditional management paradigm	New management paradigm
Scholarship of discovery (research)	Scholarship of discovery (research), scholarship of integration (synthesis), scholarship of practice (application), scholarship of teaching (pedagogy)
Logic of falsification essential for positivism (hard to apply with rigor to social theories, provides only a partial analysis of a complex phenomena); partial, reductionistic, deterministic theories	Integrated, interdisciplinary, emergence-based theories
Neoclassical economics	Reverting back to evolutionary economics, behavioral economics and institutional economics thinking

In his book *From Higher Aims to Hired Hands*,[88] Harvard Business School professor Rakesh Khurana argues that the predominant educational paradigm in the US business schools has been influenced by Harvard Business School's case-based clinical model and Carnegie Tech's quantitative scientific model, forming the foundation of the "management science" and technocratic leadership, neglecting practices based on judgement and intuition. This led to the separation of academic disciplines in business schools from more integrative and multi-disciplinary thinking and the proliferation of scholarly business journals that have been publishing academic output of little interest to practitioners. Khurana concludes that business schools have lost their societal mission and calls for a new holistic institutional context that "recognizes the legitimate economic and social interests of many members of society other than shareholders".[89] In Chapter 7, I provide some information about my own involvement in an initiative to influence changes in business schools.

Business as usual will not work anymore. Instead of just focusing on numbers, processes and structures, management needs to focus on people, their values, passion to make a positive difference, trust, higher purpose, integrity, loyalty, compassion, their need for togetherness and to be part of something bigger than themselves. Businesses have to view people as sources not as resources.[90] Resources are spent after they are used, while sources are like the sun's energy; capable of continuity and renewal. Work is supposed to be a fulfilling, purposeful and life-enhancing experience, not just a job. It is not possible to be unhappy at work and happy in life.

Thomas Kuhn[91] argued that disconfirmation of or challenging a dominant paradigm never leads to its elimination, only a better alternative does. It is only a matter of time before a critical mass of academics, business schools, practitioners and consultants accepts the new paradigm as a norm.

From the clockwork to the complex adaptive systems management

Management paradigms are traditionally based on scientific paradigms, and since the time of the Renaissance and Newton's theory, the machine metaphor has been predominant. This mechanistic metaphor describes the Universe as the clockwork, where any phenomenon is reduced to its parts, these parts are to be understood and put back together (often in new ways). It is also focused on the need for certainty, control and prediction, which prevents creativity and innovation. As discussed, this model was popularized by Frederic Winslow Taylor in his book *The Principles of Scientific Management*,[92] published more than a hundred years ago.

The machine metaphor can be seen in organizational charts, detailed strategic plans and job descriptions. Organizations are viewed as machines and people are like cogs in these machines. Individual components are viewed in isolation, with managers specifying changes and corporate plans, resisting change and reducing variation and complexity. The plans, rules and regulations are described in detail with the hope that the organizational clockwork can produce desired outcomes. When an unpredictable event occurs – for example, customers reject a new product or a competitor launches a major innovation on the market – we do more analysis, more prediction and then the next time something unpredictable happens we do the same. There are some contexts where this approach might work, but it is increasingly apparent that there are many situations where it does not. Rapid rates of change, new insights from life sciences and insufficiencies of the machine model have created a critical mass for revolution in management thinking.

An increasingly popular interdisciplinary approach is complexity science, which is radically changing perceptions on business and management. It is based on the insight that organizations, like many other living organisms, behave like complex adaptive systems (CAS). Complex adaptive systems are systems comprising individual agents that act in unpredictable ways. The agents can change and share mental models, control is dispersed throughout the non-linear interaction among them, and from such an interaction, the new behavior emerges.[93] Novelty and non-linearity cause high unpredictability of system behavior, and it is apparent that we could never predict in detail the behavior of a human system, but generally true statements about CAS behavior can be made. The sets of circumstances that cause creative emergence are often known as "the edge of chaos". In such circumstances there is not enough agreement, rigidity and certainty to make the next decision easily but there is not too much disagreement or uncertainly that would cause complete chaos. Order emerges out of the edge of chaos.[94]

Complexity theory is an overarching framework that explains the world, the living systems, organizations as social systems, as well as biological and ecological systems. It is focused on understanding life, and this is changing our perceptions about organizations, management and social change. Complexity science-based management provides an opportunity for people to work together as teams in a different, more creative, decentralized, effective and adaptive manner, leading to more innovation and business success, using the following guidelines:[95]

- When agents interact and mutually affect each other in a system, this is the source of emergence
- Agents' behaviors in a system are governed by a few simple rules
- Small changes can lead to large effects
- Emergence is certain, but there is no certainty as to what it will be
- The greater the diversity of agents in a system, the richer the emergent patterns.

Management is about changing structure, knowledge, skills and behavior according to current goals and accepting that change will happen as a result of these actions. A complex system encompasses the current system and factors (such as agents' knowledge, skills, goals and motivation) that will cause the system to adapt and transform. Management is about transforming and adapting; it has to deal with dynamic capabilities reflected in changing external environments, technology, processes and people. This implies that complexity, systems thinking and management are closely interrelated. Culture, creativity and productivity emerge from employee's interaction, co-evolution and self-organization.[96] I will discuss some specific implications for leadership style that arise from the science of complexity in the next chapter.

Organizational fitness is related to an organization's ability to adapt, thrive and survive, and management's responsibility is to help it do so. Complexity principles are highly applicable to business. Organizations in equilibrium are not responsive to changes. When faced with threat or extraordinary opportunity, organizations tend to move towards the edge of chaos, which evokes higher levels of experimentation and innovation. In these circumstances, components of organizations self-organize and new forms emerge from the interaction of individual components. If properly employed, these principles allow organizations to revitalize and thrive. Complex systems are not compatible with prediction; they are about action, experimentation, reflection and learning.

Putting the new management paradigm into action

Putting The Management Shift into action means that adaptive organizations are managed as living organisms, with non-linearity, informal networks, and interactions embedded in processes. Power and decision-making are distributed; responsibility is delegated, rather than tasks; culture is based on care, purpose, connection and trust, and communication is good in all directions.

For a number of years, I have been researching and comparing traditional and emerging management approaches. Table 1.4 shows a comparison between the two, compiled from many published sources, personal insights, my lecture notes and conversations with academics and practitioners over

TABLE 1.4 A comparison between traditional and emerging management concepts and approaches

Traditional management approaches	Emerging management approaches
Newtonian paradigm	Complexity paradigm
Machine model	Organizations as living organisms
Clockware (focusing on individual parts)	Swarmware (focusing on interactions amongst interconnected parts of an organization)
Seek comfort	Support differences
Competition	Balance competition and cooperation
Focusing on one task at a time	Multitasking
Human resources	Talent management Diversity imperative
Hierarchical linearity	Non-linearity, networks, interactions
Command and control	Distributed power, autonomy, interconnectivity
Pyramids	Networks
Manage by rules	Manage on the edge
Focus on data	Balance data and intuition
Control information and force agreement	Stay on the edge and use the "right" amount of information
Focus on formal relationships	Utilize the shadow system
Ignore tension and paradox	Embrace tension and paradox
Focus on shareholders	Focus on customers
Focus on share price, earnings, growth	Invest in future growth
Grow big (economies of scale)	Be agile (flexible, adaptable)
Plan everything in detail before taking action	Have a good enough vision, take action, learn and adapt. Balance planning and acting
Avoid risks	Balance safety and risk, take reasonable risks
No experimentation, trial and error	Be open to experimentation, learning and reflection
Know your direction in detail before action	Let direction emerge from action
Reduce complexity, simplify models	Embrace complexity
Settled and stable, maintain equilibrium	Question the status quo, start to change when on top
Authority based on power	Authority based on knowledge

Traditional management approaches	Emerging management approaches
Key leadership traits: being tough, controlling, analytical	Key leadership traits: intuition, cooperation, being forgiving, risk taking
Charismatic CEO	Courageous, humble CEO
Rank your employees	Hire self-motivated people with the sense of purpose
Control rigidly within fixed framework	Allow freedom within agreed overall (changeable) framework
Be a market leader	Find a niche and use innovation
Cutting costs	Culture based on care, connection and trust
Admire company's strength	Admire company's soul
Centralized hierarchies	Decentralized networks
Profit-making machines	Sustainable and socially responsible living systems
Employees as costs/liabilities	Employees as value creators/assets
Short average life expectancy	Long average life expectancy
Micromanaging	Delegating responsibilities
Low levels of trust and transparency	High levels of trust and transparency
Low levels of teamwork and collaboration	High levels of teamwork and collaboration
Vertical communication	Horizontal communication
Short-term financial performance	Long-term performance and making a positive contribution to the society
Profit from maximizing share prices	Profit from passion and purpose
Long lifecycles	Short lifecycles
Loyal customers	Less loyal customers
Stable prices	Unstable prices
Incremental change	Discontinuous change
Managed results	Sustainable value creation
Focus on functions and departments	Focus on cells and networks
Focus on management	Focus on leadership
Focus on power	Focus on innovation
Focus on incentives	Focus on sharing
Focus on status	Focus on purpose
Focus on rules	Focus on principles and shared values
Structure	Flow

(*continued*)

TABLE 1.4   Continued

Traditional management approaches	Emerging management approaches
"Theory X" human nature assumption	"Theory Y" human nature assumption
Inside-out hierarchical power	Outside-in value creation
Functional division	Functional integration
Centralized leadership	Distributed leadership
Leaders rule	Market rules
Top-down control	Team-based self-governance
Working in the office	Working anywhere
Working 9–5	Working anytime
Need for a good boss	Need for good colleagues
Working to earn pension	Working to fulfil purpose
Obsessing with competitors	Obsessing with customers
Power comes from hoarding the knowledge	Power comes from sharing the knowledge
Using written policies for decision-making	Using good judgement for decision-making
Focus on when, where and how the work gets done	Focus on results produced
Influence is dependent of hierarchy	Influence is independent of hierarchy, it is more dependent on knowledge and connectedness
Focus on how to get to the direction	Focus on direction
Managing for getting the work done	Leading and coaching people to create magic
Hiring to delegate	Hiring to elevate

several years. The information provided in this table is self-explanatory. Most organizations would probably use a combination of both approaches, and this table could be used as a check-list for organizations that may wish to assess the predominant management style used.

According to marketing software HubSpot's Culture Code, companies have to change dramatically the way they operate:

> Although people, business environment, technology and management insights have changed dramatically, especially in the last couple of decades, many organizations operate as if they are frozen in time,

as if the time has stopped....as if the money matters most, as if the Internet was not invented and if amazing people are just happy to keep their job.[97]

Another trend in the new management approaches is focusing more on the customer, as Andrew Mason, the former CEO of Groupon, expressed: "Have the courage to start with the customer. My biggest regrets are the moments that I let the lack of data override my intuition on what's the best for our customer."[98]

Traditionally, companies have been adopting risk avoidance, detailed planning, rules, stability and status quo. On the other hand, companies adopting emerging paradigms are open to experimentation, learning, reflection and managing on the edge. Detailed long-term strategic plans are impossible to produce due to constant changes in business environments. Managers cannot plan all details in advance – no one is that smart or has a clear crystal ball. A general direction for the future can be set, and people should be ready to adapt and evolve as environments change. In traditional management paradigms, for example, the emphasis is on cost cutting. However, no company has ever shrunk to greatness.[99]

According to the traditional management theory, the focus is on establishing order and control by a few people at the top of the organizational hierarchy. There is an emphasis on admiring a company's strength reflected in its balance sheets. In emerging management approaches, the emphasis is on admiring the company's soul reflected by its caring company culture, which will encourage creativity and innovation, love, purpose and compassion[100] and by its philanthropy, where more companies realize the power of giving back to the society. Given the rapid changes in business environments, companies are in danger of applying old solutions to new challenges; emerging management paradigms can provide many answers.

The extent of the application of emerging management practices in an organization would depend on the degree of uncertainty, dependency on knowledge and innovation, challenge faced and the magnitude of the change sought, and the extent of the use of knowledge for value creation.

If all these elements are at a high level, emerging approaches would be much more suitable than the traditional ones. For example, managing knowledge workers such as academics, software developers or medical doctors should be predominantly based on emerging management paradigms. In practice, at best, most companies would use a mixture of traditional and emerging management approaches.

Examples from the real world of business: companies implementing emerging management practices do well financially

There is growing evidence that inspirational, trustworthy companies built on authentic values, focused on a higher purpose and caring culture, experience exceptional financial performance over the long term. In short, companies that have implemented The Management Shift do well financially, sustained over the long term. In a well-known study carried out by Raj Sisodia, David Wolfe and Jac Sheth for their book *Firms of Endearment*,[101] the authors studied the financial performance of 30 Firms of Endearment (FoE), defined as firms that focus on passion and purpose and bring the interests of all stakeholder groups (including society, partners, investors, customers and employees) into strategic alignment. They found that the public FoEs returned 1,184 percent for investors over ten years (to the end of June 2006) compared to 122 percent for the S&P 500, which is about a 9 to 1 ratio.[102] Furthermore, the authors compared the performance of 30 FoEs with the performance of 11 companies identified in Jim Collins' bestselling book *Good to Great*[103] and found that over the same ten-year period, FoEs outperformed the *Good to Great* companies by a ratio of 3.6 to 1. They have also updated the data to cover the 15-year period between 1996 and 2011. In that period, FoEs outperformed the S&P 500 index by a factor of 10.5.[104]

An analysis of the performance of Fortune's "100 Best Companies to Work For"[105] – where criteria used includes trust, pride and camaraderie (creating a genuine sense of satisfaction amongst employees), reveals that between 1997 and 2011 these companies had three times higher stock market returns than S&P 500 companies. An organization called Ethisphere[106] is producing an annual list of the world's most ethical companies assessed in areas such as corporate responsibility, innovation that contributes to the public well-being, executive leadership and reputation track record. Since 2007, these companies have outperformed the S&P 500 by an average of 7.3 percent annually.[107]

Harvard Business School professors John Kotter and James Heskett showed in their book *Corporate Culture and Performance*[108] that companies with strong and flexible business cultures that take into consideration all stakeholders and have empowered managers, outperformed companies that did not exhibit these characteristics. They did so on revenue growth (682 percent versus 166 percent), share price increase (901 percent versus 74 percent), and net income increase (756 percent versus 1 percent). In a study of 520 companies,[109] Mary Sully de Luque and her colleagues examined the financial impact of autocratic versus visionary leadership based on values and purpose. They found that over time companies led by visionary leaders significantly outperformed those led by autocratic, financially focused leaders.

According to John Mackey and Raj Sisodia,[110] the reasons inspirational, conscious companies do well financially include: high sales (they have superior acceptance by customers), margin mirage (they seek partnership with innovative, inspirational partners), lower marketing costs (they have many loyal customers), lower employee turnover and higher engagement (employees personal passions are aligned with the company's purpose), and lower administrative costs (they eliminate non-value added expenses).

I compiled my own list of inspirational companies that have shown tendency for embracing the new management paradigm in their practices (see Appendix 1), which I selected from the following sources:

1. Companies that have implemented at least two principles of Management 2.0, as emerged from the MIX Management 2.0 Hackathon,[111] a global collaborative effort to reinvent management through crowd sourcing
2. Companies included in research described in *Firms of Endearment*[112]
3. Companies that emerged through my own crowd-sourcing-based research using more than 200,000 members at various LinkedIn groups (including Harvard Business Review, Stoos Network, Linked 2 Leadership,

Leadership Think Tank, Senior Executive Exchange and World Wide Management Consultants groups)

4. Companies identified by Beta Codex Network,[113] an open source network founded in 2008 focused on transforming organizations

5. Companies listed in the World Blu List,[114] identified through a survey completed by employees measuring scores on the freedom to fear-based continuum.

In addition to examples of companies listed in Appendix 1, there are other lists available, but in total these companies represent a very small minority in comparison to the majority of companies still managed using the old management paradigm, which is largely responsible for many problems we are facing today. One cannot help but wonder what the world would be like if the majority of organizations were genuinely authentic, trustworthy, transparent, purposeful and caring; where pyramids are replaced with networks, command and control is replaced with collaboration, and autonomy, fear and authority are replaced with higher purpose and authentic care. Imagine how people would feel to work in such organizations, how well these organizations would do financially and how many more opportunities that would give to the young generation. Wouldn't it be fantastic if such organizations became the norm rather than the exception? The Management Shift will lead to creating organizations that are fit for the 21st century, with better engagement, resilience and innovation. This will ultimately result in more economic and social prosperity for everyone.

SEVEN REFLECTION POINTS

1. Do you feel engaged and passionate about the work you are doing?
2. Do you feel you do what you were born to do and you express your life purpose through your work?
3. Can you recognize any of the problems discussed in this chapter in your organization?

4. What is the biggest problem your organization is dealing with and what can be done to address this problem?
5. Does your organization use predominantly traditional mechanistic practices or emerging management practices resulting from The Management Shift?
6. If your organization is still managed using traditional management approaches, what would be the three main changes that could be done to move your organization closer towards The Management Shift?
7. What is the ideal organization you would like to work for and why? How would working there make you feel?

chapter 2

The Need for a New Type of Leadership

This chapter provides answers to the following key questions:

- Why are traditional leadership approaches counterproductive for the vast majority of organizations?
- Why does leading for purpose, values, passion and compassion create better results?
- What is the link between complexity science and the new leadership style needed today?
- What are the key differences between traditional and emergent leadership approaches and practices?
- How do knowledge workers expect to be led?
- How can emergent leadership practices be implemented?
- What are the key characteristics of the emerging management approaches?
- What are the examples of companies successfully using emergent leadership approaches?
- What are the lessons that can be learned from these companies?

The Management Shift Requires a New Leadership Style

Leadership matters now more than ever. We live in a world of constant change, unprecedented economic and social challenges, interconnectivity, continuous innovation and increasing competition. Conventional wisdom about leadership approaches and styles needs to be un-learned as it is not serving its purpose anymore – it is detrimental for adaptability to changes and innovation, and it does not create conditions for engagement and purposeful work in organizations. This approach helped to increase productivity and efficiency in a different context, but now it is becoming a liability.

Individuals and organizations benefit from embracing a leadership style based on a new mindset, part of The Management Shift. In this approach, leaders strive to serve, to inspire others to find purpose and calling in the work they do, to unleash their passion and creativity, and to use all internal resources and intrinsic motivation to provide exceptional service. They also coach, mentor and provide enabling conditions for others to emerge as natural leaders and make decisions when they have most relevant knowledge to do so.

New leaders should be exemplars of honesty, integrity, humility, transparency and compassion. As Stephen Covey put it in his book *The 8th Habit*,[1] leaders should find their unique human voice by helping others to find theirs. They should also inspire others to achieve their full potential as described by John Quincy Adams: "If your actions inspire others to dream more, learn more, do more and become more, you are a leader."[2]

Traditional command-and-control style leadership is not only unhelpful, it can be counterproductive, causing companies to lose their ability to create value, to innovate and stay competitive. There is a growing body of research[3] showing that traditional leadership styles are inadequate for leading knowledge workers and that they stifle creativity, motivation and engagement. Professor Richard Roberts' study[4] on the causes of the financial crisis showed that hubristic, autocratic or even bullying leaders constituted one of the main causes of the financial meltdown in 2008 and earlier.

As Gary Hamel argues in his inspirational book *What Matters Now*,[5] obedience, diligence and knowledge can be bought relatively easily; they are becoming global commodities. However, to ignite the value-creating gifts of employee initiative, creativity and passion, leaders will have to create inspiring working environments. Without initiative, people will not go the extra mile to do the best work they can; without creativity they will not challenge conventional wisdom and be innovative; and without passion they will not see their work as a calling to make a positive difference in the world.

Leading for purpose, values, passion and compassion

Empowering leaders imbue their colleagues with a desire to achieve something of lasting benefit, powerfully illustrated by a quote from Tim O'Reilly: "Pursue something so important than even if you fail, the world is better off with you having tried."[6] Bill Gates did not become one of the wealthiest people in the world by pursuing profits, he pursued his quest to spark a global revolution in personal computing. As Professor Jean Lipman-Blumen[7] wonderfully puts it:

> The overarching purpose of leadership has always been the identification of noble enterprises and the invitation to supporters to engage, with the leader, in those noble missions that serve the society while creating meaning in their own lives.

As individuals and teams, we all need a purpose to be energized and inspired to do our best. Purpose makes us excited every morning about yet another day when we can be totally engaged and motivated to do work we feel we were born to do. It helps us to unleash our passion for work and overcome any obstacles; it gives us a sense of direction and it keeps us focused on doing the right thing. Purposeful work makes us use our internal resources and wisdom to produce amazing achievements, develop resilience and thrive even in times of uncertainty. The essence of finding a purpose is well expressed by the well-known management thinker Charles Handy, who described "proper selfishness" as a "responsibility for making the most of oneself by ultimately finding a purpose beyond and bigger than oneself."[8]

Organizations need purpose too, as expressed metaphorically by Ed Freeman, a trustee of Conscious Capitalism Inc.:

> We need red blood cells to live (the same way a business needs profits to live), but the purpose of life is more than to make red blood cells (the same way the purpose of business is more than simply to generate profits).[9]

Arie de Geus deploys similarly vivid metaphors in his seminal book *The Living Company*,[10] where he contrasts companies that operate like economic machines to purposeful companies that achieve greater longevity. The "Economic" companies are managed using traditional leadership approaches; they are managed primarily for profit; they exist to produce maximum results (wealth) with minimum resources for a smaller inner group of investors and managers. People are regarded as extensions of the capital assets, they are managed by hierarchical control, and there is no sense of community for employees. Whilst assets and Return on Investment (ROI) are important, employees of such companies trade their expertise and skills for money and they feel little loyalty, trust or passion for their work, and this is not a thriving environment for innovation. The "Economic" companies are

> like a puddle of rainwater – a collection of raindrops, gathered together in a cavity or hollow. They remain in their position, at the bottom of the cavity. When it rains, more drops may be added to the puddle... Paradoxically, this stability may lead to vulnerability. Puddles of rainwater cannot survive much heat. When the sun shines and the temperature heats up, the puddle starts evaporating. In fact, most puddles have a very short lifespan.[11]

On the other hand, companies based on purpose and organized on the ethos of communities have much greater longevity, and they emulate a flow of a river.

> No one drop of water dominates the company for long... The river is a self-perpetuating community, with component water drops that enter and leave... A company, by initiating rules for continuity, and motion of its people, can emulate the longevity and power of the river.[12]

The need for purpose, community, respect for people and decentralization features prominently in the ideas proposed by legendary management thinker Peter Drucker, who stated that "an organization is an organ of the society and fulfils itself by the contribution it makes to the outside environment",[13] leading to a belief that great companies could stand among humankind's noblest inventions.[14]

Some of the key premises of a new leadership approach are that leaders follow their inner voice instead of the pursuit of power; that they show compassion for all stakeholders, including customers, employees, investors, partners, suppliers and the communities they serve; that they do good while they do well, have a strong sense of connectivity at all levels, make this world a better place and inspire others to do the same.

The need for such a mindset is recognized by a growing number of business leaders. For example, Tim Sanders, a former chief solutions officer at Yahoo!, proposed the idea that love is a key strategic asset of a company.[15] Kevin Roberts, head of ad agency Saatchi & Saatchi, suggests that brands are reaching a higher level of existence as "lovemarks".[16] Timberland's mission is "to make the world a better place".[17] Similarly, the purpose of Brand Velocity Inc., an Atlanta-based management consultancy, is to help "people successfully reinvent their organizations in a way that makes the world a better place".[18]

From traditional to emergent leadership

So, what does it mean in practice to move away from the traditional towards the new, emergent leadership style? There is a large body of research on the *what* and *why* of new, emergent leadership practices, describing what needs to be done to lead organizations differently from conventional approaches and why this is so important, especially now.

Emergent leadership is defined as a new leadership approach that brings more innovation and profit through distribution of formal power and decision-making, interaction through informal networks and experimentation and learning. The main underlying concepts are that leadership is about facilitating and enabling rather than directing and controlling, and that more work is accomplished through learning by doing rather than by formal instruction. It also means encouraging experimenting and allowing good attempts (and tolerating mistakes) instead of target setting, planning and controlling – this leads to more innovation and better performance. This new approach is also about creating new knowledge by sharing information across functional boundaries and interacting across networks. Trusting that people will do the right thing, instead of controlling their behavior and imposing decisions on them, unleashes their full potential, which will lead to more profits.

When an emergent leadership culture is implemented, employees are intrinsically motivated to perform well, a strong team culture is developed, and levels of stress and absenteeism are reduced.[19] What does this mean to leaders? By giving away formal power, leaders will get more power back, as more will be achieved with less effort. This will make the leader's life easier, with less stress and burnout. Most importantly, leaders will develop more motivated, innovative and energized employees.

Emergent leadership produces strong results and is suited for a world changing as fast as ours. This observation is not new, but too few organizations actually translate it into action, meaning conventional leadership and management approaches based on linear hierarchies – reflecting an organizational culture based on rules, command and control and formal relationships – are still very much the norm.

Many different labels are used to refer to emerging leadership approaches. When I conducted an extensive literature search on this subject a few years ago by reviewing around one thousand articles and books on this subject,

I discovered concepts and terms that convey the essence of new leadership approaches. Some of these terms include: conscious leadership, shared leadership, complexity leadership, energy leadership, positive leadership, network leadership, distributed leadership, tribal leadership, collective leadership, collaborative leadership, participative leadership, democratic leadership, self-organizing leadership, adaptive leadership, enabling leadership, empowering leadership, energizing leadership, transformational leadership, relational leadership, principle-centered leadership, value-based leadership, new leadership, appreciative leadership, spiritual leadership and open leadership.

An analysis of the key concepts and ideas behind these different labels for a new leadership reveals that there are many similarities amongst these approaches. They all advocate moving towards more empowering and democratic practices that lead to better engagement and more innovation. The key differences between traditional and new, emergent leadership approaches are summarized in Table 2.1. This information can be used as a checklist to assess whether your organization is heading towards emergent leadership approaches. In my experience, most leaders would adopt a combination of both approaches, but there would be a tendency for either a traditional or emergent approach to dominate.

Following an extensive review and synthesis of the literature on emerging leadership approaches[20] that mainly deal with the *why* and *what* of these new approaches, I focused my research efforts on the *how*, analyzing how companies can implement the new management paradigm and new leadership approaches in practice. This is largely the focus of this book. In another international study, my co-authors and I demonstrated with two practical examples in knowledge intensive companies[21,22] how reducing control and increasing freedom for employees can dramatically improve results, where trust, responsibility and innovation are key enablers.

In knowledge organizations specifically, emergent leadership is not about delegating tasks and monitoring results; it is about imbuing the entire workforce with a sense of responsibility for the business. Emergent leadership is living, distributive and communicative. It focuses on ques-

TABLE 2.1   A comparison between traditional and emergent leadership

Traditional leadership	Emergent leadership
Traditional top-down leadership	Shared, distributed leadership, leadership as emergent collective action
Leaders lead by command and control	Leaders support autonomy, collaboration and self-organized communities of passion
Direction is provided by hierarchical leaders	Direction emerges from complex network activity
Key leadership traits: being tough, controlling, analytical	Key leadership traits: being inspirational, intuitive, cooperative, compassionate
Leaders provide centralized direction	Dispersed visions are supported
Leaders control around core strategic vision	Control is dispersed around complex interactions amongst employees, actions are guided by a shared vision
Change is an incremental movement, led by a formal leader	Change is created by the movement that emerges from interactive dynamics
Centralized coordination for alignment with strategic direction	Decentralized coordination of adaptive functions to encourage emergence and innovation
Leading for equilibrium and stability	Leading for change and adaptability
Searching for order and avoiding chaos	Accepting some chaos that will lead to homeostasis
Leading for reduction of conflict	Leading for creation of enabling conditions for innovation and engagement
Reliance on best practices and total control	Embracing exploration, experimentation and trial and error
Supporting unified views	Encouraging creativity from differences
Influencing directly	Influencing indirectly through empowerment and inspiration
Implementing comprehensive change programs	Enabling emergent conditions for change
Delegating tasks	Delegating responsibilities
Leading for following rules and regulations	Leading for pursuing passion and values
Centralized decision-making on the basis of a formal position in organizational hierarchy	Decentralized decision-making on the basis of knowledge, decisions emerge through interactions
Leading based on fear and obedience	Leading based on inspiring initiative and creativity
Leading based on information control	Leading based on trust and transparency

(continued)

TABLE 2.1   Continued

Traditional leadership	Emergent leadership
Leaders support reward mechanisms based on formal positions	Leaders support reward mechanisms based on contribution/meritocracy
Leaders lead for the pursuit of profit	Leaders lead for the pursuit of purpose
Power is concentrated at the top of an organization	Power is distributed
Employees give allegiance to formal leaders	Employees give allegiance to values, principles and code of conduct
People are led as objects that help profit maximization	People are led as individuals that help an organization achieve its higher purpose
Giving information and directions without justification or "buy-in"	Sharing detailed information and getting feedback and buy-in
Using self-assessment	Utilizing and acting on feedback
Delegating and blaming when things do not go well	Leading by encouraging everyone to be a leader
Focusing on the left brain analysis for decision-making	Using whole brain thinking and intuition for decision-making
Emotionally disconnected leaders	Utilizing social/emotional intelligence
Stable power positions	Respecting employees, seeing everyone as equal
Performance monitoring and evaluation	Energizing employees through inspiring great performance
Expect allegiance to a formal leader	Expect allegiance to code of ethics, principles and values
Hindering development of mutualism through control	Building mutualism
Leadership as monologue	Leadership as dialogue and interdependence
Formalization of sources of innovation	Enabling interactions for emergence of creativity and innovation
Imposing rigid procedures, rules and regulations	Allowing flexibility with procedures, rules and regulations

tions rather than answers. As will be shown in Chapter 4, the individual continuum of developmental levels goes from "lifeless" to "limitless", whilst organizational continuum spans from apathetic to unbounded. Emergent leadership approaches help individuals to operate with a limitless mindset and it helps organizations to achieve unbounded culture. This results in a sustainable performance grounded in inspiring, purposeful and innovative organizational culture, cooperative relationships, and engaged, passionate and intrinsically motivated employees.

This is echoed by leading management thinkers Peter Drucker and Tom Peters. According to Peter Drucker, "leadership is lifting a person's vision to high sights, the raising of a person's performance to a higher standard, the building of a personality beyond its normal limitations",[23] whilst according to Tom Peters, "leadership is about nurturing and enhancing".[24] If more leaders were to exhibit such a mindset, many economic and social challenges we are facing today would be addressed, and the future prospects for the young generation would be more hopeful.

Complexity science and leadership

Many of the emerging leadership approaches listed in the previous section are rooted in complexity science, including complexity leadership, shared leadership, distributed leadership, collective leadership, collaborative leadership, participative leadership, democratic leadership, self-organizing leadership, network leadership, adaptive leadership and enabling leadership. Models that I shall describe in Chapters 4 and 5 were also developed on the basis of complexity theory, in addition to others.

The key premises of complexity theory were described in Chapter 1. To summarize, it is based on the understanding that organizations behave like complex adaptive systems (CAS), comprising autonomous individuals or groups who act in unpredictable ways. Control is dispersed throughout the non-linear interaction among the agents and from such an interaction, the new behavior or new modes of operating emerge.[25] Relationships between parts in a CAS and their interactions lead to creative emergence and minimum specifications yield more creativity than detailed plans delivered by traditional leadership approaches.[26] Leadership is distributed in a CAS. It is perceived as a system phenomenon and leaders can emerge naturally. Complexity leadership focuses on the dynamics of leadership as it emerges over time in all areas of an organizational system, where each interchange and interaction provides opportunities for leading, learning, growing and change.[27]

In a complex system, it is impossible to have absolute control, at least beyond some very general parameters. In this context, leaders need to give up the illusion of control and focus on setting a larger vision so that the creativity of employees can emerge.[28] Differences between emergent leaders and team members are blurred and leadership occurs in emergent, informal, adaptive dynamics throughout the organization and in the conditions of adaptive challenges that require new learning, innovation, exploration, new patterns of behavior and adjustments.[29]

The key for organizational effectiveness is in speed, adaptability, knowledge and learning – rather than efficiency and control suitable for manufacturing – sharply contrasting with the dominant paradigm in leadership theory focused on how leaders influence others towards desired objectives within hierarchical organization structures using centralized control.[30]

When leaders loosen control, more creativity and a culture of care will emerge, which will lead to better productivity. Leaders in complex adaptive systems should be accessible, respond to the needs of others, acknowledge and value people's contributions at all levels, create opportunities for people and take the time to build trusting relationships. They should be strong and have vision but also be comfortable leading with a hands-off approach.[31] Complexity science broadens conceptualizations of leadership from perspectives that are heavily invested in psychology and social psychology (for example, human relations models) to include processes for managing dynamic systems and interconnectivity.[32]

Interest in complexity-based leadership has been growing steadily and there are a number of published research studies on the subject. In perhaps one of the most influential of these, Mary Uhl-Bien and co-authors[33] argue that complexity science provides a paradigm for leadership that is more suitable for the needs of knowledge workers than the top-down, bureaucratic approach. Their core proposition is that "much of leadership thinking has failed to recognize that leadership is not merely the influential act of an individual or individuals but rather is embedded in a complex interplay of numerous interacting forces".

A growing number of management scholars argue that decentralized and shared forms of leadership will become more necessary for modern organizations, helping them to manage complexity and encourage innovation.[34] Organizations may be collectively led to establish a dynamic system where bottom-up structuration emerges to increase the long-term performance and innovation in the organization.[35] André Martin[36] argues that leadership is changing and will change even more in the near future due to the increase in complex challenges that leaders face. In a survey of 350 managers, he explored the current and future state of leadership. The results identified four trends that are driving this shift in leadership: globalization, a rise in complex challenges, a world of interruption and leadership for longevity. Leaders will need stronger collaborative skills, organizational architect ability, a more flexible style, be open and adaptable to new ideas, and be able to find examples of positive disobedience.

Others confirm that leadership agility based on complexity theory has become a much-needed competency.[37] In a study that involved 604 participants,[38] five levels of leadership agility were identified, each of which corresponds to a stage of adult ego development. The study emphasizes a need for an "integral" approach to leadership development that places emphasis both on professional skills needed in complex, rapidly changing environments and on the mental and emotional capacities that underlie these skills.

I have been researching this area for many years and have gathered compelling evidence on the need to move away from traditional top-down leadership, especially in knowledge-based organizations, which I have detailed in, for example, an article co-authored with Professor Amar and presented at the Academy of Management Conference in Boston in 2012,[39] as well as in various other articles.[40,41]

Leading Knowledge Workers is Different

The term "knowledge worker" was coined by Peter Drucker in his 1959 book *The Landmarks of Tomorrow*,[42] referring to anyone whose work is focused on generating or using knowledge. He subsequently discussed the issue of knowledge work productivity in many successive books, and the key ideas include:

- Knowledgeable workers are essential for the success of the modern economy
- People are an organization's most valuable resource and managers need to facilitate their development and training
- Every knowledge worker in a modern organization is an "executive" if, by virtue of his/her position or knowledge, he/she is responsible for a contribution that affects the capacity of the organization to perform and to obtain results[43]
- Productivity of knowledge workers and service workers has remained steady or has declined in some cases, which suggests that knowledge worker productivity is the most important challenge for management in the 21st century[44]
- Knowledge workers have to manage themselves, and they have to have autonomy
- Continuing innovation has to be part of the work and the responsibility of knowledge workers
- Knowledge work must be focused on the needs of the customer and business strategy
- Productivity of the knowledge worker is a matter of both quality and quantity
- Making knowledge workers productive requires changes in attitude, both on the part of the individual knowledge worker, and on the part of the whole organization[45]
- Knowledge is the source of wealth. If it is applied to familiar tasks we get productivity, if it is applied to new, different tasks we get innovation.[46]

For decades, many authors have been discussing the transition from the production economy, where the wealth is created from the production of goods, to the knowledge economy, where most value is created through use of knowledge or intellectual capital.[47] We are now witnessing another new trend – a rapid transition from the knowledge economy to the creative economy,[48] where ideas, creativity, innovation and responsiveness to changes are becoming crucial for wealth creation.

Indeed, Nobel Prize Winner Joseph Stiglitz, in his very informative article published in *Vanity Fair*,[49] argues that the US economy is going through a shift towards a creative economy, where both manufacturing and service are important. The driving force is innovation, and organizations are agile, continually offering new value to customers and delivering it sooner than normally expected.[50] Organizations focus not on short-term financial returns but rather on creating long-term customer value based on trust.[51]

A growing number of companies have made this management shift. For example, at W.L. Gore every employee can refuse any request; at Pfizer employees can outsource the least stimulating part of their jobs.[52] Small teams at Whole Foods Market food stores have a lot of decision-making authority[53] and at Google employees are permitted to spend 20 percent of their time on innovation related to their personal interests and passions.[54]

One of the foremost management thinkers, Gary Hamel, provides an eloquent summary of the change:

> Everyone gets heard, Commitment is voluntary, Power is granted from below, The tools of creativity are widely distributed, Capability counts more than credentials and titles, Individuals are richly empowered with information, Authority is fluid and contingent on value-added, Resources are free to follow opportunities, Ideas compete on an equal footing, Communities are self-defining and Decisions are peer-based.[55]

Knowledge workers: what do they want?

It is apparent that knowledge workers have special requirements, needs and aspirations and they share certain characteristics. They are highly skilled, intrinsically motivated, they do not want to be led and ignore corporate hierarchy.[56] They should be treated as associates or partners rather than as subordinates, and they need an organizational culture where authority is based on knowledge, not on formal power.[57] They have high mobility and they need to have responsibility for their own productivity;

they have to manage themselves, have autonomy and they learn fast. In *The Drive: The Surprising Truth About What Motivates Us,*[58] Daniel Pink argues that in an economy driven by ideas and creativity, financial incentives are no longer enough. Drawing on four decades of scientific research on human motivation, Pink demonstrates the mismatch between the evidence and much business practice. While carrots and sticks worked successfully in the 20th century, that is the wrong way to motivate people for today's challenges. It is much more effective to give workers a sense of purpose, mastery and autonomy over their time and their tasks. This is explained by our deeply human need to own our lives, to learn and create new things, and to do better by ourselves and the world.

Knowledge workers are not satisfied with work that is only a livelihood. They come up with new ideas and products, new ways to distribute them, and new ways to organize the company to best use these innovations. Their work time and activities tend to be less structured, so they need flexible working arrangements. They resist any interference with their work and respond to questions rather than to being micromanaged, as by definition they should know more about their task than their boss. They need to believe in what they are doing, have their say in their own management and to feel they are treated fairly. They may be reluctant to share their process precisely because they value it.[59] Organizations should encourage knowledge workers to have complete power over their task because these workers need knowledge to accomplish it and only they have full control over the essential knowledge. Because they have a key individual role to play in the functioning of their organization and are involved in complex problem-solving, they ask for the sharing of power[60] and should get it.

Knowledge workers can subtly but effectively withdraw or reduce their cooperation, or increase their share of the value they add to the organization.[61] Firms that want to stay competitive in the creative economy need to develop leadership capability to optimize and retain their human assets. This results in a shift in power whereby workers exercise an upward influence on the leadership relationship.[62,63] They cannot be led in the traditional way, especially because no one manager can have a collective understanding of the functions to be able to lead the complex task in such organizations.[64] As Gary Hamel summarizes,[65] at the time when leadership is more important than ever, leaders seem to be scarce. This seems to be a problem of traditional pyramidal structures that demand too much of too few and not enough of everyone else. We live in a world of complexity and complex organizations that require too much from too few people up top who don't have the intellectual diversity, the bandwidth capacity and the time to make critical decisions.

Leading knowledge workers for innovation in the creative economy

As shown in the above section, the special characteristics of knowledge workers imply that they cannot be led using traditional leader–follower approaches. They need to be managed in a culture where power is distributed, which is the main premise of complexity theory as discussed earlier in this chapter.

In his *Forbes* post "Leadership in the Three-Speed Economy",[66] management author and founder of the Stoos movement[67] Steve Denning argues the economy is an aggregate of three very different economies: the Traditional Economy, Financial Capitalism and the Creative Economy. Each of these economies is going at its own speed, with its own dynamic, very different trajectories and different leadership challenges. The Traditional Economy is focused on producing goods and services; it includes large companies such as GE or Walmart, which mainly practice the hierarchical bureaucracy of traditional management focused on efficiency and control, and it is in decline. Financial Capitalism comprising financial institutions continues to run on shaky fundamentals, often disconnected from the real economy. On the other hand, the Creative Economy is focused on delighting customers by mobilizing whole ecosystems that deliver continuous innovation and mass customization. It is booming despite the Great Stagnation since 2008 and it attracts the top talent. The prosperity of this economy has been accomplished not just from technology but from the fundamental changes in the way these organizations are led. The new leadership paradigm needed for the Creative Economy involves a "fundamental shift in how leaders think, speak and act in the workplace". The Creative Economy "thrives on the ethos of imagination, exploration, experiment, discovery and collaboration".

For a number of years I have been involved in a project on "Leading Knowledge Workers", in collaboration with Professor Amar Dev Amar from Stillman Business School in New Jersey. We have reviewed and synthesized an extensive literature on this subject, including more than 400 articles and books,[68] and the key findings revealed that:

- Leading knowledge organizations, where most value is created through creation and use of knowledge, is not the same as leading traditional organizations
- In the knowledge-based organization, where a variety of specialized, unre-lated or little-related tasks are executed, it is unlikely for one individual to effectively carry out the leadership responsibilities. Therefore, a knowledge organization will benefit if the formal leader eschews power and creates an environment of shared leadership
- In any organization where power use is low, such as a knowledge organi-zation, a leader with a "being in control of the outcomes" behavior, as reflected by "Internalizer" classification based on the scores on Rotter's[69] Internal-External scale, will increase one's likelihood of success
- The key source of the manager's power to lead in a knowledge organi-zation is his/her ability to create a mutualism (supportive and collabo-rative environment) that results in a benefit for all stakeholders of the knowledge work, i.e. the organization, the team members, the man-ager and others
- In a knowledge organization, lax control should be ubiquitous to build a fluid, distributed and trust-based community. Lax control of leaders and workers improves the performance and quality of outcomes of the organization
- Semblance of chaos in groups appears when a functioning leader frequently relinquishes power, which one of the other members of the group can take up. However, from chaos, a leadership homeostasis emerges and establishes an order according to which leadership becomes dormant and distributed in all group members
- Because of the practice of shared leadership in knowledge organizations, it may be detrimental to the organization if workers gave their allegiance to individuals, such as the current leaders. Instead, the workers should

avow their allegiance to a set of principles and values, such as the ethics, professional codes, legal codes, and the organizational mission and vision.

On the basis of this research we developed a model showing the individual and group process contexts in implementing leadership for innovation in organizations,[70] as shown in Figure 2.1. For effective leadership of knowledge workers, at the individual level, it is important to shed and unlearn the traditional leadership process (as well as the mindset), refrain from the use of formal power, adopt "Internalizer" behavior, expect and give no allegiance to individuals, and develop some tolerance for chaos. At organizational level, it is important to facilitate mutualism, devise lax control and develop a willingness to accept some chaos. Finally, it is important that leadership becomes available to all members throughout the organization. It is interesting to note that whilst diverse backgrounds and experiences of knowledge workers can facilitate creativity, it is

FIGURE 2.1 / The individual and group process contexts in leadership for innovation in organizations

important that a formal leader motivates everyone to provide leadership depending on one's skills, expertise and the situation. This requires a formal leader to relinquish formal power so that the leadership may emerge through interactions and informal networks.

Guidelines for Implementing Emergent Leadership in Practice

As a part of another project focused on implementing emergent leadership, my co-authors, Professor Amar and Carsten Hentrich, and I studied in depth how two knowledge-based organizations (CSC Germany and ANADIGICS) implemented emergent leadership practices. One result was a significant increase in profits. The key results from this study have been presented in our articles published in *Harvard Business Review*,[71] which received the Bright Idea Award from the Management of New Jersey Policy Research Organization (NJPRO) Foundation, and in the *Organizational Dynamics* journal.[72] We were astonished by the positive responses these articles received, especially from the practitioner communities. This gave us confidence that many practitioners are ready for this paradigm shift.

Drawing on the insights obtained from these two in-depth case studies, numerous consulting assignments I conducted over years in the public and private sectors, as well as extensive literature review, I have compiled the following guidelines for implementing emergent leadership practices, grouped in seven key areas as described in the rest of this section:

- Facilitating informal networks
- Organic growth based on expertise
- Developing caring organizational culture based on intrinsic motivation
- Collaboration and cross-fertilization of ideas between communities and teams
- Developing trust, allowing experimentation and tolerating mistakes
- Distribution of responsibility, decision-making and control, and voluntary leadership
- Senior management support.

These guidelines are generic and would not be equally applicable for each organization, but they provide a general guidance on different areas that could be addressed to move towards implementing emerging leadership practices. In order to provide very specific advice on actions to be taken in a particular organization, I developed the 6 Box Leadership Model, which will be described in Chapters 5 and 6.

Facilitating informal networks

There is an increasing understanding of the importance of informal networks, shaped by informal leaders and the most influential employees. Informal Network Analysis identifies the key nodes (informal leaders) in the informal network, with the assistance of specialist software, asking questions such as "To whom do you typically turn to get information in order to get your work done?" and "Who do you rely on to get input to complete your work?" Asking questions such as "Who knows what?" could be useful for information on relevant expertise; the knowledge and expertise of new recruits can be publicly advertised and displayed throughout an organization, and Wikis can be used for brainstorming and collaborative development of innovative ideas, projects and so on. Implementing changing staffing practices so employees spend some time working in different teams, offices, even geographical locations could build connections between teams/offices, support collaboration, innovation, decision-making and winning of new contracts.

Understanding that how people fit into networks is a matter of intentional behaviors (which can be influenced) rather than personality (which cannot be changed) means managers can then focus more on behavior than personality to find key nodes in the network. Key nodes – influential individuals – in the network do not focus exclusively on how to get things done, but on how to build relationships. They take time to systematically build their network. Leaders should allow this time in the work plans and training initiatives. Less connected workers should be encouraged to collaborate with better connected ones. Network development should be incorporated in organizational routines, processes, staffing initiatives and training activities.

In addition to using technology to support informal networks and collaboration, organizational context can be changed to support informal networks. For example:

- Formal organizational (top-down) structure (including strict rules and regulations) can impede informal networks, which can become insufficiently flexible to respond to new opportunities
- Informal networks can be constrained by functional or departmental boundaries and resulting silo mentality – this can be addressed by creating time and space for cross-functional collaboration (for example, cross-functional projects can be embedded into budgets and the planning process)
- Work management practices, such as putting people on projects to work together to leverage the effects of collaboration can be cost effective (for example, two people working on a six-month project that would take one person one year to complete)
- The value of relationships that develop outweighs the costs, and people have better morale, motivation, productivity and effectiveness when they collaborate
- Employee management practice (as part of HR strategy) could foster informal networks by, for example, hiring people who have demonstrated collaborative skills in the past or rewarding collaborative efforts
- Changing organizational culture by leaders publicly praising collaborative efforts, rewarding those who help others.

Organic growth based on expertise

Allowing organic growth based on expertise is another useful strategy. Leaders should be asking employees where their passion, interest and expertise lie. They should allow groups/communities of interests (passion) to form, self-organize and pursue their interests (aligned with overall organizational strategy). Once a critical mass is achieved in these groups, the participants should have the freedom to self-select a leader, and membership in these groups should be voluntary. It is useful to design and implement a platform for sharing and creating knowledge within the communities that enables virtual collaboration, where people take flexible leadership roles for innovative topics and thus develop their leadership skills. They learn to create innovative solutions by using their individual strengths and compensating for their weaknesses through synergy. In such groups, people will be motivated intrinsically, and become more engaged and passionate about their work.

Developing a caring organizational culture based on intrinsic motivation

A caring organizational culture – where people are valued and have opportunities for learning, development and career progression, can take pride in their success, and where their voice is heard – has a positive impact on organizational outcomes. In this environment, people have autonomy to pursue innovative ways of doing their work. Putting people more into the center, soliciting their views, asking them what their personal values are, where they want to go, where they see themselves in the company, and what their mission or vision about their personal careers are will also have a positive impact on performance. This approach nurtures intrinsic motivation for performance.

Collaboration and cross-fertilization of ideas between communities and teams

As discussed earlier in this chapter, interactions and collaboration are very important for creativity and innovation. Emergent leaders should endeavor to use teamwork for most projects, ensuring communication and collaboration between diverse teams for cross-fertilization of ideas. Regular meetings for team representatives should be organized and technology could be used to support communication and collaboration.

Developing trust, allowing experimentation and tolerating mistakes

Trust is the key aspect for distribution of authority and decision-making, and it should be developed systematically though open communication, collaborative brainstorming, valuing all ideas, facilitation, support, mentoring, coaching and so on. The latest research conducted by neuro-economist Paul Zak[73] shows that the more someone is given a sign of trust the more trustworthy they are in conduct.

Using an innovative champion – who will drive the initiative and keep developing trust amongst employees – for the project is important. It is crucial to allow employees to pursue their passion, experiment with innovative ideas and tolerate mistakes if these initiatives are not successful. Innovative solutions are needed for the increasingly complex and interconnected problems organizations face and can be achieved by allowing experimentation with new ideas and accepting mistakes. If mistakes are not made, it means that not enough is done and there is no experimentation with new ideas. When Sheryl Sandberg, Google's vice president, came to its co-founder Larry Page to apologize for a mistake that cost Google several million dollars, he responded: "I am so glad you made this mistake, because I want to run a company where we are moving too quickly and doing too much, not being too cautious and doing too little. If we don't have any of these mistakes, we are just not taking enough risks."[74]

Distribution of responsibility, decision-making and control, and voluntary leadership

Opportunities are missed if decision-making is too slow, if employees do not know where to turn to get a decision made, and if the cost of getting a simple decision approved is excessive. The risk is that an organization can become too reliant on too few decision-makers who probably do not have adequate knowledge and experience about day-to-day business operations. Allowing employees to volunteer decision-making if they have adequate knowledge and expertise will lead to faster and better decisions. Routine decisions can be delegated to administrative staff, while less routine decisions should be distributed and delegated to adequately experienced and qualified staff.

Executives often have limited understanding of informal networks around them. Investing time and effort to systematically understand these networks will help to distribute responsibility and decision-making. This is particularly crucial for strategic networks working on, for example, new product development, cross-functional partnerships, core processes and so on. Delegation of responsibilities instead of tasks leads to better performance. This shows employees that they are trusted to do their work well. By contrast, just delegating tasks can lead to micro-managing, which is disengaging, especially for knowledge workers.

Senior management support

Senior management support for implementing emergent, distributed practices is crucial. Fostering collaboration, communicating openly, praising success, rewarding team performance, focusing on people and developing a caring, purposeful culture are some of the strategies required. Rewarding groups rather than individuals and creating an environment based more on collaboration and shared responsibility leads to better performance, though individual contributions also need to be acknowledged.

When should emergent leadership style be implemented?

As discussed in this chapter, emergent leadership is particularly important for fostering innovation in knowledge-based organizations. Other, more specific conditions include situations when:[75]

- Business operates in a field that requires highly diverse knowledge, competencies and skills, which a small group of people at the top do not possess
- An entrepreneurial attitude is required among all members of the workforce to meet the requirements of business agility and to enable new market initiatives
- Creativity among the workforce needs to be enabled to drive innovation consistently
- Business is based on highly qualified knowledge workers
- The talent of each individual needs to be integrated in a way that activates intrinsic self-motivation and self-organization
- New market initiatives need to be started quickly and to be brought to the customers for a competitive advantage

- A high-quality culture, where highly qualified individuals give their best to achieve the maximum customer value, works as a differentiator in the market and needs to be implemented
- Building long-lasting relationships of trust among employees, managers, customers and partners is viewed as a basis for sustainability of the business
- Employee engagement is a key differentiator of the business, delivering high-quality products and services and surpassing customer expectations
- Command-and-control management style has been seen to cause reduced employee motivation, loss of talent and lower customer satisfaction.

New Leadership in Practice

In this last section of this chapter I have collected some examples of companies that have implemented emergent leadership practices. These advanced management practices have made all these companies not only a desirable place to work but they all also enjoy a sustainable financial performance.

Semco

Semco's world renowned CEO Ricardo Semler has transformed a small Brazilian family business into a highly profitable manufacturing, services and high-tech company using a democratic leadership style. He took over the business from his father in 1980 and the company has since grown to become 40 times larger, with profits increasing from US$4 million to US$160 million in over 20 years of Semler's leadership.[76] Some of his innovative management practices include:[77,78]

- There is an absence of formal organizational charts. Leaders are created only by the respect of the led. When organizational charts are needed, they are drawn in pencil and destroyed after use
- When people are hired or promoted, others in that unit can interview the candidates
- Workers make decisions previously made by their bosses
- Everyone has access to the company's books

- Shop-floor workers set their own productivity targets and schedules
- Working hours are flexible and every employee has a responsibility for setting and keeping track of them
- Employees can change and adapt their working environment in any way they want, and everyone can wear what they like at work
- Causing any pressure, fear, insecurity or disrespect to an employee is not acceptable
- Change is embedded in the organizational culture
- Participation and involvement are encouraged; everyone should make their voice heard
- Twice a year every employee evaluates their boss.

In designing innovative management practices for Semco, Ricardo Semler considered profound questions such as:

> Why are we able to answer emails on Sundays, but unable to go to the movies on Monday afternoon? Why can't we take the kids to work if we can take work home? Why do we think we are equipped to choose schools, doctors and mayors, but don't trust our capacity to lead ourselves at work? Why do we think intuition is so valuable and unique- and find no place for it as an official business instrument? Why do we agree that living well is living every moment, without reinforcing past or future – but then spend most of our work lives dealing with historical data and future budgets?[79]

HCL Technologies

When Vineet Nayar became CEO of Indian IT consultancy HCL Technologies in 2005, he started implementing a number of innovative management practices, such as:

- As employees create value for customers, employees come first and customers second. The traditional pyramid is inverted and managers at the top have to earn support and confidence from employees
- A culture of change is created by trust achieved through transparency
- Every employee rates their boss, their boss's boss and results are posted online
- The role of CEO is to ask questions, see others as a source of change and enable the organization to be self-run and self-governed. This makes

employees feel like the owners, makes them excited about their work and focused on innovation
- Electronic "tickets" are used to flag anything that requires action in the company, because employees who are secure and happy (in a caring culture) can better focus on customer success and would want to stay. This is based on the understanding that the best employees are the hardest to retain
- Strategic partnering with customers is formed and risks are shared.

During the first year of Vineet Nayar's leadership, both the retention rate and share value more than doubled. Performance indicators for HCL Technologies in the first four years of the new leadership style revealed that 70 of all major deals secured by HCL Technologies were won against the Big Four global IT companies, the number of customers grew 500 percent, employee attrition fell by almost 50 percent, there was a 70 percent increase in employee satisfaction according to an independent external survey, and revenues and operating income were increased 300 percent.[80]

Brand Velocity Inc.

Brand Velocity Inc. is an Atlanta-based management consultancy set up in 2001 by its CEO Jack Bergstrand, a former CIO of The Coca-Cola Company. The consultancy became a working laboratory for how to best organize for the Knowledge Age – inspired by Peter Drucker's *Post-Capitalist Society*.[81] Some of the innovative management practices implemented include:

- Using a points system instead of a hierarchical-based compensation system. The boss does not automatically earn a higher salary and incentive if he/she is not contributing as much as more junior people. Similarly, anyone in the company can earn more money than their boss and can earn equity in the company if they can successfully sell great work, deliver great work and recruit and develop a diverse group of employees who can do the same
- Compensation is calculated in a transparent way, and every employee has total access to financial statements and other corporate records
- The company implemented a "Traditionally Virtual" organizational structure. Corporate infrastructure (for example, systems such as email, time

tracking, intranet, accounting, payroll, the look and feel of business cards, and so on) is handled centrally with no variation. However, personal infrastructure (for example, phones, computers, printers, office requirements, supplies) is handled by the individual as long as decisions are secure and don't interfere with the person's ability to collaborate with others. This structure leads to more autonomy, as employees can choose and manage their own personal infrastructure and expenses. It leads to greater meritocracy, as personal infrastructure is not linked to hierarchical position in the formal organizational structure

- Brand Velocity Inc. is a commercial business with a social purpose, contractually donating a significant percentage of its revenues and operating profit to the Drucker Institute. This is consistent with its mission to help make the world a better place, through its strategy of helping the Drucker Institute achieve its socially focused mission and in its primary objective to successfully apply Peter Drucker's insights and values internally and externally, to stimulate effective management and responsible leadership
- Trust is achieved through shared values, a common process, transparent measures and institutionalized communication routines. It is also aided by the company's integrated commercial and social purpose, and its corporate value to be kind to and help one another.

Since its formation, Brand Velocity Inc. has enjoyed a significant growth, and strong levels of profitability. It was nominated for the Seven Smalls Jewels award by *Consulting* magazine[82] as one of "the hidden gems of the consulting profession".

Whole Foods Market

Whole Foods Market is a foods supermarket chain based in Austin Texas, focused on selling natural and organic products as well as protecting the environment. It was co-founded in 1978 by John Mackey, and it has experienced continuous growth, with revenue reaching more than US$12 billion at the end of 2012.[83] Core values include:

> Selling the highest quality natural and organic products available, satisfying and delighting customers, supporting team member happiness and

excellence, creating wealth through profit and growth, caring about communities and the environment, creating on-going win–win partnerships with suppliers and promoting the health of the stakeholders through healthy eating education.[84]

Some of the Whole Foods Market management practices that support these values include:

- Individual stores have sufficient authority to oversee store operations efficiently, and offer different products in partnerships with local suppliers
- Employees are encouraged to apply for promotions and available jobs for which they are qualified, which results in higher skill retention and decreases the need for supervision
- Each store values the team members and their extensive knowledge of the products
- Unlike their product offerings, employee training is unified across all stores resulting in increased motivation
- Employees have access to the online "Whole Foods Market University", an information portal that provides information on the core values of the company and helps further product knowledge
- When a new team member is hired, they are assigned a mentor
- In-store "team leaders" operate instead of "managers".

W.L. Gore & Associates

W.L. Gore & Associates was established in 1958 by Bill Gore. The company is focused on creating innovative, technology-driven products from medical devices to high-performance fabrics. The company has a unique culture and management practices, including the following features:[85]

- There is an absence of traditional organizational charts, chains of command and predetermined channels of communication
- Hands-on innovation is encouraged and those closest to a project are involved in decision-making
- Teams self-organize around opportunities and natural leaders emerge

- Organizational culture is based on belief in people and their abilities, freedom, cooperation, autonomy and synergy
- Associates (not employees) are employed for general work and are guided by their sponsors (not bosses). Associates commit to projects that match their skills and everyone can quickly earn credibility to define and drive projects
- Leaders often emerge naturally by demonstrating specialist knowledge, skill or experience that advance a business objective
- Employees adhere to basic principles set by Bill Gore:
  1. Fairness to each other and everyone with whom one comes into contact
  2. Freedom to encourage, help and allow other associates to grow in knowledge, skill, and scope of responsibility
  3. The ability to make one's own commitments and keep them
  4. Consultation with other associates before undertaking actions that could impact the reputation of the company.

W.L. Gore & Associates has grown continuously and currently has almost 7,000 employees in 24 countries, with annual sales close to US$2 billion, based on its reputation for good quality and innovative products.

CSC Germany

CSC Germany, a division of the leading global IT consulting and services firm, decided to empower employees and as a result of this managed to boost morale, engagement and productivity. After experiencing poor financial and market performance, the division realized in 2007 that a move away from a command-and-control style of leadership could reduce bureaucracy, improve communication and innovation, and boost performance and profits. Starting in the Enterprise Content Management unit, comprising 60 employees, the division implemented a new corporate strategy for decision-making, as the previous emphasis on hierarchy had slowed down the process.[86] The following practices were implemented:

- Whilst leadership had previously been focused on delegating tasks and monitoring results, the new priority is on instilling a sense of shared responsibility and motivation to succeed by freeing staff to work in teams on topic areas (known as "communities", working in areas such as innovation or strategy) according to what they feel best matches their interests and strengths

- Through the practice of "mutualism", community members take decisions collectively through discussion; they also agree their own community leaders, democratically and on a shifting basis as they see fit
- It became apparent that values such as trust, responsibility and innovation are far more likely to motivate staff than numerical goals or measurements. Achieving the numerical goals did happen, but as a result of leadership that engages and empowers staff rather than dictates
- A formal organizational structure with clear reporting lines remained in place, but it was overlaid by an informal structure of the communities based on talents and skills. The whole focus shifted towards forming an environment based on collaboration and shared responsibility
- The distribution of responsibility, decision-making and control, as well as the mentoring and coaching system that was set up to support this strategy, lead to more motivated and energized employees. Perhaps paradoxically, leaders realized that while it may not initially be easy to give up power, more power and influence are gained subsequently by letting go.

The impact on profits has been very impressive, leading CSC Germany to extend the practices to another unit – IT Architecture. For the first year of the new leadership paradigm, the profit margin target achievement was 151 percent, and for the following year it was 238 percent. The overall long-term target achievement over the period was 205 percent. The staff grew by 13 people during the first year, representing an increase in resource utilized of 36 percent for that year, and the resource utilized grew a further 18 percent in the subsequent year.

When CSC Germany's senior management extended the strategy to the IT Architecture unit, results were even better. Utilization target for that unit was 93.5 percent in the first year. Only six months after implementing the new leadership culture, 295 percent of the performance target was achieved.

Zappos.com

Zappos.com is an online shoe and apparel shop based in Henderson, Nevada. It was founded by Nick Swinmurn in 1999. This hugely innovative company has enjoyed steady growth, achieving over US$1 billion in annual sales only nine years after it was established. In 2009, Amazon purchased Zappos.com for 10 million Amazon shares, worth almost US$928 million at the time. Its success is based on a unique company culture that is well illustrated by its CEO Tony Hsieh: "Personally I cringe at the word 'leader'. It's more about getting people do what they're passionate about and putting them in the right context or setting. They're the ones doing the hard work."[87] Examples of management practices implemented in Zappos.com include:

- There is a non-hierarchical, flat organizational structure
- A lot of decision-making is decentralized
- People interact with each other at all levels, develop friendships, and managers spend about 20 percent of their time socializing with people they manage
- Delighting customers is central to the culture. They offer 365-day return policy with free shipping both ways, 24/7 customer phone lines, live online help, and customer product ratings
- The focus of the culture is the happiness of employees and customers, and creating a place for work that is fun
- The main premise is that employees will achieve success by being given freedom and focusing on culture and happiness rather than sales targets and financial goals
- Zappos will pay new hires $2,000 to quit on their first day to weed out employees who may not be the right fit or have the passion required for the job
- Employees are expected to be humble, innovative, learn and grow continuously, have open and honest communications and be passionate about their work
- The interview process is long and sometimes even the CEO participates in order to ensure the culture fit of a new employee.

The above examples of successful companies that have implemented emergent leadership practices show that it is possible to do well financially whilst doing good for all stakeholders: employees, customers, shareholders, suppliers, communities and the environment. There are thousands of less well-known companies all over the world that have moved away from traditional hierarchical management and leadership practices and achieved The Management Shift, but unfortunately they still represent a minority. With a growing evidence base about the benefits of emergent leadership practices, and increasingly louder pleas from people who understand the benefits, there is a hope that in time such inspirational companies will become the norm. This would lead to many benefits for individuals, organizations, communities and entire societies.

SEVEN REFLECTION POINTS

1. If you are the leader, do you feel you inspire and energize others to achieve amazing outcomes?
2. If you are the leader, what three changes could you implement or what three initiatives could you take to inspire your colleagues even more?
3. Do you feel your boss is leading using traditional or emergent leadership approaches?
4. If you are led by a leader using traditional leadership approaches, how does this make you feel?
5. Can you recall a situation where either you or someone else used a traditional leadership approach that created a specific problem? Could this situation be avoided in the future by using a different leadership style?
6. Can you envisage the benefits of implementing some of the emergent leadership approaches discussed in this chapter in your organization?
7. If you could lead any organization, which organization would that be and why? How would that make you feel?

3

Insights from the Leading Management Thinkers: from the *Why* and *What* to the *How*

KEY INSIGHTS FROM THIS CHAPTER

This chapter provides answers to the following key questions:

- Why are the *why*, the *what* and the *how* of The Management Shift so important?
- Is there a consensus amongst the key management thinkers on the key management trends emerging?
- What are the key emerging trends in the area of strategy that lead to better results?
- Why do traditional approaches to strategy not work anymore?
- Why does short-term profit maximization lead to problems over the longer term?
- What are the key emerging trends in the area of innovation?
- Why is experimentation so important for innovation?
- How can a focus on people and culture lead to more innovation?
- What are the key ideas emerging in the area of engagement?
- How can employees become more engaged when they find their higher purpose?
- What leadership styles foster innovation and engagement?

The *Why*, the *What* and the *How* of The Management Shift

Management innovation, or The Management Shift, has been attracting the attention of many leading management thinkers and practitioners for decades. Whilst in the past, big radical ideas for moving away from traditional management approaches have been rather isolated efforts to make a positive difference, in the last few years the number of books and articles focusing on management innovation has been increasing steadily.

This chapter provides a summary of the key ideas on management innovation from the leading management thinkers that are related to the ideas presented in this book. The amount of published work on management innovation is growing continuously as we are approaching the tipping point for such a momentous shift and it is beyond the scope of this chapter to provide a detailed guide. My aim is to raise the awareness of the leading edge thinking and illustrate how this thinking supports and complements my work presented in this book.

The *why*, the *what* and the *how* of The Management Shift are important. The *why* is about the purpose; it is about the reasons for moving away from traditional management approaches and implementing emerging management practices. In an organizational context, the *why* is the reason for an organization to exist, and this is a very powerful driving force. The *what* of management innovation is about describing new management approaches that organizations need to implement to achieve sustainable value creation for all stakeholders. The *how* is about how to implement these new management approaches in practice, turn theory into practice, and put knowledge into action.

The importance of the *why* was discussed in Chapter 1, where I considered how important it is to focus any work and business on a higher purpose which is the driving force for excellence and success. The importance of *why* is also well illustrated in a widely known book by Simon Sinek, *Start with Why*,[1] showing how most successful organizations start with purpose, and then figure out what they need to do and how to achieve that purpose.

The *what* of management innovation has been discussed in Chapter 2 and it will be addressed in this chapter as well as in Chapter 4, where a 5 Level Emergent Leadership Model will be presented. The *how* of management innovation will be presented in Chapters 5 and 6 where the 6 Box Leadership Model and its practical application will be explored.

Most management scholars focus on the *why* or the *what* of management innovation, and examples of *how* to actually implement emerging management practices are rather rare; this is one of the key contributions of this book. The moral philosopher Dov Seidman argues in his book *How*[2] that due to the digital revolution everyone operates within a totally transparent world, where openness, ethics, connection and collaboration are crucial. In such an environment, how companies conduct their business is crucial. That includes how they treat their customers, employees, suppliers, society and the environment. Profitability depends on trust, purpose, reputation and values and these should be embedded in everything a company does. This view is reinforced by many other scholars, as will be illustrated in the next section.

Leading Management Thinkers Sing the Same Tune

As part of my academic research, I have been involved in reviewing relevant management literature for more than two decades. I have supervised many PhD students, who have helped me learn what I could not discover on my own. I am also honored and privileged to have a large professional network, which includes some of the leading thinkers whose books are also included in this review. I learn a lot from conversations with them. In addition, as part of my research for this book, I looked at the Thinkers50 lists[3] published in 2003, 2005, 2007, 2009, 2011 and 2013, where 50 leading management thinkers were listed for those particular years. I then searched for their key publications, reviewed their main ideas and selected those that I thought were most relevant for the purpose of this book. Another useful source of information has been the blog by management author Steve Denning[4] on *Forbes*.

As this book is mainly aimed at practitioners, I did not use academic articles extensively for the review presented in this chapter. However, the key themes and findings presented here are firmly supported by academic literature, as evidenced in the synthesis of extensive academic literature I produced in collaboration with Professor Amar from Stillman Business School in New Jersey.[5,6]

I grouped the key ideas reviewed in this chapter into sections related to Strategy, Innovation and Engagement, as these categories cover the main drivers for organizational success.

The perception of strategy is changing

Traditional corporate strategy literature is largely based on Michael Porter's notion of sustainable competitive advantage. Whist there are obvious advantages of competing in ways that others cannot imitate, the competitive landscape is changing fast and there are few companies today that can maintain competitive advantage sustainably. This is largely caused by the digital revolution, globalization, unpredictability of competitors, the increasing power of customers, fewer barriers to entry and constant changes in business environments. As Rita Gunter McGrath shows in her book *The End of Competitive Advantage*,[7] as competitive advantages disappear in less than a year for many companies, they need to constantly start, keep refining and exploiting many "transient competitive advantages" at once. A portfolio of such temporary advantages can enable companies to sustain a strong position over a long time. This view is echoed by other authors including Richard D'Aveni,[8] Kathleen Eisenhardt[9] and Yves Doz.[10] Other trends influencing the area of strategy include focusing on adaptability and resilience,[11,12] transparency,[13,14] networking, collaboration and acting globally.[15,16]

An important aspect of the shift in thinking on strategy is the notion that delighting customers should be the key strategic priority. The idea was advocated by Peter Drucker decades ago, when he stated, "There is only one valid definition of a business purpose: to create a customer",[17] but it has only recently started to receive the wider attention it deserves. For example, Roger Martin, in his book *Fixing the Game*,[18] argues that some of the remedial steps to repair the American capitalist system should include: putting the customer first, rethinking executive compensation and making boards accountable. Similarly, Steve Denning,[19] Ranjav Gulati,[20] Frederic Reichheld and Rob Markey,[21] amongst many other authors, state that firms need to become customer-centric. This is particularly important as, with more widespread use of social technologies, customers have more power than ever and can broadcast their opinion of any business to a far-reaching network, as shown by Charlene Li in her book *Open Leadership*.[22]

Long-term orientation of organizational strategy is another important emerging trend. This means that, in addition to focusing on providing value to customers, companies need to focus on values and higher purpose,[23,24,25] do good for the society along with making profits[26,27] and move away from maximizing shareholder value as the main reason for the company's exist-ence.[28] In his book *Post-Capitalist Society*,[29] Peter Ducker warned that man-aging a company to maximize shareholder value means "damaging if not destroying the wealth-producing capacity of the business". He believed that an organization should define "an organizational purpose that goes beyond next quarter financial results and goes beyond maximization of shareholder wealth". When employees believe in a higher purpose that is at the core of everything the company does, they will do their best at work. This is the essence of the *why*.

Rosabeth Moss Kanter, summarizing interviews of more than 350 key executives in major corporations all over the world, provides encouraging evidence that businesses that are agile, reactive to market changes and responsive to customers' needs are also progressive and socially responsible human communities.[30] They simultaneously create innovation, profits, growth and social good, which is great proof that companies can do well whilst doing good.

Mass-scale innovation or transformations of markets become possible using digital platforms and eco-systems of partners, as described by Nicholas Vitalari and Haydn Shaughnessy in their book *The Elastic Enterprise*.[31] For example, Google operates as a platform interconnected with an eco-system of Search Engine Optimization (SEO) services. SEO services integrate different platforms such as Google, Twitter and Facebook and this relationship is effective as well as mutually dependent. Free knowledge flows, liberalization, improved technology and collaboration are transforming the modus operandi of many organizations, as related by John Hagel III et al. in their book *The Power of Pull*.[32]

In summary, the key emerging ideas in the context of strategy include:

- *Transient competitive advantage instead of competitive advantage* – as discussed in Chapter 1, a useful metaphor is running an organization as a sailing boat with adaptable strategy rather than as a less maneuvrable supertanker
- *Long-term orientation* – moving away from focusing on share price maximization on a quarterly basis will lead to better financial performance over a longer period, and will allow organizations to give more back to the community
- *Focus on customers* – focusing on providing value to customers instead of share price maximization will lead to higher share prices, increased profit, growth and so on, as customers are the only reason for a company's existence
- *Focus on higher purpose* – using a higher purpose as the driving force for business will lead to better financial performance over the longer term, in addition to making this world a better place. What more could any organizational leader want to achieve?
- *Building alliances amongst stakeholders* – collaborative work with customers, suppliers and other stakeholders leads to more value creation and improved innovation. This can be achieved at a national and, more increasingly, a global level.

Innovation as the lifeline for organizations

The importance of innovation for sustainable organizational wealth creation is obvious and well documented. According to Michael Porter, "Innovation is the central issue in economic prosperity".[33] Similarly, in his book *Circle of Innovation*,[34] Tom Peters maintains that innovation has to become a top-line obsession. In a Harvard Business School blog on innovation,[35] Scot Kirsner claims that whilst in the past explorers searched for the famous city of El Dorado where everything was made of gold, today innovation is the new El Dorado for organizations. This is well illustrated by Barack Obama:

> …cutting the deficit by gutting our investments in innovation and education is like lightening an overloaded airplane by removing its engine. It may make you feel like you're flying high at first, but it won't take long before you feel the impact.[36]

However, the level of innovation is not determined by the amount of money spent on Research & Development. It is determined to a large extent by organizational culture, mindset of employees and their interactions, leadership style and organizational processes that foster innovation. These are all captured in the 6 Box Leadership Model, as detailed in Chapter 5. The importance of people aspects for innovation is echoed by Steve Jobs, who said:

> Innovation has nothing to do with how many R&D dollars you have. When Apple came up with the Mac, IBM was spending at least 100 times more on R&D. It's not about money. It's about the people you have, how you're led, and how much you get it.[37]

When I researched the key ideas on innovation emerging from the leading management thinkers, few names stood out from the rest. Harvard Business School Professor Clayton Christensen's work provides some of the most influential ideas around innovation. In his classic book *The Innovator's Dilemma*,[38] he identifies the problem of disruptive innovations (an example might be digital photography which, as quality and resolution have improved, has marginalized traditional photography), which usually emerge at the low end of markets, seemingly unprofitable and unpromising, but in time can cause many successful companies to fail if they ignore such disruptive innovation. In his subsequent book *The Innovator's Solution*,[39] Clayton Christensen and his co-author Michael Raynor offer advice on how to recognize and react to disruptive innovations that lead to a new value proposition. An interesting idea proposed in this book was that resources, processes and values are foundations of organizational capabilities. This idea was further explored and developed when the 6 Box Leadership Model was created.

In his more recent book *The Innovator's DNA*,[40] Clayton Christensen and his co-authors Jeff Dyer and Hal Gregersen identify five skills that comprise the innovator's DNA. They include: practicing associative thinking by making connections among various ideas from different areas (I refer to this as "connecting the dots"); asking questions; observing what people do, how they do it and why; networking with diverse people (this point is important as complexity theory explains how innovation emerges from interactions amongst people with different backgrounds); and experimenting with ideas (I have seen in many companies the benefits of trial and error, assuming mistakes are forgiven).

The importance of experimentation for innovation is well explained in Seth Godin's book *Poke the Box*.[41] The key premise is that one should experiment with the new idea when "the cost of being wrong is less than the cost of doing nothing". To make the new idea successful, one should "have the guts and passion to ship". That says it all: the best ideas will not succeed if the innovator does not have the courage, the belief in success and the passion to launch the idea to the market. Without taking some risks it is not likely that an amazing product or service will be conceptualized and successfully launched. In his book *The Silver Lining*,[42] Scott Anthony shows how the risk of innovating can be reduced by experimenting quickly, cheaply and strategically. Similarly, Vijay Govindarajan and Chris Trimble argue in their book *The Other Side of Innovation*[43] that each innovation should be viewed as an experiment driven by hypothesis, and the focus should be on learning quickly and inexpensively.

Another trend in innovation is co-creation: collaborative or open innovation. Fuelled by advances in technology and globalization, collaborative innovation efforts are everywhere. As C.K. Prahalad and M.S. Krishnan explain in their bestseller *The New Age of Innovation*,[44] to foster innovation, organizations should seek expertise everywhere, both within an organization and throughout the world. This is echoed by Vijay Vaitheeswaran in *Need, Speed and Greed*,[45] where he shows how innovation is now becoming more open and effective and how democratization has changed its processes. In his book *Open Innovation*,[46] Henry Chesborough shows how the open innovation model allows new ideas to emerge from outside the organization, utilizing teamwork with industry peers as well as collaboration with customers and suppliers. Similarly to open innovation, Crowdstorming is the latest trend described by S. Abrahamson et al. in *Crowdstorm*,[47] whereby online space is utilized for mass brainstorming, problem-solving and innovation, which is similar to mass-collaboration *Macrowikinomics* advocated by Don Tapscott and Anthony Williams.[48] As customers are increasingly using social technologies they can amplify positive and negative messages about products and services they receive. To keep pace with today's connected customers, every company needs to become a connected company and engage and collaborate with employees, partners and customers, changing how work is done.[49]

A counter-intuitive idea gaining momentum is to do a "Reverse Innovation".[50] As the world economy shifts, the nature of innovation is also changing. So, instead of focusing on innovation in developed countries, companies create new products for and in emerging economies and then they sell these products in developed markets as well (for example, Renault designed a low-cost version of its model Logan for Eastern European markets, which then later sold in Western European markets).

An important aspect of innovation is the predominant leadership style in an organization. Not every leadership style is conducive for innovation. In general, traditional leadership styles based on hierarchical command and control will stifle innovation. Emergent leadership approaches based on autonomy, transparency, openness and collaboration will lead to more innovation as well as better engagement. I compared and contrasted these leadership styles in detail in Chapter 2. For the purpose of this chapter, I have selected a few ideas from authors focusing on leadership and innovation. For example, in their book *Leading for Innovation and Organizing For Results*,[51] Frances Hesselbein, Marshall Goldsmith and Iain Somerville argue that trying to control everything is the certain way to stifle innovation. Diversity as well as collaboration – rather than competition – between business units is essential for innovation. As every great idea requires a period of incubation, it is normally the CEO's task to protect the start-up until it is mature enough to go to the market. Innovation is a culture rather than an event, so organizations and leaders fostering an innovative culture will experience more benefits of innovation.

To complete this review of ideas in the area of innovation, I have selected a few publications that advocate the application of Eastern philosophies. We can be truly innovative and achieve amazing things in life if we practice integrative thinking, have an open and inquisitive mind, integrate different disciplines and focus on the whole brain thinking.[52] The authors of *Jugaad Innovation*[53] argue that the Jugaad (the Hindu term for a clever solution in the situation of adversity) attitude allows someone to achieve almost anything with few resources, if determination and ingenuity is used. The key ideas of this approach include: seeking opportunities, doing more with less, thinking and acting flexibly (with an open mind), keeping things simple and following the heart (I would add, following intuition as well). This "bottom-up" approach to innovation is in contrast to the Western structured, top-down R&D approach.

Embedding innovation in organizational culture and processes is a very effective way to generate many concurrent innovative ideas. In the bestselling *Ninja Innovation*,[54] Gary Shapiro argues that executives could learn from the ancient Japanese martial arts warriors *ninjas* and utilize their ethos, strategies and tactics to achieve business goals and foster innovation. The key elements of this approach include: focusing on victory, building the right team, taking risks, preparing for battle by being focused and disciplined, being flexible in strategic planning, being ethical, knowing innovations have positive influence beyond the company's boundaries, surprising competitors, and being aware that you should "innovate or die".

There is also a growing number of published works on utilizing the Buddhist philosophy for fostering innovation.[55,56] This is articulated by

Juliette Melton of IDEO, one of the world's leading design consultancies. Speaking at the second annual Buddhist Geeks Conference (which examines the intersection between the Western technology-focused world and the ancient philosophy of Buddhism), Melton said that in the process of innovation she uses Buddhist philosophy which helps her to be mindful and pay attention to the present moment, being with what is and being open to change. She related the R&D process of prototyping to the Buddhist practice of non-attachment, emphasizing how innovators must stay open to the reality of the design process, even when 499 ideas end up on the floor.[57]

In summary, the key emerging ideas related to innovation include:

- *Awareness of the growing importance of innovation* – in the increasingly global, complex and changing business environment, innovation is the lifeline for most organizations
- *Awareness of the importance of people and culture for innovation, not just R&D investments* – embedding innovation in organizational culture and processes, and fostering an innovative mindset amongst employees are important enablers for innovation
- *Awareness of the power of disruptive innovation* – disruptive innovations, often facilitated by changes in technology, need to be recognized and action taken to achieve transient competitive advantage
- *Awareness of the type of leadership style needed for fostering innovation* – traditional command-and-control based leadership style stifles innovation and creativity. Emergent leadership approaches based on autonomy and collaboration enable innovation
- *Awareness of the importance of experimentation for innovation* – taking some risks, experimenting with new ideas quickly and inexpensively, and giving time and resources to employees to try new ideas enable more innovation
- *Collaborative or open innovation* – with globalization and developments in technology, organizations should search for and utilize expertise everywhere, within and outside the organization as well as anywhere in the world

- *Reverse innovation* – instead of focusing on innovation in developed countries, companies could create new products for and in emerging economies and then sell these products in developed markets as well
- *Application of Eastern philosophies to innovation* – applying aspects of Eastern philosophies, such as mindfulness, flexibility, openness to change, embracing risk and focusing the mind on success, to innovation can lead to an increase in innovation.

Unleashing engagement and passion for work

Given all the challenges that organizations are facing today, from complexity, unpredictability, pace of change to globalization and competition from emerging markets, building highly engaged workplaces is becoming more important than ever before. At the same time, the latest Gallup research study[58] on global engagement shows that currently only 13 percent of employees worldwide are engaged in their jobs. According to a study conducted by management consultants HayGroup,[59] UK workers are the least engaged among Western European countries and 82 percent of UK C-level executives regard low levels of engagement as one of the greatest threats facing their business.

Engagement is a behavior (i.e. it can be influenced) that employees exhibit at work to a greater or lesser extent.[60] To make people more engaged an organization needs to create an environment in which employees will feel happy, passionate, inspired, valued and motivated to do their best beyond just doing their job. All global statistics show that very few organizations are able to create such an environment.

Why is it so important to have engaged employees? Engaged employees are consistently and continuously emotionally invested in and focused on creating value for organizations; they feel passionate about the work they are doing and feel proud to work for their organization. Engaged employees have higher morale and are more productive, they are loyal, more creative and innovative and, most importantly, they are prepared to "go the extra mile" to delight a

Engaged employees are prepared to "go the extra mile"

customer. In the next few paragraphs I have summarized some of the latest thinking around engagement.

One of the good practices to engage employees is to get them involved in strategic planning. If they are involved in planning the battle, they will battle the plan. This is echoed by Jim Haudan in his book *The Art of Engagement*".[61] When organizations announce new strategies without engaging employees, these strategies almost always die quickly. It is much better to enable employees to discuss new strategies openly, where they can safely voice their ideas.

One of the powerful driving forces for engaging people is to find the meaning and purpose in the work they are doing. In his book *Meaning, Inc.*,[62] Gurnek Bains argues that employees want their work to be significant and to make a contribution to society. They have a sense of meaning when their activities relate to something purposeful and they connect their values and beliefs to what their organization is doing. Similarly, Jeremy Kourdi and Jacqueline Davies[63] claim that successful HR strategies for engaging employees include developing talent, providing flexibility, offering consistent guidance and pursuing meaningful goals. This is important as employees want growth, fair treatment and the sense that they make a difference. In their book *The Why of Work*,[64] Dave and Wendy Ulrich show how people can coordinate their actions to create purpose for themselves, value for stakeholders and hope for humanity by identifying their strengths, establishing a culture of values, instilling flexibility and resilience and adding meaning to their work.

Leadership style is crucial for engaging employees. Traditional leadership approaches based on hierarchical command and control will be very disengaging. By contrast, emerging leadership approaches based on autonomy, distribution of authority and decision-making, collaboration and transparency will help create an engaging work environment. As Dan Pontefract effectively argues in his book *Flat Army*,[65] command and control is obsolete and fosters employee disengagement, whilst the "flat army" approach draws on openness, sharing, harmony and trust – fostering engagement.

Leaders should engage in meaningful conversations, and even storytelling,[66] with employees to engage them and bring new opportunities,[67] to instil values, to help employees envision a successful future, and to collaborate and share knowledge. They should also motivate employees to believe in a better tomorrow and help them pursue this vision,[68] and even "enchant"[69] employees using trust, honesty and openness to change their "hearts, minds and actions" and support a good cause. The most successful leaders gain more power and inspire engagement by granting power to their subordinates;[70] they use a sense of purpose to motivate their employees to go beyond the call of duty[71] and to transmit positive emotions.[72]

In their *Harvard Business Review* article "Creating the Best Workplace on Earth",[73] Rob Goffee and Gareth Jones present the findings of their research on what employees require to be most productive. The key six findings include: letting people be themselves; transparent communication; magnifying people's strengths; standing for more than shareholder value – standing for something meaningful; deriving meaning from daily activities; and having rules people can believe in – moving away from bureaucratization. Employees can improve performance and engagement by focusing on their strengths[74,75] as well as focusing on their "Mojo"[76] or positive engagement that comes from the joy and meaning that people derive from each activity. This is in line with "The Progress Principle",[77] which says that "of all the positive events that influence inner work life, the single most powerful is progress in meaningful work."

Meaning, appreciation and support will lead to better engagement as well as more joy and creativity at work. Furthermore, companies that pay attention to their employees' physical, emotional, mental and spiritual needs are more successful than those that don't, and fulfilling employees' spiritual needs is achieved by finding meaning in their work.[78] As Chip Conley says in his book *Peak*,[79] when you find the heart of your business and your calling, your entire working life becomes a peak experience. Focusing on higher purpose also applies to sales professionals, as described by Lisa Earle McLeod in her inspirational book *Selling with Noble Purpose*.[80] Most successful sales leaders succeed because "a noble sales purpose" (NSP) motivates them to improve their customers' lives and make a positive contribution, and that brings meaning to their work.

In summary, the key emerging ideas related to engagement include:

- *Awareness of the growing importance of engagement* – with global engagement figures at very low levels and with a plethora of evidence on the detrimental effects of unengaged employees, increasing employee engagement is crucial for the sustainable prosperity of any organization
- *Awareness of the importance of a nourishing culture for engaging employees* – it is apparent that an organizational culture based on care, trust, joy, openness and autonomy plays a crucial role in fostering employee engagement
- *Nurturing employees' strengths* - focusing on and nurturing the talents of employees will support engagement
- *Awareness of the importance of finding meaning and higher purpose to inspire engagement* – finding a higher purpose greater than any individual employee and finding a meaning in any job will lead to better engagement
- *Awareness of the need to use emerging leadership approaches to inspire engagement* – emerging leadership approaches based on autonomy, distribution of power and decision-making, collaboration and transparency will create an environment that will support employee engagement.

Common Themes Emerging

Most leading thinkers passionately advocate the need for new management approaches and a new mindset. They might be using different terms but the essence of the message is the same. They recognize that traditional management approaches do not work anymore and that the time has now come for a major shift in the way organizations are managed. Many leading management thinkers are passionately calling for a different reality that will lead to a different future and more prosperity for everyone.

It is apparent that the key principles of emerging management form the common denominator that connects different approaches and views from leading authors. Some of these new principles include: collaboration, openness, trust, autonomy, experimentation, distribution of authority and decision-making, higher purpose and meritocracy. Many authors provide examples of organizations that live and breathe new management practices, and some are providing evidence on the qualitative and quantitative (financial) benefits[81,82] of embracing these new management approaches.

Companies are moving away from focusing on efficiency towards co-creating value through alliances with suppliers, partners and customers. Hierarchical command and control is being replaced by communication, collaborative value creation, innovation and shared responsibilities. In *What Matters Now*,[83] Gary Hamel summarizes well what is needed in organizations to survive today: values (including trust), innovation (that should be a responsibility of every individual), adaptability (that leads to evolutionary advantage), passion (rising human spirit at work) and ideology (based on freedom and self-determination).

The common themes emerging from the literature were also articulated at a gathering of leading management thinkers at the Global Peter Drucker Forum 2013.[84] The themes were summarized well by Steve Denning in a *Forbes* article:[85]

- Most large and important organizations are in trouble, mainly because of the way they are managed. Line structures do not work anymore, and "fear-based environments" inhibit innovation
- New, better organizational forms are emerging, including self-organizing learning networks that create value, as well as open, creative and adaptive ecosystems that foster collaboration and innovation
- Companies should not be managed exclusively on the basis of monetary values; they should also focus on purpose and people
- Managers should become enablers of self-organizing teams and networks, inside and outside the organization
- Working in short iterative cycles, allowing autonomy and experimentation and getting direct feedback from customers

- Values and principles such as transparency, continuous improvement, sustainability, innovation and meeting customers' needs are becoming increasingly important
- Communications are becoming interactive and multi-dimensional, horizontal communication is becoming more important and mutual respect for viewpoints and expertise are paramount.

If most organizations become genuinely authentic, trustworthy, transparent, purposeful and caring, replacing pyramids with networks, command and control with collaboration and autonomy, and fear and authority with higher purpose and authentic care, many of the global economic problems we are now facing will be diminished. People will become happier, more engaged and more passionate about their work; there will be more innovation and value creation for all stakeholders. Wouldn't it be wonderful if such organizations became the norm rather than the exception?

There is no doubt that the world of management is changing rapidly, and The Management Shift on a large scale is inevitable. There is an overwhelming consensus about this shift amongst the leading management thinkers. There is agreement about the importance of the *why* – a higher purpose that drives exceptional value creation. There is also agreement about the *what* of management innovation, and this has been summarized in this chapter. However, the *how* of management innovation is still in its infancy and this is the main contribution of the next three chapters of this book.

SEVEN REFLECTION POINTS

1. Does your organization use a transient competitive strategy approach? If so, what are the benefits experienced?
2. Does your organization have long-term orientation or is it focused on short-term maximization of profit?
3. Is focusing on delighting customers the core part of your organizational strategy?

4. Do you or your boss use an appropriate leadership style to foster innovation and engagement?
5. Is there a caring culture in your organization? If so, what benefits do you and others experience as a result of this culture?
6. Do you feel engaged at work? If so, could that be because you have found the higher purpose in your work?
7. Do you feel your organization nurtures its employees' strengths? If so, what benefits have you experienced as a result of this practice?

4

The Emergent Leadership Model: From the Stagnating to the Unbounded Culture

This chapter provides answers to the following key questions:

- How are individual consciousness and organizational cultures interconnected?
- What are the five levels of individual development?
- What are the typical emotions, keywords used, energy levels, thought and language patterns of employees and leaders at each level of individual development? (This chapter describes five levels of development for individuals and organizations.)
- What are the five levels of organizational culture development that correspond to specific individual levels?
- What is the typical behavior of leaders and employees at each organizational level?
- What are the work implications and organizational outcomes at each organizational level?
- Why is it so important for individuals and organizations to move from Level 3 to Level 4?
- What are the key triggers and processes for shifting to Level 4 culture?

Evolution of the Human Consciousness and Organizational Cultures

For many years, I have had a passion for personal development. As part of my research into this area, and its links to organizational performance, I have investigated in detail what occurs at both individual and collective levels in terms of individual mindset, behavior, beliefs and actions, leadership style and organizational outcomes. I studied various aspects of psychology, organizational behavior, complexity science, neuroscience, leadership theories, economics and so on. Based on this research, I produced the Emergent Leadership Model, which describes five levels that individuals go through during their development and corresponding organizational culture, as described in the following section. Some of the sources that have informed and influenced the development of this model include: Ken Wilber's integral theory of consciousness,[1] Jane Loevinger's stages of ego development,[2] Abraham Maslow's hierarchy of needs,[3] Spiral dynamics model,[4] Jane Loevinger's stages of ego development,[5] Susan Cook-Greuter's Leadership Development Framework,[6] Richard Barrett's Seven Levels of Consciousness Model,[7] Bruce Schneider's Energy Leadership Model,[8] Lawrence Kohlberg's stages of moral development[9] and research related to *Tribal Leadership*.[10] It is outside the purpose of this book to review all these theories and models in detail, though I have mapped the stages of some of these key models to the five levels of the Emergent Leadership Model, as detailed in Appendix 2.

The key insights from all these models and theories reveal that we, as individuals, go through different levels or stages of development during our lifetime. They are better described as a spiral ascension than as discrete steps, though for the sake of visual simplicity I represent them as stages in the Model. We cannot skip developmental levels; we can move up only one level at a time, and it usually takes years to move from one to the next. Once we are anchored at a certain level we can go back down to any lower level temporarily but we are able to bounce back.

A level that individuals in a particular organization (or part of it) are predominantly anchored at will influence organizational culture, and vice versa. As individual development levels are evolving, corresponding organizational cultures are evolving too. Any organization can have pockets of groups and cultures at different levels, though a predominant organizational culture will have a large influence on the success of an entire organization, as discussed later in this chapter.

The relationship between individuals and organizational culture can be explained by the concept of a *holon*. This concept was coined by Arthur Koestler in his book *The Ghost in the Machine*.[11] A holon is something that is at the same time both a whole and a part. Holons exist simultaneously as self-contained wholes in relation to their subordinate parts as well as dependent parts when considered from the inverse direction. Humans, organizations and their cultures can be considered as holons. Individuals are a whole system, but also part of a larger system such as an organization, which is part of a larger system such as society and so on. As a holon is embedded in larger wholes, it is influenced by and influences these larger wholes. And because a holon also contains subsystems, or parts, it is similarly influenced by and influences these parts. Information between smaller and larger systems flows bi-directionally.

This approach enables us to appreciate that individuals and organizations are mutually dependent, and they influence each other in both directions. For example, if individuals in an organization are predominantly at a high developmental level, the organizational culture will be more conducive to high levels of engagement, performance and innovation. And similarly, if most individuals are anchored at a lower level, this healthy dynamic is less likely.

Individuals and organizations are mutually dependent

Furthermore, if we look at an organization through the lens of complexity theory and consider an organization to be a living or complex adaptive system rather than a mechanistic sum of parts (see Chapters 1 and 2), we can explain and understand the mutual interdependence of an organization and its individual components. When employees interact as human agents they will influence other agents, and new organizational forms (including culture and innovation) will emerge as a result of these interactions.

The latest insights in social neuroscience lead to similar conclusions. For example, in their influential *Harvard Business Review* article "Social Intelligence and the Biology of Leadership",[12] Daniel Goleman and Richard Boyatzis discuss what happens in the brain when people interact. They show how when leaders engage in empathetic behavior, they can literally alter the chemistry in their own and in the brains of people around them. In such interactions, individual minds become merged into a single system, and the best leaders are able to leverage the system of brain interconnectedness.

Figure 4.1 shows how individual traits, organizational culture and processes mutually influence each other. Individual values, beliefs, assumptions and mental models (individual's representations of the world and their experiences) can be changed through personal development. That leads to changes in the individual mindset, eliminating self-limiting beliefs (subjective, usually negative beliefs that can hold us back), increased emotional

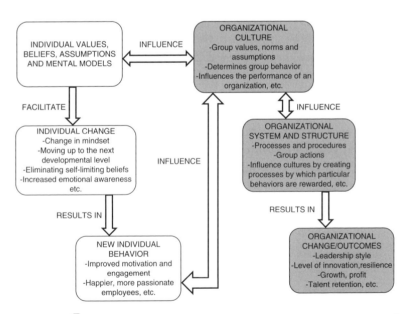

FIGURE 4.1 ╱ The interconnectedness of individual and organizational aspects of an organization

awareness (improved emotional intelligence), helping us to move up the developmental levels. This will result in new behavior of individuals, which will impact the level of engagement, motivation, level of passion for work and so on. New behavior of a critical mass of individuals will create a ripple effect, influence behavior of other colleagues and impact organizational culture. At the same time, organizational culture (reflected in organizational values, norms, assumptions, leadership style and so on) will influence individual and group behavior, which will have an impact on the performance of an entire organization. Organizational culture, systems and structure will also influence each other, which will impact overall organizational outcomes.

As it can be seen from Figure 4.1, a common practice of cutting the budget for learning and development as a response to a crisis will eventually be detrimental to organizational performance, profit, talent retention and so on. Similar outcomes can be expected when organizations focus on short-term share price maximization, as discussed in previous chapters. For most organizations, any strategy for a long-term, sustainable performance needs to take into account people and their need for development, learning and growth, as well as an understanding of the interdependencies between individual and organizational aspects. These interdependencies are further discussed in Chapter 5 where the 6 Box Leadership Model is presented as the next step in this research.

Emergent Leadership Model: Five Levels of Individual and Organizational Development

During the course of my theoretical and empirical research into various aspects of personal and organizational development, leadership theories, neuroscience, complexity theory, etc., I published a number of articles that preceded and informed development of the Emergent Leadership Model.[13,14,15,16,17,18,19] These articles include both theoretical and empirical research with various companies, which helped me to get an insight into what is happening at individual developmental levels and how this affects organizational culture and its overall performance. On the basis of all that research, I developed the Emergent Leadership Model as shown in Figure 4.2. This model is one of my contributions to the WHAT of management innovation.

The model shows how individuals and organizations go through different developmental levels. It also shows the levels of maturity of organizational culture as individuals and organizations evolve. Each level is characterized by a specific mindset, beliefs, language used, leaders' behavior and organizational outcomes. For example, at Level 1, a dominant mindset is "Lifeless" the corresponding organizational culture is "Apathetic", and not much gets done. At Level 2, individual mindset is "Reluctant" and culture is "Stagnating", and people do the minimum they can get away with. At Level 3, the mindset is "Controlled" and organizational culture is "Orderly", leadership style is based on traditional command and control, employees are micromanaged and they do what they are told to do. Levels 1, 2 and 3 correspond to traditional management, Management 1.0 or Tayloristic management.

A fundamental shift in performance, innovation and engagement happens when a critical mass of individuals move from Level 3 to Level 4. A dominant mindset becomes "Enthusiastic" and culture becomes "Collaborative". Leaders

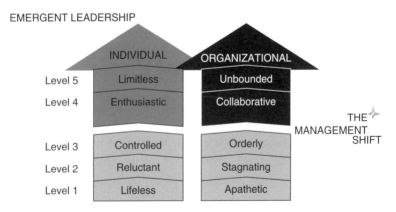

FIGURE 4.2　Emergent Leadership Model

lead by letting go, power and authority are distributed, there is a strong teamwork ethos and employees feel purposeful and are passionate about their work. This is the level where a paradigm shift (or The Management Shift) happens and the effects of emergence and interactions materialize. Employees at Level 4 can occasionally reach Level 5 where the mindset becomes "Limitless" and the culture "Unbounded" and anything seems to be possible to achieve. Levels 4 and 5 correspond to Management 2.0 or Drucker-based management, and this is where companies can experience more innovation, better engagement and more value creation. A much more detailed description of each level will be provided later on in this chapter.

As mentioned previously, over a number of years I studied various models and theories of development that helped me to develop the Emergent Leadership Model, and Appendix 2 shows my mapping of the five levels of the Emergent Leadership Model to other relevant models of development. These models have between 5 and 9 stages of development, and offer a slightly different view, focusing on different aspects of development (such as leadership skills, values, motivation, consciousness, ego, morality and energy level) and they mainly focus on individual rather than organizational levels or stages of development.

I have synthesized and incorporated the key elements from most of these models in the Emergent Leadership Model and linked individual levels to organizational levels. I decided to use five levels only for simplicity. It is interesting that after I developed this model and the first version of the description of levels, I came across research published in the book *Tribal Leadership*.[20] Based on ten years of research, and a sample of 24,000 individuals in dozens of organizations, the authors concluded that individuals and organizations go through five stages of development. This confirmed the soundness of the Emergent Leadership Model.

Various theories of development confirm that developmental levels cannot be skipped, people move up one level at a time. Each level provides a new, more comprehensive mindset and an evolved world view that is integrated with previous levels. A person cannot think beyond his/her level of development. At each level, there is a typical language and set of keywords people use, and there are predominant thoughts, emotions, beliefs and actions for each level, influencing our world and experiences. Anyone is capable of being at any level at certain times up to the highest current level achieved. Cognitive development would not regress, but the self-center of gravity and focus can fluctuate amongst different levels at any time. For example, someone could be anchored at Level 4, but in a challenging situation may think, speak and behave at one of the lower levels.

As discussed, the predominant level among individuals in any organization or part of it will influence organizational culture, and every group (team, department, unit) has a predominant level of culture. It can be claimed that a predominant culture and a person's sense of self are intertwined. Each level and its corresponding culture has a typical way of speaking, behaving, leadership style, typical types of relationships people form and typical organizational outcomes (such as growth *vs* stagnation). The dominant cultural level determines effectiveness and level of performance of individuals and the entire organization.[21]

A group of individuals at a particular developmental level will outperform a similar group anchored in a lower level. The essence of advancing to the next level is giving up the language, thoughts, emotions, beliefs and actions of the current stage and adopting the language, thoughts, emotions, beliefs and actions, as well as the type of interpersonal relationships, of the next level. Coaching and mentoring could speed up the advancement to the next level. A coach or mentor should use the language of the level above during individual coaching or mentoring sessions. For example, if a person being coached is anchored at Level 3, the coach should use language of Level 4 during coaching sessions.

The key to success is to move a critical mass to Level 4 (from Level 3) and help them to occasionally reach Level 5 and stay there as long as possible. Level 5 will outperform Level 4, Level 4 will outperform Level 3 and so on. Often people at Level 3 have sudden, unexpected insights that help them move to Level 4. The way to move the performance of entire groups to the next level is to move the critical mass to the next level. That critical mass will influence the rest of the group and their actions and behavior will spread like a ripple influence through the group (or organization). According to some research,[22] a six to twelve month intervention can raise the group to the next level.

As research in neuroscience shows that emphatic leaders can affect the brain chemistry of people around them,[23] and in the process their own brain chemistry changes, it can be concluded that groups and their leaders create one another. The dominant developmental level of leaders will influence people around them, which will lead to a dominant culture for that group, and this will ultimately impact the organizational performance. An example of such influence can be found in Professor Roberts' study on the causes of the financial crisis.[24] The study concludes that one of the five key causes of the financial crisis was autocratic or hubristic leadership (typical for a Level 3 developmental level, as shown in the next section), which helped bring down entire financial institutions.

Individual levels: from lifeless to limitless

In this section, a detailed description of individual levels of the Emergent Leadership Model is provided. This description is based on my research as well as on practical experience obtained from coaching, consulting and lecturing tens of thousands of professionals over more than two decades.

Level 1: Lifeless

This is the lowest individual level and most adults will be past this developmental stage. Very few organizations would have a critical mass of employees anchored at this level. As this level is characterized by negativity, self-destruction, complete lack of confidence and motivation, fear and so on, nothing could get done and no organization could survive even short term with employees and leaders operating from this level. Table 4.1 shows a detailed description of typical emotions and energy patterns experienced at this level, the typical thought processes of employees and leaders anchored here, the type of interpersonal relationships normally developed and some of the keywords that people anchored at this level tend to use.

TABLE 4.1 Typical thoughts, emotions and behavioral patterns of employees and leaders anchored at Level 1

		Level 1 – Lifeless			
Typical Emotions	Typical Energy Patterns	Typical Thought and Language Patterns of Employees	Typical Thought and Language Patterns of Leaders	Inter-Personal Relationships	Keywords Used
• Rage • Jealousy • Apathy • Insecurity • Guilt • Unworthiness • Fear • Grief • Depression • Despair • Hatred	• Destructive • Unproductive • Negative • Draining • Catabolic • Depressing • Impulsive • Survival focused	• I feel bored at work • I am cut-off • I cannot win • I feel demoralized • I feel discouraged to make any effort • I cannot do anything useful • I cannot make any decisions • It is too late to change anything • I am overwhelmed • I am too tired • I feel useless • I feel worthless • I am disappointed • I feel so unhappy • I am so worried • I am not motivated to work harder • No one likes me • I do not like my colleagues • There is nothing I can do to change this situation • I do not make an effort in my physical appearance	• I am bored at work • I feel isolated • I cannot inspire anyone • I feel discouraged to take any initiative • I cannot achieve what is expected of me • I do not care what will happen with this company • I cannot make decisions • I feel overwhelmed • I am disappointed with my work and life in general • I do not socialize with others at work • I wish I could change my career • I spend little effort and energy to motivate others • I lack the ability to lead myself and others • I cannot get much done • I should not be in a leadership position	• Very isolated • Very little support from others • Almost no team work/ collaboration	• Whatever • Hard • Difficult • Break • Why me? • It is not fair • Can't • Do not bother • Unhappy • Anxious • Cut off

Level 2: Reluctant

When people move from Level 1 to Level 2, they still have a lot of negative thought and energy patterns, but they are able to do some work. However, they would tend to do the minimum that they have to do to get a pay check. They tend to blame others for problems, they are very reluctant to try any new initiatives, they feel stressed, tend to argue with others, do not trust others and they resist any change. Some isolated relationships do start to form at this level, however. Some organizations have groups operating at this level, but such organizations would struggle to prosper beyond short- to medium-term time horizons. Table 4.2 shows a detailed description of typical emotions and typical energy patterns experienced at Level 2, typical thought processes of employees and leaders operating from this level, the type of interpersonal relationships usually developed and some of the keywords that people might use.

Level 3: Controlled

At Level 3, people develop a traditional employee–boss relationship; they accept and expect to be micro-managed, they do what they are told to do, they accept formal power and hierarchy in the organization. They are reluctant to try any new initiatives, there is a strict division between formal leaders and followers, and leaders tend to use an authoritarian, command-and-control leadership style. At this level, there is often a presence of a "Star" mindset based on big egos of charismatic leaders. The mindset is focused on words such as "I", "me" and "mine". Any teamwork that is happening at this level is usually controlled by a formal leader. Work gets done at this level, targets and Key Performance Indicators (KPI) are often met because of a "carrot and stick" management style, but most employees tend to be disengaged, have little or no passion for work and innovation is not thriving. Most organizations have many employees and leaders anchored at this level. They can do fine on a short-term to medium-term horizon, but it is unlikely that such organizations thrive on a long-term basis. Table 4.3 shows a detailed description of typical emotions and energy patterns experienced at Level 3, the typical thought processes of employees and leaders operating from this level;

TABLE 4.2 Typical thoughts, emotions and behavioural patterns of employees and leaders anchored at Level 2

			Level 2 - Reluctant		
Typical Emotions	**Typical Energy Patterns**	**Typical Thought and Language Patterns of Employees**	**Typical Thought and Language Patterns of Leaders**	**Inter-Personal Relationships**	**Keywords Used**
• Feeling overwhelmed • Disappointment • Doubt • Worry • Blame • Discouragement • Anger • Revenge	• Destructive • Unproductive • Negative • Draining • Catabolic • Judgemental • Sarcastic	• What is the point of trying? • My life is difficult • This is not going to work • I easily engage in conflict at work • I am annoyed by my work environment • I often argue with my colleagues • I demand attention from my colleagues • I feel frustrated at my work • I am impatient with my colleagues • I feel very stressed • I resent going to work • I resist any change • I tend to blame others for my disappointments • I feel lonely at work • I feel demotivated to make any effort • I would rather be somewhere else • I feel lethargic • I have no impact on decision-making • My ideas do not make an impact • I feel drained most of the time • I make some effort in my physical appearance • I am not supported by my boss • I am not supported by my colleagues	• There is no point in trying too hard to achieve good results • I tend to argue with my employees • I focus on problems rather than on solutions • It is frustrating to work in this company • I resent working with my employees • I am impatient with my employees • I feel drained when I am at work • I wish I had chosen a different career • I am impatient with my employees • Nothing can be achieved without great effort • Innovation is not central for our organization • We do not have a common view as to how the work should be done • I am very directive when dealing with my employees • I am unable to get results that are sustainable • My employees are likely to become unproductive, unhappy and give up • I am detached from my emotions	• Mainly isolated, occasional relationships with like-minded people • Team work and collaboration are almost non-existent	• Autocratic boss • Try • Can't • Give up • Quit • Resent • Difficult • Conflict

TABLE 4.3   Typical thoughts, emotions and behavioral patterns of employees and leaders anchored at Level 3

		Level 3 – Controlled			
Typical Emotions	Typical Energy Patterns	Typical Thought and Language Patterns of Employees	Typical Thought and Language Patterns of Leaders	Inter-Personal Relationships	Keywords Used
• Contentment, Boredom • Pessimism • Frustration • Irritation • Impatience • Pride • Egocentric	• Dominating • Self-centered • Borderline, moving between positive and negative • Unstable	• My boss is autocratic • I feel demotivated to take any initiative • I should be in charge • I should take control • I cannot delegate as no one is as capable as I am • I do not have enough time to complete all my tasks • I feel tired and drained • When is this place going to change? • I feel stressed and anxious • I am micromanaged • I cannot take responsibility for my ideas • My opinion is not being heard • I have to follow orders • There are many changes needed here • Who is going to lead the changes?	• I am better than others • I am a high achiever • I am in charge • I need to be in control • If they underperform, I might have to sack them • I cannot delegate work as they are not as capable as I am • I am so overworked • I am worried about becoming burned-out • I achieve best results by telling employees directly what they need to do • My leadership style is very traditional, based on formal power and control • I am impatient and frustrated • I do not tolerate mistakes • My employees' are trying hard to do as I tell them	• Self-centered • Any teamwork is controlled and directed by a "Star"	• I • Me • My • Doing • Have • Controlling boss • Great • Star • Power • Ego • Control

(continued)

TABLE 4.3 Continued

		Level 3 - Controlled			
Typical Emotions	Typical energy patterns	Typical Thought and Language Patterns of Employees	Typical Thought And Language Patterns of Leaders	Inter-Personal Relationships	Keywords Used
		• This place might never get sorted out • I would benefit from changing my employer • I do make some effort in my physical appearance • I do not express my ideas easily • I feel manipulated by my boss • I am unable to make decisions that are within my competencies • I am fearful of making mistakes • I am not encouraged to experiment with new ideas • I do not make connections with others easily • This place is driven by formal power and control	• I search for order • I manage by control or authority • I tend to blame others for mistakes • I do not encourage experimentation as risks might be too high • I do not share important information easily as it provides a source of my power • My employees are fearful of me • I have to manage conflict at work		

the type of interpersonal relationships usually developed, and some of the keywords that people use.

Level 4: Enthusiastic

A fundamental breakthrough for individuals and organizations happens when Level 4 becomes dominant. People become enthusiastic, happy, motivated, creative, engaged, empathetic, passionate about their work and focused on making a difference for the customers and the world. They develop a collective mindset based on collaboration and teamwork. This is where the emergent leadership style occurs; power and authority are distributed, decisions are made on the basis of knowledge rather than formal hierarchical position, and natural leaders can emerge depending on situation, skills and knowledge. The mindset is focused on "we", "us" or "ours"; people are intrinsically motivated, as volunteers are, and experiment with new ideas; innovation is embedded in organizational DNA, and work becomes fun. The authors of *Tribal Leadership* state that the transition to this level (or stage) often happens when people experience some kind of epiphany, and the average age when this happens is around the mid-forties. I have found that when focused self-development efforts are supported with coaching, this transition can happen much earlier and I have seen many examples in practice of this happening at different ages.

Interpersonal interactions are very important at this level. People form informal networks and there is a strong sense of community. Companies that have many groups operating at Level 4 can expect good performance and prosperity, including on a long-term basis. Although such companies are still in a minority today, it is encouraging to see that their numbers are growing – especially in areas where knowledge and innovation are crucial for survival – and more companies are adopting the emergent leadership style and employing employees with a Level 4 mindset, having learned that being stuck at Level 3 is detrimental for innovation, engagement and productivity.

Table 4.4 shows a detailed description of typical emotions and energy patterns experienced at Level 4, the typical thought processes of employees

TABLE 4.4   Typical thoughts, emotions and behavioral patterns of employees and leaders anchored at Level 4

		Level 4 – Enthusiastic		
Typical Emotions	Typical Energy Patterns	Typical Thought and Language Patterns of Employees	Typical Thought and Language Patterns of Leaders	Inter-Personal Relationships	Keywords Used
• Enthusiasm • Eagerness • Happiness • Positive expectation • Belief, optimism • Hopefulness • Pride • Acceptance	• Constructive • Productive • Positive • Energizing • Anabolic • Uplifting • Inspiring • Genuine	• We are great as a team • We can achieve great results • I am creative • I am eager to achieve • I am enthusiastic about my work • I am motivated to give my best performance • I am optimistic about my career and life in general • I have a purpose in my life • I respect myself and others • I am supportive of my colleagues • I empathize with others • I enjoy helping others • I enjoy working in this company • I look for opportunities for continuous development • I am striving for high achievement • I socialize and connect with others • I experience a strong team culture • I feel energized when interacting with my colleagues • I am glad I have chosen this career • I make a difference in the world by serving others • I have highly positive and invigorating energy • I feel confident I can achieve great results at work • I am connected to others • Work is fun for me	• We can achieve great results as a team • We are finding opportunities in all challenges • I help others to identify shared values and aspirations • I understand that power is abundant, the more I give the more I get back • I feel happy and fulfilled at work • I am motivated to give my best performance • I respect myself and others • I empathize with others • I let others make important decisions on the basis of their knowledge and experience • I have a strong connection with mine and other people's emotions • I feel inspiring • I encourage and receive good performance from others • I am perceived as a role model by my colleagues • I have a good intuition and use it to make decisions and generate ideas • I am humble • I am keen to continuously improve my skills and abilities • I tolerate mistakes	• People form informal networks • There is an awareness of community • Importance of teamwork and collaboration • People are making good eye contact when communicating	• We • Our • Team • Us • Trust • Transparency • Autonomy • Positive • Secure • Strong • Delighted • Community • Commit • Value • Purpose

and leaders operating from this level, the type of interpersonal relationships usually developed and some of the keywords that people typically use.

Level 5: Limitless

The objective for many individuals and organizations is to be firmly anchored at level 4. Occasionally, however, individuals and teams can temporarily reach and tap into the power of Level 5. All of the traits of Level 4 are present at this level but to these is added a concept of limitless potential, where people believe that anything is possible to achieve. People reach the energy level of collective consciousness at this level and, through collaboration, achieve what was thought to be impossible. They have a strong intuition, purpose and passion to make a difference, feel energized and excited to work with others; they are connected to their deep inner wisdom and are able to achieve amazing, almost miraculous outcomes. Very few teams and companies reach Level 5, but when they do they often produce new inventions, launch new disruptive innovations or achieve a breakthrough in the new markets. Table 4.5 shows a detailed description of the typical emotions and energy patterns experienced at Level 5, the typical thought processes of employees and leaders operating at this level, the type of interpersonal relationships emerging and some of the keywords used.

Organizational levels: from apathetic to unbounded

A critical mass of individuals operating at a particular level will influence organizational culture and vice versa. Such influence will spread throughout an organization (or its part) like a ripple and determine organizational outcomes. Organizational culture is a powerful driving force for any organization, determining its outcomes and longevity.[25] Different levels can exist within the same organization, but the predominant level will naturally have the biggest impact on the prosperity of the organization. For example, in one of the organizations I researched, in the R&D department the predominant culture was at Level 4, which was very important for fostering innovation; but in the manufacturing department, the dominant

TABLE 4.5 Typical thoughts, emotions and behavioral patterns of employees and leaders anchored at Level 5

		Level 5 – Limitless			
Typical Emotions	**Typical Energy Patterns**	**Typical Thought and Language Patterns of Employees**	**Typical Thought and Language Patterns of Leaders**	**Inter-Personal Relationships**	**Keywords Used**
• Joy • Wisdom • Empowerment • Freedom • Love • Appreciation • Passion	• Constructive • Productive • Positive • Energizing • Anabolic • Uplifting	• People have unlimited potential • We are making a global impact • I am striving for excellence in everything I do • We are all connected • We can achieve anything • I have great awareness of myself and others • I am fulfilled at my work • Everything is perfect as it is • I feel great love for myself and others • I feel I do what I was born to do • I am fully connected to my inner wisdom • I am looking for opportunities for continuous self-development and personal growth • I have no ego • Life is great • I am striving for excellence • I have a "can do anything" attitude • I believe anything is possible to achieve • I feel very energetic • I am normally free from stress and anxiety • I have a very large network of friends and colleagues • I make an effort in my physical appearance • I passionately put my heart and soul into my work • I find my life purpose in my job • I make a difference in the world by serving others • I do not take anything personally	• I inspire people to achieve their unlimited potential • We are making a global impact • We can achieve what other people thought cannot be done • We are all connected • I have great awareness of myself and others • We form ever growing networks • I am living a fulfilled life • I inspire and receive top performance from others • There is a sense of community at my workplace • I have close bonding with my co-workers • We are free to express creativity • I feel I do what I was born to do • I am inspiring and energizing others to give exceptional performance • There is no place for ego in this workplace • I release control • I show a strong empathy to others • I have a very strong connection with mine and other people's emotions • I see everybody as equal to me and others • I know what I am passionate about and my life purpose	• People form ever growing informal networks • There is a strong awareness of community • Importance of teamwork and collaboration	• We • Our • Team • Achievement • Fantastic • Perfect • Trust • Transparency • No boundaries • Have • Purpose • Values

culture was Level 3 to ensure meeting the production targets and quality requirements through increased control, whilst there were some elements of Level 4 that facilitated some empowerment and engagement.

At each of the five levels, it is possible to observe the typical behavior of leaders and employees, the work implications in terms of performance, engagement, innovation, work atmosphere and overall organizational outcomes. The boundaries between levels are usually fuzzy, and as the next level is approached it is possible to find some elements of both levels within the same culture. I have described below what typically happens at each level from the organizational culture perspective.

Level 1: Apathetic

At this level the culture is "Apathetic"; leaders are not engaging or inspiring and are detached, employees are lethargic and this is reflected in very low performance, engagement, isolated employees and lack of team culture. Organizational culture is based on fear, and stagnation is prevalent. No organization in the private sector could survive long term at this level. According to research published in *Tribal Leadership*, about 2 percent of organizations operate at this level, and the typical example given for this level is a prison service. Table 4.6 shows information about the typical behavior of leaders and employees, and the work implications and organizational outcomes at Level 1.

Level 2: Stagnating

Organizations anchored at this level have a "Stagnating" culture. They get more work done than at Level 1 but this is still at a minimum level. At level 2, autocratic leaders lead through fear and formal authority, employees are disengaged and do the minimum they can get away with. Relationship-based conflict is frequent, organizational values are not strong or even widely known. There is a short-term focus, and long-term prosperity of such organizations is very unlikely. According to findings in *Tribal Leadership*, about 25 percent of US organizations that were researched for this book operate from this level, which is quite astonishing. In my own experience, many organizations have elements of Level 2 and Level 3 organizational cultures, some are between Level 3 and Level 4, and few are established at Level 4. Table 4.7 shows information about the

TABLE 4.6   Typical organizational outcomes at Level 1

	Level 1 - Apathetic		
Typical Behavior of Leaders	Typical Behavior of Employees	Work Implications	Organizational Outcomes
• Little effort and energy is spent to motivate others • Lack of ability to lead yourself and others • Not much gets done • Completely detached from emotions • Working in a crisis mode • Has many limited beliefs and weaknesses • Should leave the company • Should not be at leadership position	• Pessimistic/depressive mindset • Disengaged • "Cannot do" attitude • Very low level of consciousness • Very low level of performance	• Victim mentality, lethargy • Nothing gets done, people are focused on problems • Social networks almost nonexistent • Employees are isolated, socially alienated and unhappy • There is no team culture, people are alienated from organizational concerns and values, people form isolated groups that operate by their own rules • People think about leaving • Low quality of interpersonal relationships • Unattractive physical environment • Disengaged employees • No flexibility with procedures, rules and regulations • There is a high level of fear or stress in the workplace • Relationship-related working conflict happens often	• Imploding energetically • Constant stagnation • Bankruptcy

TABLE 4.7 Typical organizational outcomes at Level 2

	Level 2 - Stagnating		
Typical Behavior of Leaders	**Typical Behavior of Employees**	**Work Implications**	**Organizational Outcomes**
• Aggressive, command-and-control leadership style • Key leadership traits: being tough, controlling, analytical, demotivating • Leaders provide centralized direction • They can get some work done on a short-term basis but the results are not sustainable • Detached from emotions • Leading for equilibrium and stability • Leading for reduction of conflict • Expect allegiance to a formal leader • Power concentrated at the top of the hierarchy • Leaders hinder development of high level of trust	• Demotivated employees • They would rather be somewhere else • Lethargic with no sense of urgency • No accountability • Have no impact on decision-making • No motivation to be innovative • Imploding creativity and innovation • Low level of consciousness • Employees do make some effort for physical appearance • Employees are likely to become unproductive, unhappy and give up	• Conflict, fights, defiance • Isolated and/or weak social networks • Employees are disengaged • People are disconnected from organizational concerns and values • Team culture is almost non-existent • Physical environment is not attractive • There is a lot of arguing, burnout and stress • People show no initiative or passion for work • People do not care about organizational outcomes • Culture embodies disappointment, unmet needs and repressed anger • Little flexibility with procedures, rules and regulations • There is a substantial level of fear or stress in the workplace • Working conflict happens regularly	• Risky position • Stagnation • Short-term focus • Absence of innovation • Fighting for survival • Concerned about finances only

typical behavior of leaders and employees, and the work implications and organizational outcomes at Level 2.

Level 3: Orderly

This is a traditional, predominant level where culture is "Orderly". At this level, traditional leadership style is used, based on hierarchical command and control, bureaucratic organization, standardization, specialization, order, rules and regulations, formal power and authority. Chapter 2 provides more details about this leadership style. At this level, micromanagement is the norm, employees do what they are told to do, work gets done, targets are normally met and organizations can keep surviving and in some cases even do well on a longer term basis. However, culture at this level inhibits innovation, creativity, engagement and passion for work. Employees rarely feel purposeful, empowered or intrinsically motivated. According to *Tribal Leadership*, about 49 percent of organizations operate from this level. Table 4.8 shows information about the typical behavior of leaders and employees, the work implications and organizational outcomes at Level 3.

Level 4: Collaborative

A breakthrough in performance, innovation and engagement happens when organizations move a predominant culture from Level 3 ("Orderly") to Level 4 ("Collaborative"). At this level, enterprises reinvent themselves[26] and The Management Shift, the shift from old to new management (i.e. from Management 1.0 to Management 2.0), is achieved. Cooperation and collaboration increase, creativity and innovation emerge, more is achieved with less effort, employees are engaged and intrinsically motivated, and there is a strong team culture. Direction emerges from complex network activity, exploration and trial and error are embraced, and there is flexibility with procedures, rules and regulations. This is in line with the key ideas from the leading management thinkers as described in Chapter 3. This is the level where the management paradigm shift happens and a whole new way of thinking, doing and being (described in Chapter 1) materializes.

TABLE 4.8 Typical organizational outcomes at Level 3

	Level 3 - Orderly		
Typical Behavior of Leaders	**Typical Behavior of Employees**	**Work Implications**	**Organizational Outcomes**
• Command-and-control driven • Very traditional • Impatient and frustrated • They achieve employee motivation through their need to be liked rather than being productive • Some connection with emotions is achieved • Searching for order • Avoiding chaos • Managing by control • Delegating and blaming • Giving information and directions without justification or buy-in	• Employees do not take responsibility for their ideas • Employees feel their opinion is not being heard • Employees have to follow orders • They feel many changes are needed • They think how long they need to stay • Employees make some effort for physical appearance	• Domination of egos • Taking responsibility • Many employees feel demotivated • There are isolated groups providing high performance • Some social networks are established • Some team culture exists • There is some flexibility with procedures, rules and regulations • People are engaged with more energy and commitment but this is focused on personal gain and achievement • Efforts are focused on personal interests • People tend to form two-person relationships • People resist sharing information • There is often a culture of fear or stress • Unproductive (relationship-based) conflict happens occasionally	• Reasonably stable in short term • Lack of growth • Lack of sustainable innovation • Focus on quantitative measures of success not people

At this level, emergent leadership occurs (as described in Chapter 2), focused on: intuition, cooperation, risk taking, emotional awareness, leading for change and adaptability, distributing authority and decision-making on the basis of knowledge. To use Lynda Gratton's analogy from her book *Hot Spots*,[27] at this level "Hot Spots" emerge fuelled by igniting purpose and eagerness for cooperation. Organizational outcomes at this level include reinvention, accelerated project completions, sustained growth, increased innovation, more resilient and adaptive organizations, better knowledge worker retention. According to *Tribal Leadership*, about 22 percent of organizations operate at this level. One of the purposes of this book is to help increase this percentage for organizations worldwide through the 6 Box Leadership diagnostic (described in Chapter 5), which was developed to identify the bottleneck for shift between Levels 3 and 4. Table 4.9 shows information about the typical behavior of leaders and employees, and the work implications and organizational outcomes at Level 4.

Level 5: Unbounded

All characteristics of Level 4 culture are included in this "Unbounded" culture as well, although they are even more prominent at this level. Even more innovation, engagement and value creation can be achieved as employees reaching this level believe anything is possible. At this level, purpose, challenge, mastery, autonomy,[28] trust,[29] transparency[30] and team spirit are ignited at the highest level. It would be very difficult for any organization to sustain this level permanently, but some teams/ organizations anchored at Level 4 can occasionally reach this level and achieve what had been thought to be impossible. According to *Tribal Leadership*, fewer than 2 percent of organizations operate at this level. Table 4.10 summarizes information about the typical behavior of leaders and employees, and the work implications and organizational outcomes at Level 5.

TABLE 4.9   Typical organizational outcomes at Level 4

Level 4 - Collaborative			
Typical Behavior of Leaders	Typical Behavior of Employees	Work Implications	Organizational Outcomes
• Opportunities are found in all challenges • Shared values and aspirations are identified and aligned • Three-person relationships are established • Strategy for exceptional performance is built • Control is released to a large extent • Empathy is shown to others • Words are used carefully to get best out of people • There is a strong connection with emotions • Leaders are inspiring, expecting and receiving greatness from others • Lead more by presence than by action • Role models • Have good intuition and use it to make decisions and generate ideas • Powerful but humble • Knows his/her level of excellence and is still interested in growing • Takes actions to improve without ego blocks • Leadership as emergent collective action • Key leadership traits: intuition, cooperation, being forgiving, risk taking • Leading for change and adaptability	• Looking for opportunities to help others • Striving for high achievement • Socializing and connecting with others • Developing strong team culture • High level of consciousness • Employees make an effort on physical appearance • Employees put their heart into their jobs • Employees find their life purpose in their job • They make a difference in the world by serving others • Nothing is taken personally • Highly positive and invigorating energy • People feel empowered, confident, courageous and connected to others • Employees have fun working • There is a concern for environmental issues • There is a desire to give back to society	• Widespread cooperation, collaboration, creativity and innovation • High level of trust • Strong social networks • Focus on service and making a difference • Employees are very motivated to perform well • Strong team culture • Loyal employees • Attractive physical environment • Employees have identified personal values that are aligned with organizational values • Change emerges from interactions • Decentralization facilitates emergence and innovation • Direction emerges from complex network activity • Embracing exploration, trial and error • Flexibility with procedures, rules and regulations • There is a free flow of information • There is very little fear or stress • Unproductive (relationship-based) conflict is rare	• Implementing The Management Shift • Sustained growth • Organizational reinvention • Talent retention • Strong market position • Widespread innovation • Focus on qualitative measures of success and people rather than quantitative • Strong financial performance

TABLE 4.10 Typical organizational outcomes at Level 5

Level 5 - Unbounded			
Typical Behavior of Leaders	Typical Behavior of Employees	Work Implications	Organizational Outcomes
• Inspiring and energizing others to give exceptional performance • Releasing control • Values are crucial • Strong empathy to others • There is a very strong connection with emotions • Leaders see everybody equal to them and others • Totally engaged in a task or activity yet completely detached from the result – this is unlocking true power and potential for leaders and others • Completely passionate about what he/she is doing • Having an ability to unlearn traditional leadership paradigm • Accepting some chaos that will lead to homeostasis • Leading by encouraging everyone to be a leader • Identifying and raising energy level of employees	• Striving for excellence • Feel enlightened • "Can do anything" attitude • Very energetic • Looking for opportunities for continuous self-development and personal growth • Very high level of consciousness • Employees make an effort on physical appearance • Employees put their heart and soul into their jobs • Employees find their life purpose in their job • They want to make a difference in the world by serving others and giving back to the society • Nothing is taken personally • There is a substantial concern for environmental issues	• No obstacles or problems are perceived, only opportunities • "Wow" moments are experienced • High levels of creativity, trust and innovation • Very strong social networks • Values and aspirations are central • Employees believe they have unlimited potential • Anyone can work with anyone • Employees have clearly identified personal values that are aligned with organizational values • Ability to contribute to global concerns is developed • Employees are wise and highly motivated to provide top performance • Very strong team culture • There is a common belief that fulfilment is achieved through serving others • Physical environment is attractive • Considerable flexibility with procedures, rules and regulations • There is almost no fear or stress • Working conflict is almost non-existent	• Thriving • Sustainable high performance • Strong growth • High levels of innovation • Occasional "miraculous" innovations and achievements • Rising profits • Focus on people and qualitative measures of success rather than quantitative • Manifestation of pure leadership and inspiration • Making history

Reaching Levels 4 and 5 Culture

Triggers for shifting to Level 4 culture

There are various triggers that make the shift to an emergent leadership style and Level 4 culture either necessary or an aspiration for organizations anchored at Level 3. I researched a number of organizations where this shift happened,[31] and some of the main triggers that emerged from interviews, observations and literature include:

- Change in business focus and/or change in corporate values – an organization can initiate a change program for changing business focus or corporate values, even if it is doing well at the moment. Such initiatives can be illustrated by a quote from one of the executives in a company that has achieved a shift to Level 4:

  > There was a big change program initiated. The new corporate strategy was about a more collaborative culture, a more emotional side of things. It was all based on corporate values, which put the people and the knowledge workers at the centre of gravity and the business focus on customers. It is all about more effective, more efficient processes, which are more flexible

- *Poor financial and market performance* – organizations experiencing poor financial and market performance might have no other choice than to work on changing culture as well as strategy and business processes
- *Unpredictability of the operating environment* – organizations operating in highly unpredictable and volatile environments would benefit from moving to Level 4 culture as this would result in better resilience, more agility and a more efficient response to changes
- *Lack of a formal leader* – in some cases a formal leader might not be available any more, and in the formal power vacuum that results, new initiatives for change can often get started. This might lead to self-organization of knowledge workers, as illustrated by this quote from an executive experiencing such a situation:

Because the old director left, and we didn't have a new one, we sat together as a team of managers and decided we needed to change now and we don't need the king on top of us. And then one of the managers took on the role of director, but we agreed prior to that, that we wanted to set it up differently, and we did

- *Inadequate engagement/motivation/energy* – if employees are not sufficiently engaged and motivated, changes are needed to ensure sustainable performance of overall organization. Shifting to Level 4 would result in better engagement and overall performance
- *Untapped potential of the team prior to change* – in some cases the potential of people is not realized for various reasons and that could be a trigger for change, as illustrated in this quote from one of the companies I researched:

The team was in a very poor state. Profit margins were really low. And we said, "It's not the market. It's not that we have people that don't have skills, it's the type of management, people don't get involved as much as they can be", and the impact was amazing when we changed that and helped people to achieve their potential

- *Slow or problematic decision-making* – slow and inefficient decision-making processes can have a very negative impact on performance, as illustrated by this executive:

If you need to make a decision, which you can't make yourself because of rules, you have to approach your boss. And you have to wait for the decision that the senior person makes. Usually that senior person or your manager doesn't have enough information to make the right decision. So usually he/she calls you back, requires more information, and so on... and you almost end up making the decision yourself anyway. If I'm in the position that I have the best information and the competencies to make the best decision, why shouldn't I make it? Even if it is not dependent on my position but dependent on the best information, and competency I've got to make this decision

- *Poor communication* – lack of communication is normally very detrimental for individual and organizational performance. This could be another trigger for culture change. The importance of communication is shown in this quote from one of the executives participating in a change program:

  > Before [the] new form of leadership, basically people weren't communicating that much. The expertise is very distributed, and usually you only have the manager or the top level director, who claims to have all the knowledge about what the team can do and what the customer wants, and there was not so much interaction going on. This impeded performance

- *Economic crisis* – this can be a power trigger for change, as organizations that stay stuck at Level 3 without a sustainable attempt to change could experience substantial difficulties, especially if they are knowledge based and depend on innovation.

Some of the outcomes of shifting to Level 4 culture

There are many benefits that individuals and organizations can experience once they move to Level 4 or achieve The Management Shift. I was involved in a number of empirical and theoretical studies that looked into the effect of culture change and implementing emergent leadership approaches (at Level 4).[32,33,34] Some of the key outcomes that were discovered in these studies are shown in Table 4.11, together with some illustrative quotes obtained from executives being interviewed.

Moving up the individual levels

Leaders as well as internal and external coaches can help individuals to move up to the next level. If more individuals reach a higher developmental level, the whole organizational culture will eventually shift to the next level. Leaders need to understand and recognize the language, emotions, thoughts, beliefs, actions and types of interpersonal relationships at each level. They need to listen, and to observe the clues that indicate who is at

TABLE 4.11   Key outcomes of moving to Level 4 culture

Key Outcomes of Moving to Level 4 Culture	Illustrative Quotes
Retention of the key talent	"People do not want to leave because of the caring culture, empowerment, support through coaching and networking, and they are also proud of the success."
Emergence of new forms (for example, informal organizational structures not deliberately designed by senior management)	"New forms have emerged through this process, such as informal networked-based structure that was imposed over formal structure. This structure gets the work done, enables solving of any problem, it facilitates communication and collaboration and leads to better performance and profits."
Unleashing the potential of team members	"With increased intrinsic motivation, morale and enthusiasm, the full potential of teams was unleashed and the level of innovation and profit increased as a result."
Improved performance and innovation	"There are various outcomes related to people realizing their potential. You have shorter decision cycles, you make better decisions, you are more innovative, you make fewer mistakes, and your profit figures grow. All our KPI indicators went up very rapidly six to seven months after we introduced the new leadership model. All the things that we were measured against quantitatively show very good numbers, such as the billability, the direct cost margin, resource growth."
Increase in profit	"The profit was increased by 240 percent by the second year. Also the unit of 34 employees outperformed another unit of 70 employees led traditionally."
Increase in billability and utilization	"Both billability and utilization have increased significantly as a result of this new leadership initiative."
No need for sales support for the follow-up work	"We have a few of these things where customers themselves just buy the job that we have done. Things just happen. You don't have to aggressively sell yourself when you have happier people, making better jobs, creating more … better buy-in from the customer, this creates values. But it's not predictable."

(continued)

TABLE 4.11   Continued

Key Outcomes of Moving to Level 4 Culture	Illustrative Quotes
Many decisions made in parallel, more quickly by most competent people	"We were able to make a lot of decisions in parallel, and people that had the best competency to make these decisions were actually making them. I think that's one of the key aspects."
Improved quality and quantity of decisions	"We were able to make a lot of decisions in parallel, and [allow] people that had the best competency to make these decisions. As a result the quality and quantity of decisions improved."
Improved customer satisfaction	"Because of the improved decision-making process, customer satisfaction was improved and we have been gaining repeated business."
Greater level of flexibility, agility and resilience	"Due to parallel decision-making, we had a greater level of flexibility and agility and this also created a greater level of trust from our customers."
Creating new partnerships	"So, we had a greater level of flexibility and also created a greater level of trust from our customers, because when you make better decisions and make better decisions for your customers, you create better results for your customers, and that also creates better partnerships."
More engaged, motivated and productive workers, with improved behavioral system	"I think there were many changes which were not really obvious, because they happened on the level of individual behavior. I'd say, how they behave, interact with the customer, interact with each other, share more knowledge, are more open, have more trust in relationships – these are the small changes that happened on an individual level, and in combination they create these very large effects."
Reduced stress	"New culture, shared responsibility, coaching and mentoring process, opportunities to grow and contribute on a equal basis – all this has energized and motivated people and as a result the stress has reduced."
Improved loyalty to organization due to a caring culture	"The staff retention rate improved, people became more loyal to the organization as they appreciated the caring culture and would not go to work elsewhere even for a higher salary."

which stage. They should move up the levels to reach at least Level 4 and help others to move up, one level at a time. Leaders should understand and speak all five levels without losing any of their own development – and this is the key to effective leadership.

Over many years of my coaching and consulting experience, working with many individuals and organizations, I developed and tested many techniques and processes that can help individuals move up levels. In addition, I developed assessment tools to determine at which level an employee or leader is anchored. I also run workshops focused on helping individuals to understand and apply the 5 Level Emergent Leadership Model and to learn how to move up the levels themselves and help others to do so. More information about these workshops is available at the website: *www.themanagementshift.com*.

The next step: moving an organization from Level 3 to Level 4 for a breakthrough in innovation, engagement, value creation and overall organizational success

I cannot emphasize enough how important it is to reach Level 4 and achieve The Management Shift, individually and then collectively. A whole new world of possibilities opens up when this happens for individuals, organizations and entire societies. Gerald Jampolski, the author of *Love is Letting go of Fear*,[35] reminds us that letting go of fear (pertinent to Levels 1 to 3) brings us to a better mindset (at Level 4 and Level 5), where we aim to give to receive. We give our compassion, purpose and creativity to colleagues, customers, society and mankind and receive more contentment, a more purposeful life, prosperity, compassion, joy, inspiration, self-actualization, etc. The thoughts, emotions and language we use, and the actions we take create a ripple effect, positive at higher levels (4 and 5) and negative at lower levels (1 to 3).

We have the choice. We can work consciously towards anchoring ourselves and our organizations at Levels 4 and 5 and, as emergent leaders, create powerful positive ripples that will go way beyond what might be imaginable at our current level of awareness. On my journey of discovery, once I developed the 5 Level Emergent Leadership Model, I started thinking that moving individuals up the levels is very important as this will improve people's lives and will eventually impact the entire organizational culture. This will bring many benefits but will take time, possibly years. I then started thinking: how can we move an entire organization from Level 3 to Level 4 in a shorter period of time? At that point, I decided to do more research and investigate how that could be possible. In this process, I read widely, did some more empirical research and also went back to many interdisciplinary projects I was involved in during many years of my academic career. This is how the 6 Box Leadership Model was created, as described in the next chapter.

SEVEN REFLECTION POINTS

1. What is the dominant level you are anchored at?
2. If your dominant level is below Level 4, what can you do to shift to the next level?
3. How would your life change if you shift and anchor yourself at one level higher?
4. What can you do to help others in your organization move one level higher?
5. At what level is the predominant organizational culture anchored in your organization?
6. If it is below Level 4, can you think of five actions that can be taken to move your organizational culture closer to Level 4?
7. If your organization is anchored at level 4, what can be done to tap into Level 5 as often as possible?

chapter 5

The 6 Box Leadership Model: An Organizational Body Scan

This chapter provides answers to the following key questions:

- How was the 6 Box Leadership Model created to help organizations achieve The Management Shift?
- What is the philosophical thinking behind the 6 Box Leadership Model?
- What are the other key organizational diagnostic tools? How does the 6 Box Leadership Model compare to these other tools?
- What are the key factors that drive innovation, engagement and value creation in an organization?
- How was the online 6 Box Leadership diagnostic tool developed and tested empirically?
- What are the additional three frameworks used in the 6 Box Leadership diagnostic that enable looking into the same data from four different perspectives?
- What are the key results from the statistical analysis of the reliability of the online diagnostic tool?
- What are the key processes used in implementing the 6 Box Leadership diagnostic?
- What are the benefits obtained from the 6 Box Leadership diagnostic in various organizations?

Moving Organizations from Level 3 to Level 4: The Creation of the 6 Box Leadership Model

Many leading management thinkers, such as Peter Drucker,[1] Charles Handy,[2] Henry Mintzberg[3] and Gary Hamel,[4] have recognized the need for The Management Shift, to move away from mechanistic models of management towards distributed leadership and decision-making, a collaborative culture and more social orientation of businesses. A recent synthesis of a large body of the literature on leading knowledge workers[5] reveals that in order to foster innovation in knowledge-based organizations, a different leadership style is needed, based on horizontal rather than vertical leadership, where power and authority are distributed on the basis of knowledge. This was discussed in more detail in previous chapters. I have also discussed that there have been more publications describing *what* organizations should do than on *how* they can make changes.[6]

Once I created the 5 Level Emergent Leadership Model, I started thinking about *how* organizations can be helped to move from Level 3 to Level 4 in a sustainable way, attending to organizational aspects including culture. I have always been keen to bridge the gap between theory and practice and I have focused my academic work on applied research that can create an impact in practice. That has led to extensive consulting experience, which in turn helped me with my academic work. In his book *Management: Tasks, Responsibilities, Practices*,[7] Peter Drucker wrote that ideas must be turned into action. This view is succinctly and memorably stated by Soichiro Honda: "Action without Philosophy is a lethal weapon and Philosophy without action is worthless."[8]

Philosophical thinking behind the 6 Box Leadership Model

I mentioned in Chapter 3 my belief that we can be truly innovative and achieve great things if we move away from the silo thinking and mindset, think holistically, have an open and inquisitive mind, integrate different disciplines and focus on whole brain thinking.[9] One of my role models, the "father of management" Peter Drucker, is a perfect example of such thinking. His diverse interests in subjects from management, social sciences, religion, philosophy, literature, history, to economics, statistics and Japanese art enabled him to be very prolific and innovative in his thinking. These interests also enabled him to "connect the dots" and see things from an integral perspective.

Another example is Ken Wilber's integral theory[10] or Theory of Everything, offering an approach "to draw together an already existing number of separate paradigms into an interrelated network of approaches that are mutually enriching".[11] It has been applied in a variety of different domains such as integral art, integral ecology, integral economics, integral politics, integral psychology, integral spirituality, and many others. Researchers have also developed applications of this theory in areas such as leadership,[12] coaching and organizational development.

My mindset is very much integrative. I thrive when I can "connect the dots" and bridge the gap between different disciplines, between theory and practice or between different groups of people working on a similar cause (more information about my "connecting the dots" actions will be provided in Chapter 7).

Reviewing existing organizational models

At the time that I started working on the development of the 6 Box Leadership Model, I had already completed extensive research into individual development models. This was used for the development of the Emergent Leadership Model, as described in Chapter 4. In addition, I had already been researching emergent leadership theories for several years, resulting in several publications.[13,14,15] This research is in line with research published in the articles "Leadership in the Plural"[16] and "Leadership in Organizational Knowledge Creation: A Review and Framework",[17] which synthesized a large body of academic research on emergent leadership approaches discussed in previous chapters. In addition, I have had years of experience in researching change management approaches and models,[18, 19, 20] such as Business Process Reengineering,[21,22] Process Innovation,[23] Total Quality Management,[24] Just-in-Time[25] and Knowledge Management.[26]

The next step in my research was to conduct a further study of organizational change models and see if any of the existing models could be used to help organizations to move from Level 3 to Level 4. Table 5.1 summarizes the key characteristics of all five levels of the Emergent Leadership Model and shows that the shift from Level 3 to Level 4 is crucial to transcend the traditional leadership approaches that cause many problems for individuals and organizations, as discussed in previous chapters.

The shift from Level 3 to Level 4 is crucial and requires change at both individual and organizational levels. This chapter focuses particularly on the organizational aspects of change in the 6 Box Leadership Model. There are many organizational change theories, frameworks and models,[27] and there is not the space in this book to review them all in detail, but I shall present an overview.

In the organizational context, change management is defined as "the process of continually renewing an organization's direction, structure and capabilities to serve the ever-changing needs of external and internal customers".[28] There is a consensus amongst researchers that many organizational change theories and approaches are contradictory and mostly lacking empirical evidence,[29] and change initiatives tend to be reactive,

TABLE 5.1   Key characteristics of levels in the Emergent Leadership Model

Level	Key Characteristics
Level 5 **EMERGENT**	Unlimited mindset, strong team cohesion, unbounded culture, inspirational leaders, strong sense of purpose and passion for work
Level 4 **EMERGENT**	Enthusiastic mindset, team ethos, collaborative culture, distributed/horizontal leadership, unleashed purpose and passion for work
THE MANAGEMENT SHIFT	
Level 3 **TRADITIONAL**	Controlled mindset, orderly culture, command and control/vertical leadership, micromanaging, self-centered relationships
Level 2 **TRADITIONAL**	Reluctant mindset, stagnating/blame culture, disengagement, autocratic leadership, overwhelmed employees
Level 1 **TRADITIONAL**	Lifeless mindset, apathetic/fear-based culture, isolated and disengaged employees and leaders

discontinuous and often triggered by organizational crisis.[30,31] At the same time, change is an inevitable feature of organizational life,[32] in the same way as it is for individuals. Given the dynamics of the current business environment, it could be claimed that a primary task of management is to lead and facilitate organizational change,[33] something that affects all organizations in all industries.[34,35] Interestingly, various research studies report a failure rate of around 70 percent for change programs.[36,37]

Whilst there is a consensus on the importance and inevitability of change for organizations, there seems to be a lack of empirical evidence in support of the different theories, models and approaches.[38] As the next step, I started focusing my research effort on finding organizational change models that are supported by empirical research and have been implemented in practice. I compared these models with the 6 Box Leadership Model, and a summary of this investigation is provided in Appendix 3. All these models provided valuable insight and contributed to my understanding of what a good organizational change framework or tool might look like. They are all based on empirical research, have their usability for different purposes, and are widely known. However, I concluded that none could be used for helping organizations specifically to move from Level 3 to Level 4. I had to develop a new model.

Thematic analysis of relevant research

The next phase in the development of the 6 Box Leadership Model was to search for factors pertinent for Level 4 organizations; factors that are proven to have a positive impact on organizational performance, innovation and engagement. I had completed many theoretical and empirical projects that dealt with these issues, and I had supervised a number of PhD dissertations that investigated different aspects of organizational performance. I started thinking about how I could bring all this knowledge and these insights together from an interdisciplinary perspective to create a new model.

I then started doing an exploratory (content-driven) thematic analysis with coding.[39] Coding is a way of indexing or categorizing the text in order to establish a framework of thematic ideas about it.[40] Thematic analysis is often used in qualitative research for examining themes within data. As I had to deal with large data sets and was searching for categories to emerge from data, I judged that this was the most suitable research method.[41] Qualitative data analysis involves analysis of text, pictures or sounds, and in this case there was a large volume of text.

In addition to the large volume of literature that I reviewed, I reviewed the data collected from various interdisciplinary projects I was involved in as researcher or research supervisor over a period of more than 15 years. The theoretical research consisted of a review and synthesis of more than 1,000 research articles, while the empirical research included projects with more than 23 case studies, involving more than 300 semi-structured interviews. Many of these case studies were in-depth, longitudinal case studies, carried out over a period of two to three years. The empirical research also involved a survey of 88 organizations and more than 6,000 respondents. Appendix 4 shows a description of the six phases of thematic analysis that were followed in this stage of research.

This process resulted in the holistic framework with 130 themes, or factors, that drive value creation in organizations. These factors were grouped into six categories and this is how the 6 Box Leadership Model was created, as shown in Figure 5.1. The right side of the model (with economic and process-related factors) includes Strategy, Systems and Resources, which broadly correspond to the notion of Resources, Processes and Value in Christensen's RVP Framework.[42] The left side of the model captures people-related dimensions, including Culture, Relationships and Individuals.

Appendix 5 shows an overview of the key projects that form the foundation of the 6 Box Leadership Model, research methods used in these projects, key findings, examples of key outputs and the link of each project to the six boxes of the 6 Box Leadership Model. Most of these projects were interdisciplinary, investigating various aspects of value creation in organizations that lead to improved performance, innovation, resilience and engagement. Some of the insights were also obtained from

6 BOX LEADERSHIP

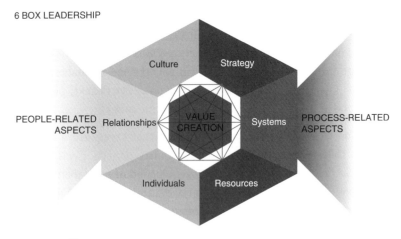

FIGURE 5.1 / The 6 Box Leadership Model

my participation in Gary Hamel's Management Innovation eXchange (MIX) Management 2.0 Hackathon. Although the output from this Hackathon (which was a global collaborative effort, involving hundreds of management thinkers and practitioners, to re-invent management principles) was not explicitly validated by further research, there are many research studies that validate individual principles of Management 2.0 that emerged from this project. Appendix 6 shows examples of some of the key factors that create value in organizations in each of the six areas that emerged from the final stages of the thematic analysis, together with sources of information for each factor.

Development of an online questionnaire

Following the development of a framework with factors that drive value creation in organizations, the next step was to develop an online questionnaire to assess the extent to which organizations have implemented factors pertinent to Level 4 organizations, to understand what is preventing them from moving to Level 4 and to discover hidden strengths and weaknesses in the areas of Culture, Relationships, Individuals, Systems, Strategy and Resources. The first version of the questionnaire consisted of 105 questions that captured the key factors from the framework. Over the period of the next two years, which was a pilot phase, this questionnaire was used in ten organizations (four in the private sector and six in the public sector). At the same time I continued theoretical research, collecting empirical data and thematic analysis. That led to the next phase of this project, where I produced the final version of the framework with 150 factors (examples of the factors are shown in Appendix 6). Subsequent to that, a new online assessment tool was developed, comprising the final 120 questions in the online survey.

For each question (Likert[43] item), a six-point Likert scale with equidistant categories (where the range of answers is from 1: strongly disagree to 6: strongly agree) was used to eliminate the neutral option. The software also allowed qualitative comments by survey respondents, which is useful for comparing the qualitative data with the Likert scores. The questions with the highest aggregate scores indicate the key strengths, and the lowest scoring questions help to identify bottlenecks in each of the six areas of the model. Average Likert scores are used to identify to what extent respondents agree or disagree with statements (Likert items) that relate to factors pertinent to Level 4 organizations. For methodological purposes, a mixture of positive (typical for Level 4 organizations) and negative (typical for organizations with dominant culture below Level 4) statements were used, and scores for negative questions were inverted for aggregation purpose.

This diagnostic tool enables quantification of qualitative aspects of an organization that are rarely measured. As Peter Drucker said, "What's measured improves".[44] The key idea behind this diagnostic tool is to use it like an organizational body scan, and discover hidden strengths and weaknesses in an organization. In order to move to Level 4 and experience more value creation, innovation and better engagement, companies can use this diagnostic tool to help them take an action that would leverage their strengths and address weaknesses or developmental opportunities. This new version of the tool has been successfully used in 11 additional organizations in the UK, USA, Norway and South Africa. All these companies experienced various benefits from the diagnostic process. More information about the practical application of the 6 Box Leadership diagnostic tool is provided in Chapter 6.

Appendix 7 shows an example of an online data input in the Culture section of the questionnaire using an online tool, and an example of the demographic data input.

Mapping 6 Box Leadership Questions to the Additional Three Frameworks

In the next phase, the original 120 questions (grouped in six boxes) were regrouped and mapped according to three additional frameworks for further analysis. During the process of my research and practical experience, I had come across several other frameworks focused on management reinvention, and I thought it would be a good test of the original 120 questions to map them to other frameworks that follow the same paradigm and useful to then consider the same data from different perspectives. The additional three frameworks I selected were: Reinvention Framework, Management 2.0 principles and the key ideas of Peter Drucker.

First additional mapping: Reinvention Framework

The Reinvention Framework[45] was created by Jack Bergstrand, combining years of his research in social science and business experience in large and small organizations. Influenced by Peter Drucker's work on knowledge-worker productivity,[46] this framework consists of four key knowledge-work productivity areas:

1. Envision
2. Design
3. Build
4. Operate.

This framework and associated online tools have been used in many organizations to improve knowledge-work productivity and to facilitate sustainable enterprise reinvention. Organizations that have a balance in all four areas have better knowledge-work productivity.

As the underlying paradigm behind the Reinvention Framework is aligned with the findings of my research and philosophical thinking, I decided to map the 120 questions from the 6 Box Leadership Model to the four phases of the Reinvention Framework. Unsurprisingly, the 120 questions fitted very well within the phases of the Reinvention Framework, with 30 questions within each phase. This enabled cross-checking of the results and the ability to ascertain if an organization completing the 6 Box Leadership survey has any issues with knowledge-work productivity. The same data could be looked at from different perspectives.

Second additional mapping: Management 2.0 principles

During the course of this research, I had the privilege to have a leading role in Gary Hamel's 2012 Management 2.0 Hackathon, conducted within the Management Innovation Exchange (MIX) community. More information about this global collaborative experience will be provided in Chapter 7.

As outlined in Chapter 1, the Management 2.0 Hackathon resulted in the following 12 principles:[47]

1. Openness
2. Community
3. Meritocracy
4. Activism
5. Collaboration
6. Meaning
7. Autonomy
8. Serendipity
9. Decentralization
10. Experimentation

11. Speed

12. Trust.

Although the actual results of this Hackathon were not subjected to further research, the underlying paradigm was closely aligned to my research, and so, as with the Reinvention Framework, I mapped the 120 questions from the 6 Box Leadership Model to the 12 principles of Management 2.0. Unsurprisingly again, the questions fitted in well and ten questions were mapped to each principle. Using this mapping, the 6 Box Leadership diagnostic enables assessment as to what extent an organization has implemented Management 2.0 principles and which are the strongest and weakest principles, depending on average scores obtained for each principle.

Third additional mapping: the key ideas of Peter Drucker

As the founder and CEO of the Drucker Society London, I have the privilege to be associated closely with the Drucker Institute and the work of the pioneering management thinker Peter Drucker. His ideas are closely associated with my research and thinking. As illustrated in Table 1.2, when I mapped the key ideas of Peter Drucker to Management 2.0 principles, the similarities were clear. The logical next step was to map these ideas to the 120 questions from the 6 Box Leadership Model.

Following my research into Peter Drucker's books,[48,49,50,51,52,53,54] eight key ideas from his work were selected, and all 120 questions were mapped into groups related to these ideas:

1. Productive organization/decentralization
2. Respect of workers/employees as assets
3. Knowledge-work productivity
4. The imperative of community
5. Focus on serving customers
6. Responsibility for the common good
7. Focusing on core competencies/properly executing business processes
8. Management by balancing a variety of needs and goals.

Using this mapping of the 6 Box Leadership questions enables assessment of the extent to which an organization is managed using Peter Drucker principles and which are the strongest and weakest principles, depending on average scores obtained for each idea. An organization with high scores (> 60 percent) could be considered to be managed more in line with Peter Drucker or Management 2.0 principles or paradigm than according to Tayloristic or Management 1.0.

Statistical Analysis

After producing the final version of the diagnostic tool and following further empirical testing, statistical analysis has been performed on a random sample of 456 data sets, using Statistical Analysis System (SAS)[55] software. The main objective was to check the reliability of the final questionnaire and check the correlation between the data. The key results are summarized and discussed briefly below.

A questionnaire reliability test, using the Cronbach Alpha coefficient, was performed to check the internal consistency. The Cronbach Alpha coefficient is commonly used as an internal consistency estimate of reliability of test scores. It increases as the intercorrelations among test items increase. Values close to 1 indicate very high reliability and close correlation among sets of items within a group.

As can be seen in Table 5.2, for all six groups of questions (S1–S6) Cronbach Alpha values show good to excellent consistency.

TABLE 5.2   Cronbach Alpha coefficients for measuring internal consistency

Variable	Cronbach Alpha Coefficient
S1- Culture	0.885921
S2 - Relationships	0.847409
S3 - Individuals	0.812090
S4 - Strategy	0.875722
S5 - Systems	0.938309
S6 - Resources	0.828690

Appendix 8 gives examples of other statistical tests, such as a normal distribution test, correlation between groups of questions and regression analysis, conducted.

The Process of the 6 Box Leadership Diagnostic Development: A Summary

In summary, the following nine steps within the process of the development of the 6 Box Leadership diagnostic tool have been taken:

1. Development of an initial framework with 130 factors (grouped in six areas: Culture, Relationships, Individuals, Strategy, Systems, Resources) that drive value creation in organizations based on more than 15 years of empirical and theoretical research using a thematic analysis with coding
2. Development of the online questionnaire with 105 questions
3. Empirical testing of the online questionnaire on ten organizations
4. Development of the final framework with 150 factors that drive value creation in organizations, based on additional research and further thematic analysis[56] with final coding
5. Development of the final version of the online questionnaire with 120 questions
6. Producing mappings of 120 questions to additional three frameworks: Reinvention Framework, Management 2.0 principles and the key ideas of Peter Drucker
7. Development of the new 6 Box Leadership software platform for data collection and analysis, with enhanced functionalities that include all four mappings of 120 questions
8. Empirical use of an online diagnostic tool in 11 additional organizations
9. Statistical analysis of a data sample to determine reliability of the questionnaire and data correlation.

The original basis for the 6 Box Leadership Model was more than 15 years of research, but it took a further four years of intensive research and practical work to complete the above nine steps. Prior to that, it took almost two years of research to develop the 5 Level Emergent Leadership Model presented in Chapter 4.

Using the Four Mappings in Practice

The final version of the 6 Box Leadership diagnostic tool using four different mappings enables data collected to be analyzed in four different ways. This provides a comprehensive insight into what is happening within an organization. Hidden strengths and weaknesses are uncovered so that specific, tailor-made action can be taken for maximum benefit and impact. A specific Action Plan, based on the highest and lowest scores in each of the six areas, is designed and discussed within an organization, and it is decided what actions will be taken to leverage strengths and address weaknesses or developmental opportunities. For most projects, particularly those for larger organizations, data is usually separated in different samples to provide an insight into differences within the group.

For example, data can be separated per department, geographical location, managerial level, etc. It is always interesting to see how different the obtained results are between different managerial levels. The pattern I observed is that the scores from the higher management levels tend to be higher than scores from the lower levels and qualitative comments often confirm that what senior managers think is happening in an organization is not always the case.

For all four mappings of the 120 questions that drive value creation, innovation and engagement in organizations, questions (factors) that elicit an average score below 40–50 percent are considered an indication of areas of possible weakness or a potential developmental opportunity, and scores above 60 percent are considered as a strength that should be leveraged further. Scores are relative for a particular organization, and relatively high scores in one organization could be considered as low in another organization that has higher average scores in all areas.

Appendix 9 gives an example of aggregate scores obtained by a company using all four mappings. Average scores for each mapping are displayed as well as ten most frequently used keywords in comments provided by survey participants. Some average scores obtained for questions in the Culture section of the 6 Box Leadership Model are also shown.

Standard process for implementing the 6 Box Leadership diagnostic

In a typical project where this diagnostic tool has been used, the following process is implemented:

- Initial meeting with the executive group is organized to ascertain the current issues faced, the main purpose of the project and to determine a sample size. In smaller organizations (up to 200 employees) all employees are invited to take part in the survey. For larger organizations, a representative sample from all managerial levels, departments or functional units is selected. Data can be separated according to any demographic variable and samples can be separated according to company-specific criteria, which enables useful comparisons
- A link to the questionnaire is sent to all participants in the survey. Once the data is collected, a software system produces reports with the raw data and a PDF file of the aggregate report
- Raw data is analyzed and a company-specific report is produced highlighting all the key strengths and developmental opportunities. On the basis of that report, an Action Plan is produced
- The report and Action Plan are presented to the executive group (and that might involve a wider selection of employees) and it is discussed which items from the Action Plan are of the highest importance and which individual and organizational actions could be taken to address action points on a short- (within one month), medium- (between two to six months) and long-term (more than six months) basis. This results in specific recommendations for action that are then normally discussed widely with all employees, often using a social media tool to facilitate this discussion. This leads to the creation of a list of the final action points that are being implemented in practice
- Once the action points are implemented, their impact is monitored every three to six months, feedback is obtained, further action is taken,

and in some cases the diagnostic process is repeated 12 to 18 months later and scores are compared with the original scores. Further action is then taken depending on the new scores. This process involves a combination of incremental and continuous improvements that lead to value creation and various (often unpredictable) benefits.

The 6 Box Leadership diagnostic could be used to achieve Jim Collins' Flywheel Effect[57] – the additive effect of many small initiatives and changes makes them act on each other like compound interest. Complexity theory explains a similar phenomenon – even small changes can result in a big, unforeseeable impact.

Some examples of output, projects and benefits obtained

The 6 Box Leadership diagnostic has been used in more than 20 organizations worldwide, in public and private sectors, in small organizations with a dozen employees and large corporations with tens of thousands of employees. In my experience, all companies that have used the 6 Box Leadership diagnostic tool so far have obtained numerous benefits, both expected and unexpected. Table 5.3 gives examples of some benefits obtained in a sample of organizations that used this diagnostic tool for transformation and improvement. Several other, more detailed case studies will be provided in Chapter 6.

Benefits from changes that were implemented as a result of the 6 Box Leadership diagnostic tool can be expected and unexpected, qualitative and quantitative; they may be subtle, incremental or substantial. The results from the diagnostic show the areas in which an organization is operating according to Level 4 management (these are the areas of strengths, with scores above 60 percent) and which areas need to be addressed to get the whole organizational culture to Level 4 and achieve The Management Shift. As discussed before, this will lead to many positive ripple effects for all stakeholders. The next chapter will present four detailed case studies to further illustrate the practical usability of the 6 Box Leadership Model for value creation, and to show how research can be turned into action.

TABLE 5.3   Examples of some of the 6 Box Leadership projects and obtained benefits

Type of organization	Examples of benefits obtained from the 6 Box Leadership survey
FTSE100 company, UK	This large retail company has been going through a company-wide performance improvement initiative and the 6 Box Leadership survey has been done to facilitate this project. The results obtained revealed several key areas that the company needed to address to improve overall performance and improve enabling conditions for innovation and engagement. These results were used for the development of the subsequent stages of the performance improvement initiative. Since this project was completed, this company experienced a 33% increase in revenue and an increase in net profit of 213%
Central government department, UK	The 6 Box Leadership survey has been done in all departments of the central government unit. The results obtained informed the Executive Board of the key strategic areas that this organization needs to focus on to improve performance and innovation, and some of these results were used for a new strategic focus. The results of this analysis were also used to design a tailored three-year-long senior management development program, where key areas for improvement discovered through the 6 Box Leadership analysis were addressed directly. Finally, it has been decided that the 6 Box Leadership Model will be used as a framework for development of a new HR strategy for this organization
Media company, South Africa	The 6 Box Leadership survey has included all employees of this SME. The results have revealed some fundamental problems in several areas (boxes), which led to the decision by the Managing Director to sell the company. He said: "This is a very accurate assessment of the business. I was impressed. It highlighted some fundamental problems with the business." The company was sold a few months after the survey was completed
Vocational training company, UK	The 6 Box Leadership survey was conducted in HR and IT departments of this major vocational training company, supported by the UK government. The results provided a valuable insight into key areas for improvement, which will provide enabling conditions for better performance and innovation in these two departments. These areas were subsequently addressed and were also used to design an internal leadership-training program for the key executives
IT training company, UK	The 6 Box Leadership survey was conducted across the entire organization, where interesting dynamics amongst various national training centres were revealed. These results were used by the CEO to initiate a number of changes to improve performance of some of the lower performing training centres, as well as introducing company-wide initiatives to improve connectivity and collaboration between different parts of the organization

National Health Service (NHS) organizations, UK	Four projects have been conducted in various parts of the NHS to discover key drivers for performance and key areas for improvement. All projects provided valuable insights for these organizations, as reflected, for example, in the statement of the Chief Executive of one of the Integrated Primary Care Commissioning organizations: "Confirming what was working well for us and discovering what was really driving our success has proven to be very enlightening. Equally, being able to see the organization through our staff's perceptions and linking this to our culture, strategy and processes has been very valuable. We now have a holistic perspective through which to help sustain and enhance our performance, engagement and patient outcomes"
An academic department, UK	The Leadership survey was conducted in an academic department of a UK university to discover the key blockages to innovation and engagement. Following a feedback session, a plan was developed to address key blockages that the department could address internally to improve academic output. This has resulted in more innovative ideas, new projects and new communities of passion formed by academic staff, involving both internal and external communities

In summary, the 6 Box Leadership Model provides assistance to managers to enable more value creation and implementation of the emerging management approaches that will lead to more innovation, better performance and engagement in the organizations they manage. It enables an organization to discover hidden areas of strengths, hidden dependencies and blockages to performance; it uncovers developmental opportunities and helps organizations to systematically turn potential into results and turn staff engagement insights into value drivers. Overall, the 6 Box Leadership diagnostic helps organizations to achieve The Management Shift – a shift in management paradigm (and that includes new ways of thinking and being) and a shift in management practices. The results are far-reaching for individual employees, the individual organization and the society of which they form a part.

SEVEN REFLECTION POINTS

1. What is the importance of managing organizations holistically as living organisms?
2. If you look at the list of some factors that drive innovation, engagement and value creation in organizations, which of these factors are strong and which are weak in your organization?
3. In which ways could you leverage the strengths and weaknesses in your organization?
4. If the 6 Box Leadership diagnostic was conducted in your organization/department, what level of scores would you expect to get in each of the key six areas?
5. How would you address individually and organizationally any problematic areas that might emerge?
6. Do you think your 6 Box Leadership scores might be comparable to the scores of your competitors?
7. If you had a chance to do the 6 Box Leadership diagnostic in your organization, how would you like the data to be separated (for example, per managerial level, per department, per geographical location, etc.)?

6

The 6 Box Leadership Model in Action: Practical Examples

This chapter provides answers to the following key questions:

- How can knowledge be put into action by using the 6 Box Leadership diagnostic for The Management Shift?
- How can the 6 Box Leadership diagnostic be used in small, medium and large organizations, in public and private sectors operating in different cultures?
- How can the 6 Box Leadership diagnostic be used to facilitate development of a growth strategy?
- How can the 6 Box Leadership diagnostic be used to facilitate innovation and engagement of employees?
- How can the 6 Box Leadership diagnostic be used to improve customer service?
- How can the 6 Box Leadership diagnostic be a life-changing experience?
- How is the 6 Box Leadership diagnostic different from other organizational diagnostic tools?
- Why is the 6 Box Leadership diagnostic considered to be *the* tool for The Management Shift?

Application of the 6 Box Leadership Model in Practice for The Management Shift

The 6 Box Leadership Model has been proven in practice, with more than 20 organizations worldwide benefiting in various ways from this diagnostic and associated Action Plans. As Peter Drucker said: "The knowledge that we consider knowledge proves itself in action. What we now mean by knowledge is information in action, information focused on results."[1] The knowledge behind the 6 Box Leadership Model has been proven in action repeatedly.

As shown in Chapter 5, there is a standard process followed in all projects, from eliciting specific organizational objectives and requirements, conducting a survey and analyzing the data, to creating an Action Plan and overseeing its implementation. Implemented actions at individual and organizational levels have resulted in various changes, improvements and in many cases major transformations.

In this chapter, I have selected four case studies that will illustrate in more detail how the 6 Box Leadership Model and associated diagnostics have been used in the private and public sectors, in small, medium and large organizations, in different parts of the world. It would be far too lengthy to present and discuss all results obtained in each example, so I have selected some of the key findings for illustrative purposes and shown how the results obtained from the 6 Box Leadership diagnostic were translated into action and transformation.

The first example I selected for this chapter relates to a small management consultancy based in the US. The main objective of the 6 Box Leadership diagnostic was to help this company design a new strategy for growth. The result was substantial growth achieved within 18 months of the project's completion. The second example is a medium-sized insurance company based in the City of London. The objective of the project was to look into ways to improve innovation and engagement. The diagnostic uncovered various strengths and developmental opportunities that formed the basis for further action. As a result, this company implemented a more tailored and employee-focused approach to training and development. A further positive outcome was the development of a new, more proactive approach to charitable giving. The third example presented relates to a large NHS Trust in the UK. The 6 Box Leadership diagnostic was used as a part of the large organizational change program; it facilitated development of a new strategy and resulted in various initiatives for improving employee engagement and customer service. The final, fourth example selected for this chapter relates to a division of a medium-sized Norwegian IT consultancy. For reasons explained later in this chapter, there was no organizational action for change implemented following the 6 Box Leadership survey, but for the executive who commissioned the survey, this project triggered a truly life-changing experience!

Example 1: The US Management Consultancy – Facilitating Strategy for Growth

This US-based management consultancy was established more than ten years ago by a C-level executive from one of the world's largest corporate brands. The company employs highly qualified and experienced consultants who have held major executive roles in large corporations. It operates in a specific niche market focusing on large companies. At the beginning of this project, the company was planning a new expansion strategy.

Amongst the other companies that had already implemented the 6 Box Leadership diagnostic tool, a number had, up to that point, predominantly been using traditional (Level 3 – Management 1.0) management practices, and the diagnostic helped them to identify bottlenecks for achieving The Management Shift (moving to Level 4 – Management 2.0). This consultancy, by contrast, had already implemented many management practices pertinent to Management 2.0 and key Peter Drucker ideas, and this was reflected in the high scores it achieved for all four mappings. The company's main objective now was to identify key strengths and developmental opportunities that it could use for growth strategy and market expansion.

As this was a small company with just nine employees, all employees were invited to take part in the 6 Box Leadership survey, and the response rate was 100 percent (in larger companies a sample of employees is normally chosen to take part in a survey).

Examples of the key results

As anticipated, all scores obtained were higher than those obtained in other projects completed up until the time this survey was conducted. Table 6.1 shows summary scores for the 6 Box Leadership mapping.

TABLE 6.1   Aggregate 6 Box Leadership scores

Box	Score
Culture	76%
Relationships	81%
Individuals	82%
Strategy	75%
Systems	79%
Resources	75%

Table 6.1 shows that high, fairly uniform average scores were obtained for all six boxes. The difference between average scores is only 7 percent. Individuals is the highest scoring box, with an average score of 82 percent, while Resources and Strategy are the lowest scoring boxes, with an average score of 75 percent.

For each of the six boxes, the highest (key strengths) and lowest (key developmental opportunities) scoring questions were identified. Table 6.2 shows an example of this analysis conducted for the Culture box. Questions annotated with a star (*) are negatively phrased questions for which original scores were inverted. Original scores are shown in brackets. The examples of key strengths in the area of Culture for this company include: ethical behavior, encouragement used instead of criticism, a caring

TABLE 6.2 An example of highest and lowest scores for questions in the Culture box

Culture			
Key Strengths		**Key Developmental Opportunities**	
Question	**Score**	**Question**	**Score**
Ethical behavior is part of our culture	98%	Employees are overworked *	55% (45%)
Encouragement is used regularly instead of criticism	95%	Employees are stressed *	43% (57%)
Our organization has a caring ethos	93%	Command and control is part of our culture *	58% (42%)
Transparency is part of our culture	93%	Senior management determines the culture *	20% (80%)
Trust is part of our culture	90%		
Employee's values are aligned with the organization's values	88%		

TABLE 6.3 Aggregate Reinvention scores

Area of Knowledge Work Productivity	Score
Envision	78%
Design	76%
Build	79%
Operate	79%

ethos, transparency and trust are part of the culture, and there is alignment of individual and organizational values. Possible developmental opportunities in the area of Culture include: potential stress and burnout issues; addressing possible elements of command and control.

Table 6.3 shows the aggregate scores for Reinvention Framework mapping. This framework shows areas of knowledge-work productivity. Organizations with good knowledge-work productivity have a good balance of scores across all four areas of the framework: Envision, Design, Build and Operate. High, balanced scores in these areas are also likely to indicate Level 4 organization according to the Emergent Leadership Model.

TABLE 6.4   Aggregate scores for the key ideas of Peter Drucker

Principle	Score
Productive organization/decentralization	66%
Respect of workers/employees as assets	80%
Knowledge-work productivity	81%
Imperative of community	85%
Focus on serving customers	87%
Responsibility for the common good	81%
Focusing on core competencies/properly executing business processes	78%
Management by balancing a variety of needs and goals	75%

The Reinvention scores obtained for the management consultancy show high, balanced scores for all four areas of the Reinvention Framework, with the difference of only 3 percent between four phases. This balance is likely to indicate a high-performing Level 4 organization. The lowest score was achieved for Design (76 percent) and the highest scores were achieved for Build and Operate.

Table 6.4 shows that high average scores were achieved for all eight key principles of Peter Drucker's work. However, there is some spread (21 percent) between the scores. The highest scoring principle is Focus on serving customers (87 percent), followed by Imperative of community (85 percent). The lowest scoring principle is Productive organization/ decentralization (66 percent), followed by Management by balancing a variety of needs and goals (75 percent).

Table 6.5 shows that high scores are achieved for all 12 principles of Management 2.0. The highest scoring principles are: Collaboration (85 percent), Serendipity (82 percent), Meaning (81 percent), Experimentation (81 percent) and Meritocracy (81 percent). The lowest scoring principles are: Decentralization (64 percent), Openness (76 percent) and Speed (76 percent). The issue of decentralization is consistent with findings from the 6 Box Leadership and Peter Drucker's ideas mappings.

TABLE 6.5   Aggregate scores for the Management 2.0 principles

Principle	Score	Principle	Score
Openness	76%	Autonomy	79%
Community	80%	Serendipity	82%
Meritocracy	81%	Decentralization	64%
Activism	78%	Experimentation	81%
Collaboration	85%	Speed	76%
Meaning	81%	Trust	78%

Overall findings for the management consultancy

In general, the management consultancy achieved very high scores for all four mappings, with few areas that could be further improved. Scores for the 6 Box Leadership Model and Reinvention Framework are more uniform than scores for the key ideas of Peter Drucker's and Management 2.0 principles. Key themes that emerged include: this company's motivated and purposeful employees are its greatest asset, which could be further leveraged by fine tuning some processes and governance structure.

The key strengths of this company achieved very high scores. In general, the key developmental opportunities were identified as questions with relatively lower scores, though for many of these questions the scores would be considered as high in other organizations that have overall 10–20 percent lower scores. Whilst there are many areas of strengths, very few developmental opportunities have scores that would indicate a major concern (below 40–50 percent).

Examples of the key strengths include: caring, transparent culture based on trust, ethical values, meritocracy and accountability; strong teamwork and collaboration ethos going across organizational boundaries; highly motivated employees, feeling happy, purposeful and passionate about their work; aligned systems and strategy; flexible working practices; alignment of information management and strategy; and good access and accuracy of information.

Examples of the key developmental opportunities for the management consultancy include: addressing possible issues of stress and burnout; addressing a possible issue of tendency for command and control; participative strategy development; improving flexibility of processes; closing gaps between stated and realized objectives; reducing hierarchical structure; improving access to training and development and mentoring processes; reducing control of budgets when appropriate; and creating enabling conditions for change.

Translating scores into action

The results of the 6 Box Leadership diagnostic were discussed with the Executive Board of the management consultancy. Some of the questions and recommendations discussed include:

How do we further develop and leverage key strengths?

Whilst key strengths are likely to make sense, what about the key developmental opportunities?

To what extent are these developmental opportunities relevant for our processes and practice?

What would be the top three developmental opportunities that could be addressed in the next three to six months that would make the biggest impact on employees and the expansion strategy?

On the basis of the survey results, an Action Plan was created and discussed with the Executive Board. The following steps were implemented:

(a) Prioritizing key strengths that need to be leveraged further

(a) Prioritizing key developmental opportunities that need to be addressed to create the biggest impact

(b) Assigning a time scale for further leveraging strengths and addressing weaknesses that were rated as highly important

(c) Designing a plan for individual and organizational action to be taken to leverage strengths and address weaknesses that were rated as highly important

(d) Implementing a plan for action

(e) Repeating the 6 Box Leadership analysis in 9 to 12 months to compare the scores and assess the impact of changes.

The above steps were implemented, and as part of this process members of the Executive Board gave their feedback on the 6 Box Leadership diagnostic and its usability. Table 6.6 summarizes some of the key comments that emerged from the feedback session, whilst Table 6.7 summarizes the key action points that were implemented. Eighteen months after this project was completed, the company doubled in size (from 9 to 18 employees) and increased revenue by 500 percent.

TABLE 6.6   Feedback on the 6 Box Leadership diagnostic from the Executive Board

"The 6 Box Leadership survey identified what are important areas to look at for value creation"
"Regarding our internal use of 6 Box Leadership, it would be helpful to both improve our operating model by doing an internal session on this, and it would serve to improve our overall knowledge of 6 Box Leadership regarding how it can improve performance and create value within an organization"
"The 6 Box Leadership is helpful for dealing with the maturity of culture and the relationship of culture to the ability to move to a more structured and process-based approach to running and growing a business"
"I think looking at the low scores around decentralization, closing the gap between stated and realized objectives and dealing with burnout/frustration issues will allow us to shape our discussions and develop action plans that can address our weaknesses and improve our strengths simultaneously"
"I can see using 6 Box Leadership on the front end of a transformation engagement (for example, to compare 'as is' with the desired 'to be' for the organization), or as a standalone offering (that may compete against less powerful 'employee engagement' offerings). Doing so would likely show gaps between where an organization is today and where its leader would like it to be"
"The even balance between the EDBO segments, the high cultural alignment among the group, and the positive relationships between individuals reflects the care we have taken to build our team. I think that is an area [of which] we should be justifiably quite proud, but [which] will be hard to maintain as we grow. It also brings up the question of where we should focus for growing our resources. Keeping our resources balanced between the quadrants might not be the best growth model depending on the future content of our work"
"Several of the identified weaknesses – mentoring, development of people and authoritative model - are natural areas of development for a small firm and one that is focused on establishing and building its market position. That said, I agree they are areas of future focus. I think mentoring is a particularly key area as we develop our resources and add resources to the firm"

Continued

TABLE 6.6 *Continued*

"6 Box Leadership compares favorably with other frameworks of this type, but it assumes that the buyer is interested in the most powerful solution"
"6 Box Leadership has better fundamentals than some other approaches"
"6 Box Leadership integrates the systems/process, strategy and resources (the hard side of culture) much more directly and efficiently"
"The link to the Reinvention Framework potentially adds a lot more of an action component than do most competing models"

TABLE 6.7   Actions taken in the management consultancy as a result of the 6 Box Leadership diagnostic

Redesigned and implemented a new Intranet site for the entire team, with enhanced social collaboration capabilities and more efficient information communication and retrieval
Updated the internal HR personal assessment process to provide more transparency to individual and team strengths, areas for development and productivity barriers
Enhanced internal accountability through documented commitments by individuals that are measurable, tied to a contribution action plan and will be proactively tracked
Looking at "What should we stop doing?", "What should we continue and build upon?" and "What should we start doing?", the management consultancy streamlined its approach to internal meetings, reinforcing an action orientation (versus a reporting orientation) and leveraging more efficient vehicles (for example, weekly two-minute voicemail updates, the new Intranet site, etc.) to keep the team informed

Example 2: The City of London Insurance Company – Engaging Employees

This award-winning City of London-based underwriting agency was established over 13 years prior to our consultancy. It is a privately owned medium-sized company that provides insurance solutions to tens of thousands of small- and medium-sized businesses. It deals only with approved insurance brokers, focusing on building policies to best suit customers based on product values such as coverage, clarity and customer focus.

The main objective of the 6 Box Leadership diagnostic was to identify hidden strengths and weaknesses and discover ways to improve performance and employee engagement. The company currently has just over

70 employees. All employees were invited to complete the 6 Box Leadership survey and the response rate was 100 percent. The project was commissioned by the Managing Director and Marketing Director and they wanted the data to be separated according to managerial level. So, the data collected was separated into three samples: Directors (D) (most senior level executives; there were six directors in this sample), Managers (M) (middle-level managers; there were nine managers in this sample) and Staff (S) (including all other staff members; there were 56 staff members in this sample).

Examples of the key results

Tables 6.8 to 6.10 show aggregate 6 Box Leadership scores for all three samples.

In this sample, high to very high scores are obtained for all six boxes, with the difference between average scores being 21 percent. Individuals is the highest scoring box, with an average score of 85 percent, and Culture is the lowest scoring box, with an average score of 64 percent.

High scores are obtained for all six boxes in this sample as well. The difference between average scores is 18 percent. Individuals is the highest scoring box, with an average score of 80 percent, and Resources is the lowest scoring box, with an average score of 62 percent.

Reasonably high and quite uniform scores are obtained for all six boxes. The difference between average scores is 7 percent. Strategy is the highest

TABLE 6.8   The 6 Box Leadership scores for Directors

Box	Score
Culture	64%
Relationships	80%
Individuals	85%
Strategy	73%
Systems	70%
Resources	73%

TABLE 6.9   The 6 Box Leadership scores for Managers

Box	Score
Culture	63%
Relationships	74%
Individuals	80%
Strategy	70%
Systems	68%
Resources	62%

TABLE 6.10   The 6 Box Leadership scores for Staff

Box	Score
Culture	62%
Relationships	68%
Individuals	68%
Strategy	69%
Systems	66%
Resources	63%

scoring box, with an average score of 69 percent, whilst Culture is the lowest scoring box, with an average score of 62 percent. It is interesting to note the differences between the scores provided by Directors and Staff. As observed in other projects, scores from senior managers tend to be higher than scores from the rest of the staff, indicating that senior managers might think an organization is doing well in all or most of the six areas but the rest of the organization might not agree.

Tables 6.11 to 6.13 show examples of the highest and lowest scores achieved in the Culture box for all three samples.

There are many questions with very high scores in the Culture box in all three samples. Key strengths were consistent for all three samples: innovation is part of the culture (D, M, S); culture focuses on delighting customers (D, M, S); employees are motivated to do their best at work

TABLE 6.11   An example of highest and lowest scores for questions in the Culture box for Directors

Culture			
Key Strengths		**Key Developmental Opportunities**	
Question	**Score**	**Question**	**Score**
Innovation is part of our culture	100%	Senior management determines the culture	13%* (87%)
Our culture focuses on delighting customers	97%	Trial and error is part of our culture	23%
Employees are motivated to do their best at work	93%	Giving back to the community is part of our culture	33%
Our culture has a sense of purpose	90%	Environmental responsibility is part of our culture	40%

TABLE 6.12   An example of highest and lowest scores for questions in the Culture box for Managers

Culture			
Key Strengths		**Key Developmental Opportunities**	
Question	**Score**	**Question**	**Score**
Innovation is part of our culture	98%	Senior management determines the culture	11%* (89)%
Our culture has a sense of purpose	96%	Command and control is part of our culture	31%* (69%)
Our culture focuses on delighting customers	87%	Employees are stressed	33%* (67%)
Employees are motivated to do their best at work	84%	Giving back to the community is part of our culture	36%* (64%)

(D, M, S,); culture has a sense of purpose (D, M, S). Examples of areas identified as developmental opportunities include: senior management determines the culture (D, M, S); trial and error does not seem to be part of the culture (D); giving back to the community does not seem to be part of the culture (D, M); command and control seems to be part

TABLE 6.13   An example of highest and lowest scores for questions in the Culture box for Staff

Culture			
Key Strengths		**Key Developmental Opportunities**	
Question	**Score**	**Question**	**Score**
Innovation is part of our culture	90%	Senior management determines the culture	24%* (76%)
Our culture focuses on delighting customers	90%	Employees are stressed	30%* (70%)
Our culture has a sense of purpose	85%	Employees are overworked	32%* (68%)
Employees are motivated to do their best at work	84%	Command and control is part of our culture	38%* (62%)

TABLE 6.14   Aggregate Reinvention scores for the three samples

Area of Knowledge-Work Productivity	Directors	Managers	Staff
Envision	68%	70%	69%
Design	72%	66%	63%
Build	73%	69%	68%
Operate	77%	72%	66%

of the culture (M, S); employees are stressed (M, S) and employees are overworked (S).

The above examples of some of the key results in the area of Culture illustrate how the 6 Box Leadership diagnostic is used in practice. The results in all six areas are too extensive to cover in detail here and so I have illustrated aggregate scores for four mappings and provided an example of the results in one of the six boxes. Table 6.14 shows the aggregate scores for Reinvention Framework mapping.

Table 6.14 shows relatively high scores achieved for all four phases of the Reinvention Framework for all three samples, although scores for the Directors sample are higher in almost all areas than scores in the other two samples. A reasonably good balance between scores for all phases was achieved. Improving this balance would lead to further improvement in performance and knowledge-work productivity.

Table 6.15 shows aggregate scores obtained for the third mapping – the key ideas from Peter Drucker.

The above results show reasonably high scores were achieved for all eight principles, with some differences between scores. The highest scoring principle for all three samples is Focus on serving customers, which was revealed in the Culture box as well. The lowest scoring principle for all three samples is Productive organization/decentralization, which indicates some centralization in management style, also revealed in the Culture box.

Table 6.16 shows aggregate scores for the fourth mapping – Management 2.0 principles.

Reasonably high scores are achieved for all 12 principles of Management 2.0. The highest scoring principles are: Serendipity (for Directors and Managers) and Experimentation (for Staff). The lowest scoring principle is Openness for all three samples, which was revealed in the 6 Box Leadership mapping in the Systems box.

TABLE 6.15   Aggregate scores for the key ideas of Peter Drucker

Principle	Directors	Managers	Staff
Productive organization/decentralization	58%	55%	57%
Respect of workers/employees as assets	76%	69%	63%
Knowledge-work productivity	75%	73%	71%
Imperative of community	76%	80%	74%
Focus on serving customers	87%	83%	72%
Responsibility for the common good	64%	65%	63%
Focusing on core competencies/properly executing business processes	74%	68%	67%
Management by balancing a variety of needs and goals	78%	70%	68%

TABLE 6.16   Aggregate scores for Management 2.0 principles

Principle	Directors	Managers	Staff
Openness	64%	60%	58%
Community	76%	68%	70%
Meritocracy	66%	64%	65%
Activism	78%	71%	64%
Collaboration	79%	77%	72%
Meaning	75%	73%	70%
Autonomy	73%	70%	61%
Serendipity	83%	80%	64%
Decentralization	63%	57%	59%
Experimentation	75%	77%	73%
Speed	76%	62%	65%
Trust	72%	69%	64%

Overall findings for the insurance company

In general, reasonably high scores were achieved for all four mappings for all three samples. There are many areas with high scores, which indicate Level 4 management, but at the same time there are areas with scores below 40 percent, which indicate a Level 3 management tendency that could be addressed further. Key themes that emerged include: the company's motivated, passionate and purposeful employees are its greatest asset, which could be further leveraged by fine tuning some processes and governance structure. Examples of the key strengths in all six areas include: innovation is part of the culture (D, M, S); culture focuses on delighting customers (D, M, S); employees are motivated to do their best at work (D, M, S); culture has a sense of purpose (D, M, S). Furthermore, work is not hampered by individuals who dominate (D); there is interaction between different teams (D, M, S); employees are passionate about their work (D, M, S); organization has the capability to recruit and retain high-calibre employees (D, M, S); the physical environment is pleasant to work in (D, S); and information management is aligned with strategy (S).

Examples of key developmental opportunities include: considering more inclusive ways to develop culture; making trial and error part of the culture; making giving back to the community and environmental responsibility part of the culture; looking at ways to reduce employees' stress and burnout; considering establishing coaching and mentoring processes and involving employees in this action; considering how experimentation could be encouraged more; and examining how employees could more regularly improve their skills (including management skills). Also, looking at how many employees over and above the senior management team could be involved in defining strategy; placing more emphasis on long-term performance than short-term results; considering how employees could be a higher priority for the organization; reflecting on how there could be a less rigid hierarchical structure; considering how there could be more flexible working practices (for example, flexitime); and changing compensation schemes more often.

Translating scores into action

Following a presentation of the survey results to the group of directors, an Action Plan was created to leverage key strengths and address key developmental opportunities. This plan and the key results were presented to all staff, and their feedback on actions to be taken immediately for the biggest impact was elicited, using the Yammer social media platform. Table 6.17 summarizes some of the key actions that have been taken following the 6 Box Leadership survey.

As can be seen from the examples in Table 6.17, a number of new actions and initiatives have been started as a direct result of the 6 Box Leadership survey. Overall consensus in this company was that the survey identified some important issues to address in order to further improve engagement and performance. Initial feedback shows that various benefits are emerging from actions taken, and a more people-focused approach is improving performance and engagement. Overall impact of the survey can be summarized by this quote from the Managing Director:

TABLE 6.17 Examples of actions taken as a result of the 6 Box Leadership survey

Issues Discovered in a Survey	Examples of Discussion	Action
INTERNAL COMMUNICATION	"Deal Of The Month (DOTM) is universally liked, and the only criticism is that we cancel it too often" "The Business Development Meeting (BDM) is generally liked, but we know that it is not scalable so the format needs a rethink" "There are some regular meetings that we can minute and share via Yammer. We have just started doing this for the Products Meeting" "We need to introduce a more formal and reliable way for all team heads to cascade the relevant information to their teams"	• G to make sure that we do the DOTM every month • G to rethink the BDM format in a post-Customer Relationship Management (CRM) environment • A to rethink the Underwriter Meeting format • A to plan more formal/uniform team leader cascading of information • Ensure that everybody uses CRM for every "biz dev" type email/phone call/meeting
GIVING BACK TO THE COMMUNITY	"People *don't* currently know what we do for charity" "Broker loyalty program provides 16 separate prizes of a £100 donation to the broker's charity of choice" "We should have a more transparent way of allocating charity funds" "If we had a Yammer Charity group and there was (a) a clearly defined pot of money and (b) a clearly defined set of charitable goals, then I am sure we would have more focus on raising extra funds and spending them *wisely*" "We should pick on a few projects each year where we can make a real difference"	• S to set up a new Yammer group, called Charity • D will kick this group off with thoughts and details of the Drucker Society London (DSL) charity • D to increase the charity budget in FY2015

| STRESS AND OVERWORK | "We are minded to employ new people as soon as we need them rather than delay, embedding a culture where we anticipate demand and employ more people accordingly"

"If you feel that your team is permanently understaffed, then either we have done a consistently bad job of anticipating demand or your team leader is not shouting loud enough!" | • Team leaders or mentor to be available to discuss any help needed for managing work or stress levels |
| --- | --- | --- |
| ON-BOARDING, TRAINING AND MENTORING | "This is one of the most important things for us to improve over the next couple of years"

"A far more complete induction process needs to be created for new joiners both generally and within their team"

"We are lacking the full suite of documentation that is required to support such a program; we need to create Underwriting Manuals for each team and A is already planning that project"

"To date we have lacked the central underwriting resource to make this happen in a more methodical way and the new project has been initiated to address this"

"We need more tailor-made training courses such as Effective Broker Communications"

"We need to organize more Lunch & Learn sessions" | • A to lead the Underwriting Manuals project
• D to lead the new on-boarding project for new joiners
• G to launch the Effective Broker Communications course
• G, A and D to build up a suite of relevant and tailored courses
• A and G to ensure regular product and NERD refresher Lunch & Learns |

The 6 Box Leadership survey was very easy to administer and came up with some very interesting findings. Perhaps most importantly, it provided the impetus for us to apply renewed vigour [sic] to the training and personal development of all staff and as a consequence we are now rewriting our training policy, making it far more *employee*-friendly, putting the onus on managers, mandating more training, and providing far more tailored courses. The survey also galvanized our approach to charity, which had previously been our best kept secret. We are now collecting a list of favoured [sic] charities from all staff and we will then have a poll to see which ones to support. We have also appointed a fund-raising champion who will be responsible for that task.

Example 3: The UK National Health Service Trust – Improving Employee Engagement and Customer Service

This NHS Trust had been established for more than ten years, to provide health and wellbeing services for a population of more than 1 million people. The Trust employs more than 7,000 members of staff working across more than 300 sites. Services are provided through various specialized networks covering a wide range of the population.

The 6 Box Leadership project was commissioned by one of the clinical directors and the Chief Operating Officer. At the time this project was conducted, the Trust had been going through a number of changes. The executive team changed with some new appointments. A new strategic plan had been developed, and the organization had been going through a Performance and Development Review process, and a Governance Audit and Staff Engagement survey. The Executive Board and heads of departments wanted to find out how the results of the 6 Box Leadership survey would correlate to other processes and data available about the organization, and how these results could be used for determining initiatives to further improve staff engagement and customer service.

It was decided to collect data using the 6 Box Leadership survey for three different samples: networks that have already implemented distributed

Examples of the key results

Tables 6.18 to 6.20 show aggregate 6 Box Leadership scores for all three samples.

TABLE 6.18   The 6 Box Leadership scores for Distributed Leadership Networks (DLN)

Box	Score
Culture	58%
Relationships	66%
Individuals	73%
Strategy	54%
Systems	54%
Resources	51%

TABLE 6.19   The 6 Box Leadership scores for Traditional Leadership Networks (TLN)

Box	Score
Culture	56%
Relationships	65%
Individuals	76%
Strategy	52%
Systems	53%
Resources	46%

TABLE 6.20   The 6 Box Leadership scores for Central Services (CS)

Box	Score
Culture	57%
Relationships	61%
Individuals	73%
Strategy	55%
Systems	52%
Resources	54%

leadership practices (DLN), networks using traditional leadership approaches (TLN), and central services (CS). Three random samples were selected from these three groups, with about 200 survey participants in each sample. Overall, 300 complete data records were obtained for three samples.

In this sample, medium to high scores are obtained for all six boxes. The difference between average scores is 22 percent. Individuals is the highest scoring box, with an average score of 73 percent, and Resources is the lowest scoring box, with an average score of 51 percent, which is not surprising given the issues around resources in the NHS.

Again, medium to high scores are obtained for all six boxes, though for most areas scores are lower than scores obtained for distributed leadership networks. The difference between average scores is substantial, at 30 percent. Individuals is the highest scoring box, with an average score of 76 percent, and again Resources is the lowest scoring box, with an average score of 46 percent.

In this sample as well, medium to high scores are obtained for all six boxes. The difference between average scores is 21 percent. Individuals is the highest scoring box, with an average score of 73 percent, and Systems is the lowest scoring box, with an average score of 52 percent.

Tables 6.21 to 6.23 show examples of the highest and lowest scores achieved in the Culture box for all three samples.

There are many common themes in the Culture box that emerged from all three samples. Key strengths included: accountability is part of the culture (DLN, TLN, CS); ethical behavior is part of the culture (DLN, TLN, CS); trust is part of the culture (DLN); employees are motivated to do their best at work (DLN); the culture has a sense of purpose (TLN, CS); employees' values are aligned with the organization's values (TLN, CS). Areas identified as developmental opportunities include: employees are stressed (DLN, TLN, CS); senior management determines the culture (DLN, TLN, CS); employees are overworked (DLN, TLN, CS); command and control is part of the culture (DLN, TLN, CS). Examples of the overall key strengths and developmental opportunities in the

TABLE 6.21 An example of highest and lowest scores for questions in the Culture box for Distributed Leadership Networks (DLN)

Culture			
Key Strengths		Key Developmental Opportunities	
Question	Score	Question	Score
Accountability is part of our culture	85%	Employees are stressed	20%* (80%)
Ethical behavior is part of our culture	79%	Senior management determines the culture	28%* (72%)
Trust is part of our culture	74%	Employees are overworked	28%* (72%)
Employees are motivated to do their best at work	73%	Command and control is part of our culture	41%* (59%)

TABLE 6.22 An example of highest and lowest scores for questions in the Culture box for Traditional Leadership Networks (TLN)

Culture			
Key Strengths		Key Developmental Opportunities	
Question	Score	Question	Score
Accountability is part of our culture	81%	Employees are stressed	22%* (78%)
Ethical is part of our culture	77%	Senior management determines the culture	27%* (73%)
Employees are motivated to do their best at work	73%	Employees are overworked	30%* (70%)
Our culture has a sense of purpose	72%	Command and control is part of our culture	33%* (67%)

TABLE 6.23 An example of highest and lowest scores for questions in the Culture box for Central Services (CS)

Culture			
Key Strengths		Key Developmental Opportunities	
Question	Score	Question	Score
Ethical behavior is part of our culture	77 %	Employees are stressed	26%* (78)%
Our culture has a sense of purpose	73 %	Senior management determines the culture	27%* (73%)
Accountability is part of our culture	73 %	Employees are overworked	33%* (70%)
Employees' values are aligned with the organization's values	73 %	Command and control is part of our culture	35%* (65%)

TABLE 6.24 Aggregate Reinvention scores for the three samples

Area Of Knowledge-Work Productivity	DLN	TLN	CS
Envision	64%	63%	63%
Design	56%	55%	56%
Build	54%	51%	54%
Operate	64%	64%	61%

TABLE 6.25 Aggregate scores for the key ideas of Peter Drucker

Principle	DLN	TLN	CS
Productive organization/decentralization	53%	50%	48%
Respect of workers/employees as assets	63%	62%	60%
Knowledge-work productivity	60%	58%	60%
Imperative of community	68%	68%	65%
Focus on serving customers	70%	66%	70%
Responsibility for the common good	67%	64%	66%
Focusing on core competencies/properly executing business processes	53%	53%	55%
Management by balancing a variety of needs and goals	51%	46%	51%

TABLE 6.26 Aggregate scores for Management 2.0 principles

Principle	DLN	TLN	CS
Openness	52%	52%	53%
Community	59%	58%	58%
Meritocracy	57%	55%	54%
Activism	66%	62%	60%
Collaboration	55%	50%	54%
Meaning	65%	64%	65%
Autonomy	59%	59%	59%
Serendipity	73%	80%	72%
Decentralization	49%	47%	50%
Experimentation	66%	67%	65%
Speed	46%	45%	45%
Trust	63%	61%	60%

six boxes will be provided below. Tables 6.24 to 6.26 show aggregate scores for the other three mappings: the Reinvention Framework, the key ideas of Peter Drucker and Management 2.0 principles respectively.

Medium to high scores were achieved for all four phases of the Reinvention Framework. There is a reasonably good balance between the scores for all phases in the three samples, with the difference of 10 percent between the four phases for DLN, 13 percent for TLN and 9 percent for CS. Improving this balance would lead to further improvement in performance and knowledge-work productivity.

Medium to high scores were achieved for all eight principles in the three samples. There is some difference between scores: the highest scoring principle for the DLN and CS samples is Focus on serving customers and Imperative of community for the TLN sample. The lowest scoring principle for the DLN and TLN samples is Management by balancing a variety of needs and goals and Productive organization/decentralization for the CS sample.

Medium to high scores are achieved for all 12 principles of Management 2.0 in all three samples. The highest scoring principle is Serendipity, for all three samples. The lowest scoring principle is Speed, again for all three samples, which means that there could be some bureaucratic barriers preventing work being completed faster, which is not uncommon in the public sector.

Overall findings for the NHS Trust

On the whole, reasonably high to medium scores were achieved for all four mappings in three samples. Key themes that emerged include: the passionate and motivated employees are the Trust's greatest asset, which could be further leveraged by fine tuning some processes and governance structure. Examples of some of the key strengths in all six areas include: accountability and ethical behavior are part of the culture (DLN, TLN, CS); trust is part of the culture (DLN); employees are motivated to do their best at work (DLN); culture has a sense of purpose (TLN, CS); innovation is part of the strategy (DLN, TLN, CS); work with customers is collaborative (DLN, TLN, CS); the organization's strategy is reviewed frequently (DLN, TLN, CS); employees form meaningful communities

(DLN, TLN, CS); there is good access to training and development (DLN, TLN, CS).

Examples of key developmental opportunities include: employees are overworked and stressed (DLN, TLN, CS); senior management determines the culture (DLN, TLN, CS); command and control is part of the culture (DLN, TLN, CS); work could be hampered by individuals who dominate (DLN, TLN, CS); coaching does not seem to be well established (DLN, TLN, CS); some employees seem to be feel unhappy at work (DLN, TLN, CS); when organizational problems arise, micro-management should not be the first response (DLN, TLN, CS); there seems to be a rigid hierarchical structure (DLN, TLN, CS); decisions might not be made by those who are most affected by them (TLN); budgets seem to be tightly controlled (DLN, TLN, CS); and it seems there are no convenient public spaces where employees can meet and interact (DLN, TLN).

Translating scores into action

Following a presentation of the 6 Box Leadership survey results to the group of directors, an Action Plan was created to leverage key strengths and to address key developmental opportunities. This Action Plan and the key results were presented to many staff members and key managers. A wide consultation and "creative discussions" took place, and directors of the key areas proposed action to be taken as a consequence. It was stated that the 6 Box Leadership survey provided "an important snapshot of an organization".

In addition, an HR Director was asked to write a report on how the findings from the 6 Box Leadership survey and the Staff Engagement survey would be used for the development of a new HR strategy. The new Chief Operating Officer is driving forward the initiative to use the findings of the 6 Box Leadership survey and other recent insights to develop a new leadership strategy and a shift of focus towards people, talents and incentives. The management team acknowledged that, as in many other NHS organizations, many staff members feel burnout, and wide consultation took place on how this could be addressed, as well as on how productivity, engagement and innovation in customer service could be improved. Table 6.27 summarizes some of the key actions that have been taken following the 6 Box Leadership survey, whilst Table 6.28 shows examples of feedback on the 6 Box Leadership diagnostic from some of the leaders of the NHS Trust.

TABLE 6.27   Examples of actions taken as a result of the 6 Box Leadership survey

Issues Discovered in Survey	Examples of Discussion	Action
ACCESS TO INFORMATION SEEMS TO BE DIFFICULT	"We need an integrated system – a single system that we can interrogate for information fast to answer simple queries from stakeholders and the media" "Teams don't have access to mobile IT systems, which is also having an impact on performance (this is linked to command and control issue)" "Performance data, and lack of its availability, has been on our risk register for some time"	• Consider possibility for integrating some of the existing systems • Work with IT to modernize IT systems and ensure that they are sufficient and more accessible • Bringing in interim resources to explore how intelligence data and systems can be bolstered as a priority
EMPLOYEES ARE OVERWORKED EMPLOYEES ARE STRESSED LACK OF COACHING/ MENTORING	"These three factors are linked" "The single list of Trust priorities is helpful, it needs to be widely accessed" "Coaching and mentoring would be very beneficial to staff" "Developing greater clarity of roles will help in motivating staff, as they will no longer be unclear of what is expected of them" "There is a need to encourage staff to take part in the Staff survey. This will help to understand what issues are causing stress and the feeling of being overworked"	• Include a capacity and capability and productivity review of the team within a new business plan • Provide access to a robust/ coaching/mentoring scheme for staff • Work on a new people-focused strategy • Develop a greater clarity of roles. This will be led and developed by the Clinical Leadership Structure • A stronger engagement strategy within networks was developed to champion success and reward acts of compassion, leadership and great care • Full utilization of Occupational Health to assist staff

Continued

TABLE 6.27 *Continued*

Issues Discovered in Survey	Examples of Discussion	Action
		• Introduced a Bouquet of the Month to reward those who have gone above and beyond their remit in the interests of service users • Started tweeting issues around good practice • Starting initiatives to ensure staff are consulted with and know they shape their own business rather than being "done to" • Growing the exit interview procedure to discover sources of stress for staff • Offering resilience training in areas of high sickness • Conducting a series of focus groups to discuss the survey findings, including soliciting ideas for change improvement • Discussing additional funding for Mindfulness and Resilience training
COMMAND AND CONTROL IS PART OF OUR CULTURE	"We need to be fully supportive of the Appreciative Leadership Programme [sic]" "Teams don't have access to mobile IT, which has an impact on information being filtered (this is related to the issue of access to information systems)" "This whole strategy is meant to better hear from our workforce and engage our workforce at a difficult time"	• Consider improving access to mobile IT for teams • Community Business Unit Service Redesign is looking at teams being more locality based and smaller to improve their autonomy • Recording monthly podcasts that document key current issues and achievements, which are widely distributed • Implementing "out and about programs" for team visits and sharing key messages, taking feedback, solving problems • Commencing quarterly away days for clinical leaders and managers

Issues Discovered in Survey	Examples of Discussion	Action
		• Commenced "Time to Shine" events as well as "Dare to Share" to encourage championing when things go right as well as learning from things that go wrong
IMPROVING SPECIALIST SERVICES	"Ownership of clinical leadership across all levels is important, as well as joint accountability between clinical and operational levels" "Measuring service user journey through care pathway is required" "Fit-for-purpose workforce based on the needs of service users, with clear succession planning and training-needs analysis for future proofing change in delivery is required"	• Clear specification and job role description has been developed • Developing comprehensive and meaningful system for the measurement of clinical outcomes • New staffing model has been completed

TABLE 6.28   Feedback on the 6 Box Leadership diagnostic from the NHS executives

"The organizational diagnostic exercise based on Professor Hlupic's 6 Box Leadership Model provided an extremely valuable perspective on how our strengths and areas for development as an organization can be exploited for the benefit of both our service users and our workforce. The findings were useful and we triangulated the data with other sources of information to enable creative and courageous conversations to take place, which has led to some new thinking about how we get the best out of our workforce, look after our staff more effectively and better engage our most valuable asset in the process of transformational change" Clinical Director
"This exercise has been both thought provoking and informative. It will inform future business planning and my own personal development" Network Director
"There was correlation between the messages from the 6 Box Leadership survey and the National NHS Staff survey. Both surveys identified the same areas of concern, and I do see the results have a value in indicating areas for further exploration and to target for improvement" HR Director

Example 4: The Nordic IT Consultancy – A Life-changing Experience

The final case study is of a division of a Nordic IT consultancy. The company operates in a niche market, employing highly skilled senior IT consultants. It offers expertise in high-end system development, integration, architecture and development of effective administrative management tools, as well as competence in developing and delivering data warehouse and business intelligence solutions. The 6 Box Leadership survey was commissioned by the Business Development Director of this particular division, employing 18 consultants. The objective of the project was to uncover hidden strengths and weaknesses that could help further improve employee engagement, given much effort was put into attracting top talent, and to get an insight into how the company could become more innovative.

All employees in this division were invited to complete the 6 Box Leadership survey and the response rate was 100 percent. As the sample size was small, data collected was aggregated in one sample.

Examples of the key results

Table 6.29 shows an aggregate of the 6 Box Leadership scores obtained for this division.

High, reasonably uniform scores were obtained for all six boxes. The difference between average scores is 12 percent. Culture is the highest

TABLE 6.29   Aggregate 6 Box Leadership scores

Box	Score
Culture	75%
Relationships	70%
Individuals	69%
Strategy	66%
Systems	64%
Resources	63%

scoring box, with an average score of 75 percent, and Resources is the lowest scoring box, with an average score of 63 percent.

Table 6.30 shows examples of the highest and lowest scores achieved in the Culture box for this division.

These scores are very high. Examples of strengths include: encouragement is used instead of criticism; trust is part of the culture; there is a focus on delighting customers; democracy is part of the culture. Areas identified as developmental opportunities include: senior management may determine the culture; making environmental responsibility and trial and error part of the culture, as well as giving back to the community.

Tables 6.31 to 6.33 show aggregate scores for the Reinvention Framework, the key ideas of Peter Drucker and Management 2.0 principles.

TABLE 6.30   An example of highest and lowest scores for questions in the Culture box

Culture			
Key Strengths		**Key Developmental Opportunities**	
Question	**Score**	**Question**	**Score**
Encouragement is used regularly instead of criticism	89%	Senior management determines the culture	42% * (58%)
Trust is part of our culture	85%	Environmental responsibility is part of our culture	44%
Employees are motivated to do their best at work	84%	Trial and error is part of our culture	47%
Our culture focuses on delighting customers	82%	Giving back to the community is part of our culture	53%
Democracy is part of our culture	80%		

TABLE 6.31   Aggregate Reinvention scores

Area of Knowledge-Work Productivity	Scores
Envision	62%
Design	68%
Build	66%
Operate	73%

TABLE 6.32   Aggregate scores for the key ideas of Peter Drucker

Principle	Score
Productive organization/decentralization	64%
Respect of workers/employees as assets	74%
Knowledge work productivity	68%
Imperative of community	69%
Focus on serving customers	65%
Responsibility for the common good	58%
Focusing on core competencies/properly executing business processes	67%
Management by balancing a variety of needs and goals	69%

TABLE 6.33   Aggregate scores for Management 2.0 principles

Principle	Score
Openness	69%
Community	78%
Meritocracy	73%
Activism	63%
Collaboration	65%
Meaning	72%
Autonomy	74%
Serendipity	59%
Decentralization	63%
Experimentation	66%
Speed	71%
Trust	67%

Relatively high scores were achieved for all four phases of the Reinvention Framework. The lowest score was achieved for Envision (62 percent) and the highest score for Operate (73 percent). The scores show a reasonably good balance between scores for all phases, with the difference of 11 percent between the four phases. Improving this balance would lead to further improvement in performance and knowledge-work productivity.

Reasonably high scores were achieved for all eight principles. There is some discrepancy between scores of 16 percent. The highest scoring principle is Respect of workers/employees as assets (74 percent) and the lowest scoring principle is Responsibility for the common good (58 percent).

Reasonably high scores are achieved for all 12 principles of Management 2.0. The highest scoring principles are: Community (78 percent), Autonomy (74 percent) and Meritocracy (73 percent). The lowest scoring principles are: Serendipity (59 percent), Activism (63 percent) and Decentralization (63 percent). The difference between the highest and the lowest scoring principles is 19 percent.

Overall findings for the IT consultancy

In general, reasonably high scores were achieved for all four mappings. As with the other three case studies presented in this chapter, a number of areas with high scores indicate Level 4 management practices, while some areas indicate Level 3 management. Scores for the 6 Box Leadership and Reinvention Framework are more uniform than scores for the Peter Drucker ideas and Management 2.0 principles. Key themes that emerged include: the IT consultancy's motivated and purposeful employees are its greatest asset, which could be further leveraged by fine tuning some processes and governance structure. Examples of the key strengths include: encouragement is used instead of criticism; trust is part of the culture; there is a focus on delighting customers and a democratic culture. Furthermore, employees are motivated to do their best and are passionate about their work; strategy emerges as employees interact; employees are empowered to make decisions on the basis of their knowledge; there is a transparent system for compensation; and there is good access to training and development.

Key developmental opportunities include: assessing whether senior management determines the culture; making environmental responsibility, trial and error, and giving back to the community part of the culture; involving employees in coaching and mentoring; finding opportunities for more interactions with other parts of the organization; ensuring that long-term performance is more important than short-term results; enabling employees to learn from each other; and there could be more convenient public spaces where employees can meet and interact.

Translating scores into action

I selected this case study as it is an interesting example of how the 6 Box Leadership diagnostic could be life-changing. As mentioned earlier, this project was commissioned by the Business Development Director. As I presented the results, it was apparent that the survey and its finding resonated very well with him. It was also apparent that he is anchored at Level 4 of the Emergent Leadership Model and was striving to maintain collaborative culture within this division. A specific Action Plan was produced and discussed on the basis of the survey results and in the next few weeks I expected to receive feedback on actions taken.

After several weeks I received some unexpected news from the Business Development Director. It turned out that the 6 Box Leadership survey exposed the differences in mindset and management approach between him and the Managing Director. It became apparent that the Managing Director was anchored at Level 3, was not interested in discussing the Action Plan and instead wanted to increase his control and formal power. As a result, the Business Development Director resigned, as he realized he could not work with a Level 3 boss and he also realized that the MD's approach would have a detrimental effect on the division.

As anticipated, this approach did indeed impact negatively on this part of the organization. During the first half of 2013, this division had employed ten new senior consultants to reach the existing total of 18 employees. The high number of new employees was one of the reasons for commissioning the 6 Box Leadership survey, as it was important to discover how employees were feeling about working in this division as well as to get an insight into how to integrate new employees, create successful teams and increase revenue. During this same period, all available consultants had been hired 100 percent of their time. All new recruits were engaged in assignments for valuable customers and the division consistently achieved a 20 to 25 percent surplus revenue per month.

The division had high scores at the individual level, as people felt that they were part of something special; they felt that they were treated well and had been part of inspiring assignments. The survey also showed a low score in the areas of knowledge sharing and community, and it was felt that this accurately represented the division's weaknesses in these areas. The Managing Director did not want to focus on these areas, and instead tried to increase his control and formal reporting processes. Following the departure of the Business Development Director during the second half of 2013, the division had three consultants unengaged for months and, at the end of the year, there was no surplus in revenue although there had been a substantial surplus in the first half of the year. At the beginning of 2014, the achieved revenue was 5 percent below expected target and two consultants were unengaged. It seems apparent that the division had lost its traction and suffered a setback in performance, and all my research and practical experience would indicate that increasing control and formal reporting instead of focusing on knowledge sharing and building communities had an important role to play in this setback.

The Business Development Director is now a very successful self-employed consultant working with some major international corporations. He told me that he had wanted to become a self-employed consultant for some time but it had never been the right time to do so. It seems the 6 Box Leadership survey played a major part in changing the life of one individual who is now spreading positive (Level 4) ripples in other, larger organizations! His view on the 6 Box Leadership diagnostic is summarized in his statement:

> I have over the last years experienced use of global surveys for identification of areas to improve our leadership. Thus, we took surveys year after year, striving to get even more knowledge about the real challenges of modern leadership. We took the 6 Box Leadership survey, and our experience was that this gave much more specific and detailed feedback to us. The 6 Box Leadership diagnostic pointed out the real status in the different aspects of our business, and told us about principles we need to adopt to be more successful. My experience tells me that general surveys can be used year after year to give an overall view, but if you want to know more, dig deeper into the challenge to be a modern leader, the 6 Box Leadership gives you the answers!

Creating Value and Positive Ripples by Using the 6 Box Leadership Diagnostic

My research and practical experience show that using the 6 Box Leadership diagnostic leads to value creation in large, medium and small companies, in public and private sectors, in companies operating in different cultures around the world. Different organizations benefit in different ways. Tangible and intangible value is created in different aspects of performance, engagement, innovation, growth, customer service and so on. As shown in this chapter, the 6 Box Leadership survey can also trigger charitable giving or cause a life-changing experience. Positive ripples are created, and they can spread far and sometimes in unexpected directions.

Positive ripples can spread far and in unexpected directions

I am often asked how the 6 Box Leadership diagnostic differs from other organizational diagnostic tools. One way of explaining this is using the T-shaped skills[2] analogy. The horizontal bar represents the breadth of the knowledge, the ability to understand multiple areas, disciplines and concepts. It represents a systemic, holistic view, multi-disciplinary cognition and cross-disciplinary competence. On the other hand, the vertical bar represents the depth of expertise, functional skill and specialist knowledge. The 6 Box Leadership diagnostic can be viewed as a horizontal bar as it encompasses a broad, multi-disciplinary view of organizational value creation and performance. It embeds a holistic, systemic view of an organization as a living organism or as a complex adaptive system where all parts are interrelated. It allows for the "whole organizational body scan", like an organizational MRI, uncovering hidden issues, strengths and weaknesses.

Most other organizational diagnostic tools are represented by a vertical bar in a T-shaped skills analogy. They normally focus on assessment of a specific, specialized domain or aspect of an organization such as values,[3] employee engagement,[4] or trust.[5] As discussed in Chapter 5, some organizational diagnostic tools assess few functional areas of an organization,[6,7, 8, 9,10] but it is important to bear in mind that some of them were developed a couple of decades ago when Level 3 or Management 1.0-based thinking was prevalent, and many of them do not include and measure people/cultural aspects of an organization.

Another differentiator for the 6 Box Leadership survey is that it is based on extensive interdisciplinary research and empirical validation. It transfers knowledge to action that results in transformation or The Management Shift – a shift in individual mindset, organizational culture and corporate consciousness. Last but not least, the 6 Box Leadership diagnostic is the *how* tool for The Management Shift. It shows how this shift and individual and organizational transformation can be achieved in practice, whilst most other management scholars focus on the *why* and the *what* of this shift.

When I recently gave a speech about this book to a group of executives, someone commented that whilst the 5 Level Emergent Leadership Model can be used as a validated governance framework in organizations, the 6 Box Leadership diagnostic is "*the* tool to use, as most change initiatives are like shooting in the dark without knowing what might work. This tool shows companies where to tap." Knowing where to tap is like the story of the large ship engine that failed. The experienced engineer tapped the engine and repaired it. He later sent a bill of $10,000 to the owner – $2 for tapping with a hammer and $9,998.00 for knowing where to tap! Knowing where to make an effort makes all the difference, and the 6 Box Leadership diagnostic shows organizations where they should make an effort to leverage strengths and address weaknesses.

It took years to develop the 6 Box Leadership Model to the current standard. However, perhaps even more importantly than the amount of work that went into this project was my drive, energy and passion to trigger positive changes for many individuals and organizations – which will, I hope, create positive ripples that spread globally.

SEVEN REFLECTION POINTS

1. Why is it so important to take action on the basis of knowledge?
2. Why do you think different organizations benefit differently from the 6 Box Leadership diagnostic?
3. Is your organization similar to any of the four case studies presented in this chapter?
4. Can you identify specific strengths and weaknesses in those case studies that could be applicable to your organization?
5. Can you see the practical usability of some of the actions taken in case studies for your organization?
6. What are the three actions that could be taken in your organization for the biggest impact?
7. Could you envisage how the 6 Box Leadership diagnostic and tailored Action Plan could help your organization to identify and leverage specific strengths and recognize and address specific developmental opportunities and bottlenecks?

chapter 7

The Management Shift is Achievable Now: A Call for Action

KEY INSIGHTS FROM THIS CHAPTER

This chapter provides answers to the following key questions:

- How do you achieve sustainable value creation through a change of mindset and inspirational management practices?
- How can positive ripples be spread beyond organizational boundaries?
- What key global networks are working towards achieving the tipping point for The Management Shift?
- Why is the future of management already here?
- How can you create The Management Shift in your organization?
- Why is taking action now so important?
- How can this book be used to take action and create positive ripples?
- Why can anyone be a leader and make a positive difference?

Achieving a Sustainable Value Creation, Innovation and Engagement Through Mindset Change and Inspirational Management Practices

According to leadership scholar Ronald Heifetz,[1] it is not possible to "move" an issue until it is ripe. That means enough people must be aware of the issue, feel it deeply, and have the incentive and the resolve to solve it. There is a lot of evidence that the time is ripe now for a fundamental shift in management paradigm and practice, that is, The Management Shift. Throughout this book, I have discussed the research and practice-based evidence indicating that this shift could be imminent, and how it is crucial for our sustainable prosperity.

The positive ripple effects will spread from the individual mindset change to entire organizations, and then to entire societies. Legendary management thinker Peter Drucker said: "Business enterprises are organs of society. They do not exist for their own sake, but to fulfil a specific social purpose and to satisfy a specific need of a society, a community, or individuals."[2] Organizations anchored at Levels 2 and 3 tend to exist for their own sake, focused on share price maximization rather than on satisfying the needs of the society or individuals. As I have shown in this book, it is perfectly possible to do well financially whilst doing good for society and nurturing happy, engaged and motivated employees, helping them to develop their full potential. Organizations anchored at Levels 4 and 5 can do that by default and achieve sustainable value creation, innovation and engagement.

As discussed in Chapter 4, inspirational management practices are embedded in Levels 4 and 5, and they play an important role in anchoring an organization at Level 4. This often involves a mindset change for a critical mass of employees – assuming that formal leaders are already anchored at this level. At Level 4, the distinction between formal and informal leaders and between leaders and managers is blurred, and anyone can assume a leadership role depending on their knowledge and skills. It helps to remember that management/leadership is about human beings, it is about "lifting a person's vision to higher sights, the raising of a person's performance to a higher standard, the building of a personality beyond its normal limitations",[3] bearing in mind the importance of values, principles, compassion, pride and humanity.[4]

The Management Shift Takes a Momentum: Examples of Groups and Networks Working on Reaching the Tipping Point

The transformation that is the subject of this book requires radically different thinking and management practices. I am trying to encourage this shift by collaborating with global management innovation movements. We can achieve a tipping point for this change only if all these movements work together to make a real difference. In the next few sections, I will provide more information about some of these movements and groups that I have been associated with, to raise the awareness of their existence and perhaps inspire readers to join these groups. There are other groups and networks not included in this section but I have selected those that I have been involved with.

The Drucker Society London

Peter Drucker's work on humanistic aspects of management has been inspiring for me for a long time, and I have been keen to promote his ideas in the UK and internationally. I was therefore honored to be invited by the Drucker Trust (run by Peter Drucker's family) to form the Drucker Society London (DSL),[5] the first Drucker society in the UK, as a chapter of the Drucker Society Europe, which organizes the Global Peter Drucker Forum. The DSL now has over 50 members from academia and business, all volunteers brought together by a common purpose: a desire to make a difference, to improve the society through more responsible management and to help young people to pursue their aspirations.

With all the challenges that organizations, institutions and societies in general are facing, developing responsible future leaders and helping young people to pursue their aspirations is crucial. This is our focus within the DSL, and we do this through running "Drucker for Future Leaders" workshops, inspiring the young generation to take action and contribute to the health of the society – and at the same time build a better future for themselves and become responsible leaders.

The Drucker Institute: thought leaders meeting on long-termism

The Drucker Institute[6] is a social enterprise based in Claremont California, focused on carrying forward the legacy of Peter Drucker and promoting his ideas worldwide. The mission statement for the Drucker Institute is "strengthening organizations to strengthen the society", which is in line with Peter Drucker's opinion that any society is as strong as the organizations operating within that society. Organizations therefore have a responsibility not just to their shareholders – as has been the case for the last 30 or so years – but to the wider range of stakeholders. Pursuing share price and short-term profit maximization has actually been detrimental for share price value, as evidenced in research by law Professor Lynn Stout,[7] management thinker Professor Roger Martin[8] and many others.

In September 2013, the Drucker Institute organized a thought leaders' meeting on encouraging more long-term thinking in the corporate community and creating a global movement away from the "maximize shareholder value" orientation.[9] I attended this meeting with about a dozen other thought leaders, which was a most inspiring event. We discussed strategies for countering the financially focused mindset in corporations, reinforcing each other's work in this area and turning our collective efforts into a genuine social movement. One of the exercises we worked on was on "connecting the dots" to create a movement of movements for management innovation, and we produced a draft map (shown in Figure 7.1) identifying the areas that need to be connected and influenced by new management paradigm.

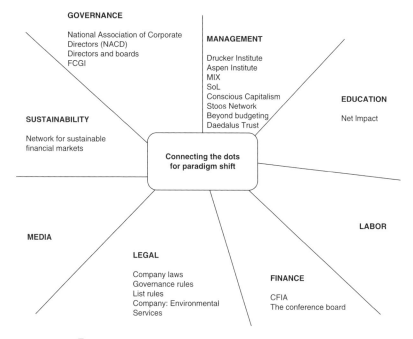

FIGURE 7.1 Examples of the areas and groups/movements to be connected for the management paradigm shift

The Management Innovation eXchange: Management 2.0 Hackathon

The Management Innovation eXchange (MIX)[10] is one of the driving forces for management reinvention. The MIX was established by well-known management innovator Gary Hamel in order to bring together a community of like-minded people connected by a common purpose – a desire to challenge the status quo of management, to reinvent and inspire the future of management. Today, the MIX has tens of thousands of members from all over the world, with diverse backgrounds: from young people still in college to senior executives and leading academics. All types of organizations are also represented at the MIX, and examples of companies involved include: Nike, W.L. Gore, Whole Foods Market and HCL Technologies.

I was involved in the Management Innovation eXchange Management 2.0 Hackathon,[11] a global collaborative effort to reinvent management. I led four different teams and we produced four management hacks: "Using 'Traditionally Virtual' organizational structure",[12] "Why points trump the hierarchy to reward contribution in knowledge organizations",[13] "Systemic/Holistic Management: Connecting the Dots with Project Monitoring 2.0"[14] and "Leading by letting go".[15] I talked about my experiences with this Hackathon in my TEDx talk in Oslo.[16]

The Stoos Network

The Stoos Network is aiming to transform organizations into learning networks where leadership is related to the stewardship of the living rather than the management of the machine. This movement was started by a few enthusiasts meeting in the Swiss town Stoos, brought together by a common desire to influence the way corporations are managed. Now, the movement has more than 1,000 members worldwide, with various satellites and events being organized. We have weekly meetings on Skype led by management author Steve Denning, where we exchange information and discuss new management innovation initiatives. In January 2013, I presented the 6 Box Leadership Model at one of the Stoos Connect events[17] in Amsterdam.

The People Cloud Thought Leadership

The People Cloud idea is based on the premise that as software is today available online thanks to the Computing Cloud, a new "cloud model" is needed to build effective teams and address the changing needs of organizations and workers. In the People Cloud, "systems" and "applications" are replaced with "people" and "problem solving", and jobs are seen as services provided to customers for value rather than as a series of tasks specified according to organizational charts. The People Cloud Thought Leadership Council,[18] based in Silicon Valley, was formed to capture the expertise on people management, innovation, leadership at all levels, optimizing talent and value-based decision-making.

Management paradigm shift: the UK initiative

On my journey to facilitate The Management Shift, I have been also associated with various groups in the UK working on management innovation, such as the Society for Organizational Learning (SoL) UK,[19] focused on cultivating organizations as living systems that fully inspire the commitment of all stakeholders, and Daedalus Trust,[20] formed to research and address the impact of the Hubris Syndrome (obsession with power) on leaders and their behavior.

Business schools: time for change

I have also been part of a group of thought leaders working on the future of education in business schools. This is a very important issue, as with the imminence of The Management Shift, business schools need to adapt the curriculum, textbooks, teaching style and their own management model to this shift and produce future leaders with Level 4 mindset and management skills. Several high-profile articles address this problem, such as that by Ian Wylie in the *Financial Times*,[21] Adrian Wooldridge's article in *The Economist*[22] and Steve Denning's article in *Forbes* magazine.[23] Our thought leaders' group has also produced an article outlining the key challenges facing business schools and the possible way forward, available at the Drucker Forum blog.[24]

The Management Shift movement

As the writing of this book progressed, I decided to start my own movement for The Management Shift. Given my large LinkedIn network, this was the obvious place to start and I created The Management Shift group[25] and invited my contacts from various networks to join. Any professional from any part of the world with any background is welcome to join as long as they have a Level 4 mindset and want to make a positive difference. This group is the place to discuss and disseminate the key ideas presented in this book, exchange relevant practical experience and help each other and others to be anchored at Level 4. The group is growing continuously, and once the tipping point is reached it will create a movement that can spread positive ripples.

The Future of Management is Here: Unstoppable Metamorphosis to a Butterfly

The future of management is already here. The Management Shift is already happening for many individuals and organizations. As Gary Hamel wrote in his landmark *Harvard Business Review* article, "Moon Shots for Management",[26] "Equipping organizations to tackle the future would require a management revolution no less momentous than the one that spawned modern industry." Similarly, in his interview for *Forbes* magazine, Don Tapscott said that we are "at a punctuation point in human history where the industrial age and institutions have finally come to their logical conclusion".[27] In the same spirit, the announcement of the Drucker Forum 2014: "The Great Transformation – Managing Our Way to Prosperity"[28] states that "It appears we have arrived at a turning point where either the world will embark on a route towards long-term growth and prosperity, or we will manage our way to economic decline. Thus the very coherence of our societies is at stake". We have no choice but to focus on long-term growth and prosperity and shift mindsets and organizational cultures to Levels 4 and 5.

In 2010, the *Wall Street Journal* Managing Editor Alan Murray wrote an article "The End of Management".[29] He declared an end to management as we know it. End of management based on corporations as bureaucracies run by bureaucrats whose priority is self-preservation and resistance to change. End of Level 3 management, which shows the inevitability of The Management Shift. Alan Murray envisions the new management model that will have to imbue in workers the drive, creativity and innovative spirit found among entrepreneurs, to move power and decision-making down the organization as much as possible, and replace traditional bureaucratic structures with something more like ad-hoc teams of peers who come together temporarily to work on individual projects. This vision is closely aligned with Levels 4 and 5 management discussed in Chapter 4.

As discussed throughout this book, both research and practice show that The Management Shift is crucial for organizations to survive, thrive sustainably, have a purposeful existence and make a wide impact. It is inevitable; it has already happened in the minds of many individuals and it is embedded in many organizational cultures all over the world.

Towards the end of writing this book I came across this quote from Trina Paulus' novel *Hope for the Flowers*.[30] "How does one become a butterfly? They have to want to learn to fly so much that you are willing to give up being a caterpillar."

All my research and consulting experience gave me many ideas on how to achieve this transformational shift from Level 3 to Level 4, at both individual and organizational levels, and I have described many practical ideas in previous chapters. But this quote captured its essence: desire. Reaching Level 4 opens endless possibilities for individuals and organizations, it provides a more joyful and purposeful existence and it creates a better world for future generations.

Creating The Management Shift in Your Organization: Call for Action

The 6 Box Leadership diagnostic can be used as one of the tools to help with this shift, but every individual can take an action that will create some positive ripples. A group of such thoughtful individuals can eventually make a big impact, as illustrated in this quote from Margaret Mead: "Never doubt that a small group of thoughtful, concerned citizens can change the world; indeed it is the only thing that ever has".[31]

I would like to ask you to think about what the world would be like if most organizations were genuinely authentic, trustworthy, transparent, purposeful and caring; where pyramids are replaced with networks, command and control is replaced with collaboration and autonomy, fear and authority are replaced with higher purpose and authentic care. Imagine how people feel to work in such organizations, how well these organizations would do financially and how many more opportunities that would give to the young generation. Wouldn't it be wonderful if such organizations became the norm rather than the exception?

In the same way that decentralized market economies outperform centrally planned and control economies, companies with decentralized organizational cultures, operating at Levels 4 and 5, outperform highly centralized, hierarchical organizations operating at Levels 1–3.[32] The shift in management paradigm and practices will lead to the creation of organizations that are fit for the 21st century, with better engagement, resilience and innovation. This will ultimately result in more economic and social prosperity for everyone.

Executives need to take action, to challenge the conventional wisdom, which we are now realizing is not so wise, and embrace emerging management practices. By focusing on a higher purpose, delighting customers, engaging employees and inspiring them to unleash their passion for work, leaders will achieve long-term financial success, satisfy shareholders, whilst making customers, employees and society happy.

The *Harvard Business Review* article "It Takes Purpose to Become a Billionaire"[33] illustrated this point well. Bill Gates did not become a billionaire because his main goal was to make a lot of money. He became a billionaire by pursuing his dream and passion to make personal computers accessible to as many people as possible worldwide. Focusing on a higher purpose instead of short-term financial gains leads to not only more sustainable financial gains, but also to doing good for society and leaving a legacy.

To take or not to take action now?

It may seem easier to carry on with business as usual. For some of you this might happen and you might never find out what opportunities you missed. You might get by carrying on as usual, and for some types of organizations that might be sufficient. If quality control, safety and security are crucial for your business, if your processes and business environment are stable, then you could continue to use traditional management approaches. You will meet targets but your employees are not likely to be very passionate about the work they are doing.

However, if you lead an organization where innovation is crucial for your survival and prosperity, if most of your employees are knowledge workers whose creativity, engagement and passion are the driving force of your raison d'être, then embracing The Management Shift is likely to be the only way to move forward and achieve sustainable long-term performance and value creation. And performance, value creation, better engagement and innovation are not the only outcomes of implementing this new management paradigm: it can help you to lead a more purposeful life.

At the entrance to the Drucker Institute, there is a large sign with the Peter Drucker quote:

> I am always asking that question: What do you want to be remembered for? Being a leader, Building a company or Bettering Society?
>
> How about all three?

So, how about you become remembered for being a great leader who embraced collaborative leadership practices, led a great organization with engaged and passionate employees – an organization that created value for all stakeholders on a sustainable basis, and at the same time bettered society and provided a better future for the young generation?

And you are more likely to be remembered not by the amount of money you earned at the peak of your career, not by the number of people you managed or how high you climbed up the ladder of an organizational hierarchy, but by the extent to which you led a purposeful life and by how many lives you have touched and made a positive impact on.

I hope this book has demonstrated that the risk of doing nothing is much greater than the risk of taking action. Deep, radical and urgent transformation is required in management practices. The conclusions of the report on the need for revolution in higher education published by the Institute for Public Policy Research are highly applicable in the context of management revolution: "The biggest risk is that as a result of complacency, caution or anxiety the pace of change is too slow and the nature of change is too incremental."[34] So, in the spirit of Peter Drucker, I would like to ask you: "What will you do differently on Monday?"[35]

How can this book be used to take an action?

This book provides knowledge on *Why* individuals and organizations need to change (described in Chapters 1 and 7), *What* needs to be done in organizations to adopt new management practices for better innovation, engagement and value creation and sustainable success (described in Chapters 2, 3 and 4), and *How* this shift can be achieved in practice (described in Chapters 5 and 6).

This book also shows how all this knowledge can be turned into action using the 5 Level Emergent Leadership Model and the 6 Box Leadership diagnostic system. This action can lead to transformational change, creating positive ripples that will go far beyond individuals and their organizations, eventually changing societies on a large scale. Without taking action, many businesses will fail and people will continue to be disengaged, unhappy at work and failing to achieve their full potential. Figure 7.2 illustrates how this book can be used to take action and achieve The Management Shift.

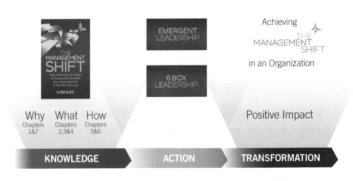

FIGURE 7.2   Using this book to facilitate The Management Shift

Key management lessons from this book

As a culmination of many years of research and consulting, this book offers many management lessons that could be used to transform individuals and organizations for sustainable success. The key lessons include:

- Organizations and societies are facing many challenges today caused mainly by outdated management practices based on traditional, hierarchical command and control
- These traditional management approaches no longer work as they were designed for predictability, stability and repeatability. Business environments today are highly dynamic and unpredictable
- The solution to the problems we are facing is emerging management approaches based on collaboration, autonomy, values and purpose
- Many individuals and organizations would benefit from embracing The Management Shift, a shift in mindset, organizational culture and corporate consciousness for sustainable success and purposeful existence
- Adopting new management practices focused on collaboration and higher purpose also leads to financial benefits
- There is a growing number of companies that have implemented inspiring management practices and are experiencing various benefits as a result of this
- Traditional leadership approaches are counterproductive for the vast majority of organizations, as they inhibit creativity, engagement and productivity, especially in knowledge-based organizations
- Knowledge workers ignore corporate hierarchy and expect to be treated as associates rather than subordinates
- Leading for purpose, values and compassion creates organizations that are far more engaging and inspiring
- There are various processes that can be used in an organization to implement emergent leadership practices, such as: facilitating informal networks; developing a caring organizational culture based on intrinsic motivation, collaboration and cross-fertilization of ideas between communities and teams; developing trust, allowing experimentation

and tolerating mistakes; distribution of responsibility, decision-making and control

- The *why*, the *what* and the *how* of The Management Shift are very important as they explain why individuals and organizations need to shift, what needs to be done and how this shift can be achieved
- There is a consensus amongst the key management thinkers on the key management trends emerging. They all agree that perceptions of strategy, innovation and engagement are changing
- The key emerging trends in the area of strategy include: the need to adopt a short-term, changeable transient competitive advantage instead of competitive advantage; long-term orientation instead of short-term maximization of profit and share price; focus on customers, higher purpose and values; and building alliances amongst stakeholders
- The key emerging trends in the area of innovation include: the awareness of the importance of people and culture, not just R&D investments for innovation, and the importance of experimentation and emergent leadership style for innovation
- The key ideas emerging in the area of engagement include: the importance of a caring culture for engaging employees, nurturing employees' strengths and finding meaning and higher purpose at work to inspire engagement
- Individual consciousness and developmental levels and organizational cultures are interconnected
- A critical mass of employees anchored at a particular level will influence the organizational culture and vice versa
- According to the 5 Level Emergent Leadership Model, the five levels of individual development are: Lifeless, Reluctant, Controlled, Enthusiastic and Limitless
- Each level has the typical emotions, keywords used, energy levels, behavior, thought and language patterns of employees and leaders
- The five levels of organizational culture development that correspond to specific individual levels are: Apathetic, Stagnating, Orderly, Collaborative and Unbounded
- Each organizational level leads to specific work implications, from surviving to thriving

- It is very important for individuals and organizations to move from Level 3 to Level 4, as this is where a breakthrough in performance, innovation, engagement and value creation is achieved
- The key triggers and processes for shifting to Level 4 culture include: change in business focus and/or change in corporate values; poor financial and market performance; unpredictability of the operating environment; inadequate engagement; slow or problematic decision-making; poor communication; economic crisis
- The 6 Box Leadership Model was created using a thematic analysis of many interdisciplinary projects to help organizations achieve The Management Shift. That led to identification of the key factors that drive innovation, engagement and value creation in organizations in the areas of Culture, Relationships, Individuals, Strategy, Systems and Resources
- The philosophical thinking behind the 6 Box Leadership Model includes a holistic, integrative worldview
- The 6 Box Leadership diagnostic can transfer knowledge into action to enable The Management Shift in small, medium and large organizations, in the public and private sectors, operating across different cultures
- Any small action can lead to large benefits and positive ripples; everyone can be a leader and make a difference
- There are various global networks working on achieving the tipping point for The Management Shift.

A few final words

My work is about turning academic knowledge into action and practice and igniting positive changes, which I have described as The Management Shift. During my career, I have learned that it is useless to try to transform any society or even a single organization if, first of all, people's hearts and minds are not transformed. To achieve a true change, there must be a transformation from within.

We always have something to give and share and an opportunity to lead. The Persian Sufi writer Farid ud-Din Attar's poem *Mantic Uttair* describes a group of birds looking for their king, the Simorg. When they meet again after many adventures, they discover that they *are* the Simorg. The king is in each of them. Similarly, the leader is in each of us, and it is our duty and honor to give and share. As Seth Godin explains in his book *Tribes*,[36] anyone can today start and lead a movement to bring together a group of like-minded people passionate about something, eager to do amazing things. You could start your own "Level 4" or The Management Shift movement in your organization and/or part of the world, and join the global Management Shift movement I started on LinkedIn. By doing so, we can all join forces to create a global impact. Every action counts, as Malcolm Gladwell explains in his inspirational book *The Tipping Point*[37] – little changes can lead to big outcomes and make a big difference.

This book will have meaning and will achieve its purpose of transforming the hearts and minds of leaders and employees, and changing organizations worldwide, if the ideas presented are lived daily. Once a critical mass of people think, behave and live their life anchored at Levels 4 and 5, many positive ripples will be created, the world will change and we can be proud of leaving a more human legacy to our children.

SEVEN REFLECTION POINTS

1. Do you think your organization is ready for The Management Shift?
2. What can you do to help this shift happen?
3. Do you feel compelled to join any of the groups and networks described in this chapter?
4. Are you going to join any of these groups and make a difference? If so, which ones?
5. How would it make you feel if you take an action and see positive ripples spreading and making a difference for individuals, organizations and society as a whole?
6. How would it make you feel to miss the opportunity to take an action and live your purpose?
7. What would other people say about you if you take a lead and inspire others to take an action and spread positive ripples?

Appendix 1

Examples of Companies that have Implemented Emergent Management Practices

TABLE A1.1   List of companies that have implemented emergent management practices

1. MIX Management 2.0 Hackathon	2. Firms of Endearment	3. LinkedIn Survey	4. Beta Codex Network	5. World Blu Survey
Atlassian, Australia atlassian.com	Amazon, USA amazon.com	Antelope Valley Transit Authority, USA avta.com	AES, USA aes.com	Axiom News, Canada AxiomNews.ca
Automattic, USA automattic.com	Best Buy, USA bestbuy.com	Biko, Spain biko2.com	Ahlsell, Sweden ahlsell.com	Barrett Values Centre, USA & UK valuescentre.com
Bank of New Zealand, New Zealand bnz.co.nz	BMW, Germany bmw.com	FAVI, France favi.com	Aldi, Germany aldi.de	Bite Studios, UK bitestudio.co.uk
Best Buy, USA bestbuy.com	CarMax, USA carmax.com	FREITAG, Switzerland freitag.ch	DaVita, USA davita.com	Boost New Media, New Zealand boost.co.nz
Brand Velocity Inc., USA brandvelocity.com	Caterpillar, USA caterpillar.com	Guidewire Software, USA guidewire.com	Dell, USA dell.com	Brandwatch, UK brandwatch.com
CEMEX, UK cemex.co.uk	Commerce Bank, USA commercebank.com	Handelsbank, Sweden handelsbank.com	DM drogerie markt, Germany dm-drogeriemarkt.de	Cedars Camps, Lebanon, cedarscamps.org
CSC Germany, Germany csc.com/de	Container Store, USA containerstore.com	HCL Technologies, India hcltech.com	Egon Zehnder International, Switzerland egonzehnder.com	Chaordix, Canada chaordix.com
Edmunds, USA edmunds.com	Costco, USA costco.com	Hindustan Unilever, India hul.co.in	FAVI, France favi.com	Collective Agency, USA collectiveagency.com
Electronic Arts, USA ea.com	eBay, USA ebay.com	HubSpot, USA hubspot.com	Flight Centre Limited, Australia flightcentre.com.au/	DaVita, USA davita.com
Evergreen Coop, USA evergreencooperatives.com	Google, USA google.com	Illinois Tool Works, USA itw.com	Google, USA google.com	Delivering Happiness at Work, USA deliveringhappinessatwork.com

Google, USA google.com	Harley-Davidson, USA harley-davidson.com	Jancoa, USA jancoa.com	Guardian Industries, USA guardian.com	Do Something Different, UK dsd.me
IBM, USA ibm.com	Honda, Japan honda.com	Joie de Vivre, USA jdvhotels.com	Handelsbanken, Sweden handelsbanken.se	DreamHost, USA dreamhost.com
IDEO, USA ideo.com	Ideo, USA ideo.com	Keller Williams Realty, USA www.kw.com/kw	HCL, India hcl.in	Dyn, USA dyn.com
Intuit, USA intuit.com	IKEA, Sweden ikea.com	Morning Star, USA morningstarco.com	Hengeler Müller, Germany hengeler.com	Explore Communications, USA explorehq.com
Kessels & Smit, the Netherlands kessels-smit.com	JetBlue, USA jetblue.com	NASA, USA nasa.gov	Herman Miller, USA hermanmiller.com	Frank, USA areyoufrank.com
MailChimp, USA mailchimp.com	Johnson & Johnson, USA jnj.com	Netflix, USA netflix.com	Ikea, Sweden ikea.com	Fusionfarm Inc., USA fusionfarm.com
Menasha Packaging, USA menashapackaging.com	Jordan's furniture, USA jordans.com	Patagonia, UK patagonia.com	Interpolis, the Netherlands interpolis.nl/particulier/default.aspx	Future Considerations, UK futureconsiderations.com
Method, USA methodhome.com	L.L. Bean, USA llbean.com	QLI, USA QLIomaha.com	Irizar, Spain irizar.com	Great Harvest Franchising Inc., USA greatharvest.com
Morning Star, USA morningstarco.com	New Balance, UK newbalance.co.uk	Rabobank, the Netherlands rabobank.com	Johnsonville, USA johnsonville.com/home.html	Greenleaf Book Group, USA greenleafbookgroup.com
Mozilla, USA mozilla.org	Patagonia, France patagonia.com	Rackspace, UK rackspace.co.uk	Kessels & Smit, the Netherlands kessels-smit.nl	Groupon Malaysia, Malaysia groupon.my
Nucor, USA nucor.com	Progressive Insurance, Malaysia progressiveinsurance.com.my	Semco, Brazil semco.com.br/en	Mondragon, Spain mcc.es	Happy Ltd, UK happy.co.uk

(Continued)

TABLE A1.1 Continued

1. MIX Management 2.0 Hackathon	2. Firms of Endearment	3. LinkedIn Survey	4. Beta Codex Network	5. World Blu Survey
Red Hat, USA redhat.com	REI, USA rei.com	Suncorp Group, Australia suncorp.com.au	Morning Star, USA morningstarco.com	Menlo Innovations, USA menloinnovations.com
Rite-Solutions, USA ritesolutions.com	Southwest, USA southwest.com	W.L. Gore, USA gore.com/en_gb	Netflix, USA netflix.com	Mindvalley, Malaysia mindvalley.com
Semco, Brazil semco.com.br/en	Starbucks, USA starbucks.com	YSOFT, Check Republic ysoft.com/	Nucor Steel, USA nucor.com	Namasté Solar, USA namastesolar.com
Southwest, USA southwest.com	Timberland, USA timberland.com	Zappos.com, USA zappos.com	Promon, Brazil promon.br.com	Nearsoft, USA nearsoft.com
Thogus, USA thogus.com	Toyota, Japan toyota-global.com		Resource Informatik, Switzerland resource.ch	New Belgium Brewing Company, USA newbelgium.com
3M, USA 3m.com	Trader Joe's, USA traderjoes.com		SAS Institute, USA www.sas.com	NixonMcInnes, UK nixonmcinnes.com
Tongal, USA tongal.com	UPS, USA ups.com		Schindlerhof, Germany schindlerhof.de	NRI Distribution, Canada nri-distribution.com
Virgin, UK virgin.com	Wegmans, USA wegmans.com		Semco, Brazil semco.com.br	Podio, Denmark podio.com
Wegmans, USA wegmans.com	Whole Foods Market, USA wholefoods.com		Snøhetta, Norway snoarc.no/	Productivity Associates, USA gotopai.com
Whole Foods Market, USA wholefoods.com			Southwest Airlines, USA southwest.com	Propellernet, UK propellernet.co.uk
W.L. Gore, USA www.gore.com/en_gb			Sun Hydraulics, USA sunhydraulics.com	Quick Left, USA quickleft.com

RoundPegg, USA
roundpegg.com

SAYS, Malaysia
says.com

Sparc LLC, USA
sparcedge.com

STATSIT, Singapore
statsit.com

Sweetriot, USA
sweetriot.com

Taf'eel Design Studio, Malaysia
tafeel.my

The Online 401(k), USA
theonline401k.com

TRAVOD, UK
travod.com

Trov, USA
trov.com

Valtech, Denmark
valtech.dk

WD-40 Company, USA
wd40company.com

Woohoo Inc. (formerly The
Happy at Work Project), Denmark
woohooinc.com

Zappos.com, USA
zappos.com

Toyota, Japan
toyota.com

Trisa, Switzerland
trisa.ch

United Supermarkets, USA
unitedtexas.com

Valve Software, USA
valvesoftware.com

Whole Foods Market, USA
wholefoods.com

W.L. Gore, USA
gore.com

WM-Group, Germany
wm-group.de

Zappos.com, USA
zappos.com

Yammer, USA
yammer.com

Zappos.com, USA
zappos.com

Appendix 2

Mapping of the Emergent Leadership Model's Five
Levels to Other Relevant Models of Development

TABLE A2.1A   Mapping of the Emergent Leadership Model's five levels to other relevant models of development

Emergent Leadership Model	Leadership Development Framework[1]	Barrett's Value Model[2]	Spiral Dynamics Model[3]	Tribal Leadership[4]
LEVEL 5	7 Ironist 6 Magician	7 Service 6 Making a difference 5 Internal cohesion 4 Transformation	8 Turquoise (Whole view) 7 Yellow (Eco systems) 6 Green (Community)	**Stage 5** *"Life is great"*
LEVEL 4	5 Strategist (POST-CONVENTIONAL)			**Stage 4** *"We are great"*
LEVEL 3	4 Individualist 3 Achiever 2 Expert	3 Self-Esteem 2 Relationships 1 Survival	5 Orange (Materialistic) 4 Blue (Authority) 3 Red (Egocentric gratification)	**Stage 3** *"I am great and you are not"*
LEVEL 2	1 Diplomat (CONVENTIONAL)		2 Purple (Rituals) 1 Beige (Survival)	**Stage 2** *"My life sucks"*
LEVEL 1				**Stage 1** *"All life sucks"*

TABLE A2.1B Mapping of the Emergent Leadership Model's five levels to other relevant models of development

Emergent Leadership Model	Energy Leadership[5]	Maslow's Hierarchy of Human Needs[6]	Loevinger's Stages of Ego Development[7]	Kohlberg's Stages of Moral Development[8]
LEVEL 5 LEVEL 4	7 Non-judgement, Absolute passion, Creation 6 Synthesis, Joy, Wisdom (SELF TRANSCENDENCE)	5 Self-actualization 4 Esteem	9 Integrated Stage 8 Autonomous Stage 7 Individualistic Stage	6 Universal ethical principles 5 Social contract orientation (POST-CONVENTIONAL)
LEVEL 3 LEVEL 2 LEVEL 1	5 Reconciliation, Peace, Acceptance 4 Concern, Composition, Service 3 Responsibility, Forgiveness, Cooperation 2 Conflict, Anger, Defiance 1 Victim, Apathy, Lethargy (SELF/SELF MASTERY)	3 Love/belonging 2 Safety 1 Physiological	6 Conscientious Stage 5 Self-aware Stage 4 Conformist Stage 3 Self-Protective Stage 2 Impulsive Stage 1 Presocial Stage	4 Authority and social-order maintaining orientation 3 Interpersonal accord and conformity (CONVENTIONAL) 2 Self-interest orientation 1 Obedience and punishment orientation (PRE-CONVENTIONAL)

Appendix 3

Key Models and Tools for Organizational Change
Compared to the 6 Box Leadership Model

TABLE A3.1 Key models and tools for organizational change based on empirical research/implementation

Model/Tool	Key Ideas	Application	Suitability/Comparison to the 6 Box Leadership Model
The Balanced Scorecard[1]	• Strategic performance management tool uses semi-standard structured report supported by automation tools • Use of financial and non-financial measures • Four perspectives measured: *Financial, Customer, Internal business processes* and *Learning and growth*	• A diagnostic tool, based on empirical research • Focused on financial stakeholders	• The Balanced Scorecard is based on a traditional management paradigm and it does not focus on the need to reinvent management and implement emerging management practices • This diagnostic tool is based on top-down management and people and culture-related aspects are not the focus of the diagnostics
McKinsey 7S Framework[2]	• Management model used as a tool to assess and monitor changes in an organization. • Based on the theory that the following seven interrelated elements need to be aligned: *Structure, Strategy, Systems, Skills, Style, Staff* and *Shared values*	• A holistic diagnostic tool based on empirical research	• McKinsey 7S model comprises some elements that overlap with the 6 Box Leadership Model • It does not provide an online questionnaire and additional mappings that the 6 Box Leadership Model provides • It is based on a traditional management paradigm though it provides a holistic view of an organization
Christensen's RVP Framework[3]	• Management model/framework that explains a foundation of organizational capabilities • *Resources, Processes* and *Values* represent key innovation capabilities • *Resources* include tangible (real estate, cash, etc.) and intangible (brands, intellectual property, channels, customer insights, etc.) assets • *Processes* include formal and informal ways that get work done. Examples include: recruitment and training, R&D, manufacturing, market research and budgeting. • *Values* include: ethics, customer demands, cost structures and risk tolerance	• Management framework based on empirical research • Used to determine organizational innovation capabilities, acquisition assessment, etc.	• RVP Framework assesses innovation capabilities • Many factors overlap with factors in the 6 Box Leadership Model, but this framework is less comprehensive and there is no online tool for diagnostics

Model	Description	Purpose	Comparison
Tribal Leadership model[4]	• Management model that shows stages at which tribes operate within organizations • The models shows that tribes operate at five stages: *Stage One* – hostile members of the tribe *Stage Two* – antagonistic members of the tribe *Stage Three* – competitive members of the tribe *Stage Four* – team working tribes *Stage Five* – tribes making a global impact	• Management model based on empirical research • Used to determine dominant stage of the organizational culture	• There is an online survey[5] with five questions to determine the stage of the culture • Coaching tips with the key action steps to building great tribes operating at higher stages are provided • Conceptually, this model is similar to the 6 Box Leadership Model, but there is no comprehensive online questionnaire to help organizations to move up to the next stage
Jim Collins' Good to Great Framework[6]	• Management framework showing how companies move from being "Good" to "Great" • Four stages (input variables) to "Greatness" include: *Stage 1:* Disciplined People *Stage 2:* Disciplined Thought *Stage 3:* Disciplined Action *Stage 4:* Building Greatness to Last	• Management framework based on empirical research • Used to determine organizational potential to become "Great" rather than being just "Good"	• There is a framework available online[7] in PDF format that can be used to assess to what extent "Good to Great" principles are followed, but there is no online calculation of scores • There are a few overlapping variables (e.g. purpose) with the 6 Box Leadership Model, but other than that both frameworks are quite different
Barrett's The Seven Levels of Organizational Consciousness Model[8]	• Model that describes the evolutionary development of human consciousness • It has been applied to individuals and organizations (as well as nations) • The seven levels are: Survival, Relationship, Self-Esteem, Transformation, Internal Cohesion, Making a Difference and Service	• Management model based on empirical research • Used to determine cultural entropy (amount of energy consumed in unproductive work) and distribution of seven levels across the Seven Levels of Organizational Consciousness Model	• There are online diagnostic tools (Cultural Transformation Tools - CTT) used to assess culture and values • Conceptually, there are some similarities with the 6 Box Leadership Model, but these tools are more focused on culture and values than on other, more broader aspects of organizational value creation included in the 6 Box Leadership Model

Appendix 4

Six Phases of Thematic Analysis Followed in this Research

Six phases of thematic analysis were followed in this research:

- *Phase 1: Familiarization with the data.* This involved reading and re-reading relevant material, note-taking and creating a list of initial codes
- *Phase 2: Generating initial codes.* In this phase the initial codes were generated and the lists of the sources of patterns were produced in table formats. Data was collapsed into labels to create categories, and inferences about the meaning of codes were made
- *Phase 3: Searching for themes.* This involved combining codes into overarching themes and producing a list of themes for further analysis. Three primary approaches were used in developing themes systematically:[1] Theory driven, Prior data or prior research driven, and Inductive (where generalizations are made from specific observations).

For example, Christensen's RVP Framework[2] was used as one source of prior research. As mentioned in Chapter 3, in their book *The Innovator's Solution*,[3] Clayton Christensen and Michael Raynor claim that resources, processes and values form a foundation of organizational capabilities. In this classification, resources include people, technology, products, cash, channels and brands. Processes include recruitment and training, R&D, manufacturing, market research and budgeting. Values include ethics, customer demands, cost structures, risk tolerance and emphasis on new opportunities. These aspects were further researched and combined with other sources of data.

- *Phase 4: Reviewing themes.* In this phase themes were analyzed to determine how they support the data
- *Phase 5: Defining and naming themes.* Each theme was defined and described, with the analysis of how these themes support the data
- *Phase 6: Producing the report.* In this phase a description of the results was produced.

Appendix 5

Background Research: Key Projects, Research Methods Used, Key Findings, Key Output and the Link to the Six Boxes of the 6 Box Leadership Model

TABLE A5.1 Key projects, research methods used, key findings, key output and the link to the six boxes of the 6 Box Leadership Model

Project	Research Method	Key Findings	Sample Outputs	Link to the Six Boxes
Leading Knowledge Workers	• Two in-depth, longitudinal case studies in knowledge-intensive organizations in the private sector • Qualitative method (context analysis), observations, semi-structured interviews (60+), documentary evidence (triangulation) • Literature review of 300+ articles	• Empirical guidelines for leading knowledge workers • Theoretical model for leading knowledge workers for innovation • Emergent Leadership Model	• Amar D. Amar, Carsten Hentrich and **Vlatka Hlupic** (2009) "To Be a Better Leader, Give up Authority", *Harvard Business Review*, December issue, 87:12, 22–4. Received the Bright Idea Award in Management of New Jersey Policy Research Organization (NJPRO) Foundation • Amar D. Amar, Carsten Hentrich, Bami Bastani and **Vlatka Hlupic** (2012) "How Managers Succeed by Letting Employees Lead", *Organizational Dynamics*, invited seminal paper, 47.1, 62–71 • Amar D. Amar and **Vlatka Hlupic** (2012) "Synthesizing Knowledge to Develop Leadership for Managing in Knowledge Organizations", presented at the Academy of Management Conference, Boston, August 2012 • Amar Amar and **Vlatka Hlupic** (2011) "Leadership Function in Knowledge Based Organizations", Proceedings of the British Academy of Management Conference, Birmingham, UK, September 2011 • Amar D. Amar, Bami Bastani, **Vlatka Hlupic** and Carsten Hentrich (2008) "'How to Manage Employees When We Cannot Use Authority: How the Theory Fits Practice Internationally", PDW presented at the Academy of Management Conference, Anaheim, USA, August 2008	• *Individuals* • *Culture* • *Relationships* • *Strategy* • *Systems*
Value Creation from Intellectual Capital	• Three in-depth longitudinal case studies in knowledge-intensive organizations in the private sector	• A framework for value creation from Intellectual Capital	• Sajda Qureshi, Bob Briggs and **Vlatka Hlupic** (2006) "Value Creation from Intellectual Capital: Convergence of Knowledge Management and Collaboration in the Intellectual Bandwidth Model", *Journal of Group Decision and Negotiation*, special issue on "Current Advances in Collaboration Process Support", 15:3, 197–220	• *Individuals* • *Culture* • *Relationships* • *Strategy*

(continued)

TABLE A5.1   Continued

Project	Research Method	Key Findings	Sample Outputs	Link to the Six Boxes
	• Qualitative method (context analysis), observations, semi-structured interviews (120), documentary evidence (triangulation) • Literature review of 250+ articles	• Factors that contribute to innovation in organizations	• Dee Alwis, **Vlatka Hlupic** and George Rzevski (2003) "Designing Organizational Memory in Knowledge Intensive Companies: A Case Study", in **V Hlupic** (ed.) *Knowledge and Business Process Management* (Idea Group Publishing), 137–53 • **Vlatka Hlupic**, Anasthasia Pouloudi and George Rzevski (2002) "Towards an integrated approach to Knowledge Management: 'Hard', 'Soft' and 'Abstract' Issues", *Knowledge and Process Management, the Journal of Corporate Transformation*, 9:0, 1–14 • Dee Alwis, **Vlatka Hlupic** and George Fitzgerald (2003) "Factors That Cause Value Creation" in L. Budin, V. Luzar-Stiffler, Z. Bekic and V. Hluz-Dobric (eds) IC Proceedings of the ITI'03 (Information Technology Interface) Conference, Croatia, June, SRCE University Computing Centre, 411–16 • Dee Alwis, **Vlatka Hlupic** and George Rzevski (2002) "Building Critical Organizational Knowledge: A Case Study", Proceedings of the ITI'02 (Information Technology Interface) Conference, Croatia, June, SRCE University Computing Centre, 293–8	• *Systems* • *Resources*
Framework for Organizational Resilience	• Online survey with 88 organizations in the private and public sectors, 6000+ respondents • Quantitative method for data analysis	• A framework for organizational resilience • Factors that contribute to organizational resilience	• Denis Bourne, **Vlatka Hlupic** and Gemma Clarkson (2011) "Organizational Resilience", Research report for Knowledge Connect Project	• *Individuals* • *Culture* • *Relationships* • *Strategy* • *Systems*

Teamwork and Change Management	• Three in-depth longitudinal case studies in knowledge-intensive organizations • Qualitative method (grounded theory, hermeneutics), observations, semi-structured interviews (88), documentary evidence (triangulation) • Literature review of 250+ articles	• A theory for leading teams in the context of change management • Human and organizational factors that contribute to the success of change management projects	• Jyoti Choudrie, **Vlatka Hlupic** and Zahir Irani (2002) "Teams and Their Motivation for Business Process Re-engineering", *International Journal of Flexible Manufacturing Systems*, 14, 45–52 • Jyoti Choudrie and **Vlatka Hlupic** (2000) "A Cross-Comparison of Re-engineering Teams Undertaking Business Process Change", *Journal of Intelligent Systems*, 10:5–6, 473–507 • Jyoti Choudrie and **Vlatka Hlupic** (2000) "Identifying and Understanding the Human and Organizational Aspects that Affect the Teams Undertaking Business Process Re-engineering", in P. Beynon-Davies, M.D. Williams and I. Beeson (eds) *Information Systems: Research, Teaching and Practice* (Berkshire, UK: McGraw Hill), 668–70. Presented at UKAIS 2000, Cardiff, April • Jyoti Choudrie and **Vlatka Hlupic** (2002) "Explaining the Development of the Re-engineering Teams using Conflict, and Communication", Proceedings of the Second International Conference on Systems Thinking in Management (ICSTM-2002), April, B4, 8–17 • Jyoti Choudrie and **Vlatka Hlupic** (2001) "Investigating Teams and Business Process Change Using Case Studies", Proceedings of the UKAIS 2001, UK Academy of Information Systems Conference, Portsmouth, UK, April, 106–15	• Individuals • Culture • Relationships
Aligning Organizational Culture and IT Systems for Organizational Change Projects	• Three in-depth longitudinal case studies in the private sector • Qualitative method (deductive testing of constructs), observations, semi-structured interviews (50), documentary evidence (triangulation) • Literature review of 200+ articles	• A framework for aligning organizational culture and IT systems for successful organizational change projects • Interdisciplinary REBUS framework for successful change projects	• **Vlatka Hlupic**, Jyoti Choudrie and Nayna Patel (2000) "The REBUS Approach to Business Process Re-engineering", *Cognition, Technology and Workplace*, 2:2, 89–96 • **Vlatka Hlupic** (2000) "Improving the Success of Business Process Change: The REBUS Strategy", in P. Beynon-Davies, M.D. Williams, and I. Beeson (eds) *Information Systems: Research, Teaching and Practice* (Berkshire, UK: McGraw Hill), 192–201. Presented at UKAIS 2000, Cardiff, April • **Vlatka Hlupic**, Nayna Patel and Jyoti Choudrie (1999) "The REBUS Approach to Business Process Re-engineering", in D. Kalpic and V. Dobric (eds) Proceedings of Information Technology Interfaces, ITI'99, Croatia, June, University Computing Centre, 475–81	• Culture • Strategy • Systems

(continued)

TABLE A5.1 Continued

Project	Research Method	Key Findings	Sample Outputs	Link to the Six Boxes
Business Process Change	• One in-depth longitudinal case study in the private sector • Qualitative method, observations, semi-structured interviews (15), iterative prototype development, documentary evidence (triangulation) • Literature review of 200+ articles	• A methodology for business process improvement through dynamic modelling • Factors that contribute to process modelling and efficiency	• Tamrat W. Tewoldeberhan, Alexander Verbraeck and **Vlatka Hlupic** (2010) "Implementing a Discrete Event Software Selection Methodology for Supporting Decision Making at Accenture", *Journal of the Operational Research Society*, 61, 1446–58 • Vesna-Bosilj-Vuksic, Vlatko Ceric and **Vlatka Hlupic** (2007) "Criteria for the Evaluation of Business Process Simulation Tools", *Interdisciplinary Journal of Information, Knowledge and Management*, 2, 73–88 • George Giaglis, **Vlatka Hlupic**, Gert-Jan De Vreede and Alexander Verbraeck (2005) "Synchronous Design of Information Systems and Business Processes Using Dynamic Process Modelling", *Business Process Management Journal*, 11:5, 488–500 • **Vlatka Hlupic** and Gert-Jan de Vreede (2005) "Business Process Modelling using Discrete-Event Simulation: Current Opportunities and Future Challenges" invited keynote paper in the inaugural issue of *International Journal of Simulation and Process Modelling*, 1:1/2, 72–8 • **Vlatka Hlupic**, Gert-Jan de Vreede and Alessandra Orsoni (2006) "Modelling and Simulation Techniques for Business Process Analysis and Re-Engineering", *International Journal of Simulation Systems Science and Technology*, 7:4–5, 1–8 • **Vlatka Hlupic** (2003) "Business Process Modelling: Potential Benefits and Obstacles for Wider Use", *International Journal of Simulation Systems Science and Technology*, Special Issue on Performance Modelling and Optimization, 4:1&2, 62–7	• *Systems* • *Resources*

Personal Development and Engagement	• Literature review of 200+ articles • Empirical research/action learning	• EXCELLENCE framework for personal development and engagement	• **Vlatka Hlupic** (2006) "EXCELLENCE©: A Holistic Model for Executive Coaching and Leadership Development", Proceedings of the 5th International Conference on Studying Leadership: Knowledge Into Action, Cranfield Management School, UK, December	• *Individuals* • *Relationships*
Management Innovation eXchange Management 2.0 Hackathon	• Collaborative, iterative development of Management 2.0 Hacks	• Principles of Management 2.0 • Management 2.0 Hacks	• Management 2.0 Hackathon – A Report (forthcoming) • Four management hacks led by **Vlatka Hlupic**: *Leading by letting go; Holistic/systemic management – connecting the dots; Using points system for reward management; Using "Traditionally virtual" organizational structure*	• *Individuals* • *Culture* • *Relationships* • *Strategy* • *Systems* • *Resources*

Appendix 6

Examples of Some of the Factors in the 6 Box Leadership Model and Sources of Data

TABLE A6.1   Examples of factors in the 6 Box Leadership Model and sources of data

Factors/Themes	Sources		
	Theory	Prior Research	Specific Observations
Culture			
Motivated employees	√	√	√
Caring ethos	√	√	√
Democratic culture	√	√	√
Higher purpose	√	√	√
Autonomy of employees	√	√	√
Distributed authority	√	√	√
Transparency	√	√	√
Accountability	√	√	√
Trust	√	√	√
Values	√	√	√
Relationships			
Collaboration	√	√	√
Effective working relationships	√	√	√
Lack of relationship-based conflicts	√	√	√
Facilitating informal networks	√	√	√
Good communication	√	√	√
Team building	√	√	√

Factors/Themes	Sources		
	Theory	Prior Research	Specific Observations
Quality of internal relationships	√	√	√
Established coaching processes	√	√	√
Established mentoring processes	√	√	√
Spontaneous interactions amongst employees	√	√	√
Individuals			
Attitude of employees	√	√	√
Mindset of employees	√	√	√
Skills of employees	√	√	√
Opportunities for learning and development	√	√	√
Motivation of employees	√	√	√
Interpersonal skills	√	√	√
Emotional intelligence	√	√	√
Alignment of individual and organizational values	√	√	√
Delegating responsibilities	√	√	√
Sense of purpose and passion for work	√	√	√
Strategy			
Collaborative development of strategy	√	√	√
Prioritizing long-term performance	√	√	√
Aligning of people and systems	√	√	√
Understanding of a strategic direction	√	√	√
Innovation embedded in strategy	√	√	√
Prioritizing people aspects of an organization	√	√	√
Working collaboratively with stakeholders	√	√	√
Avoiding micro-management	√	√	√
Managing risk	√	√	√
Focus on customer	√	√	√
Systems			
Self-organization of employees in communities	√	√	√
Distribution of authority	√	√	√
Experimenting with new ideas	√	√	√
Flexibility of processes	√	√	√
Distribution of decision-making	√	√	√

(continued)

TABLE A6.1 Continued

Factors/Themes	Sources		
	Theory	Prior Research	Specific Observations
Transparent compensation system	√	√	√
Eliminating activities that fail to add value	√	√	√
Regular feedback on performance	√	√	√
Talent retention	√	√	√
Organizational learning processes	√	√	√
Resources			
Access to resources	√	√	√
Compensation schemes	√	√	√
Sharing of resources	√	√	√
Access to information	√	√	√
Accuracy of information	√	√	√
Intellectual property rights	√	√	√
IT infrastructure	√	√	√
IT support	√	√	√
Software tools for collaboration	√	√	√
Physical infrastructure	√	√	√

Appendix 7

Examples of an Online Data Input in the 6 Box Leadership Model Online Tool

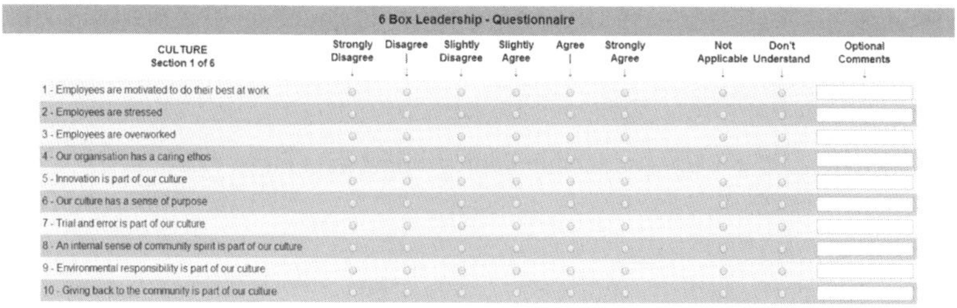

6 Box Leadership - Questionnaire									
CULTURE Section 1 of 6	Strongly Disagree	Disagree	Slightly Disagree	Slightly Agree	Agree	Strongly Agree	Not Applicable	Don't Understand	Optional Comments
1 - Employees are motivated to do their best at work	○	○	○	○	○	○	○	○	
2 - Employees are stressed	○	○	○	○	○	○	○	○	
3 - Employees are overworked	○	○	○	○	○	○	○	○	
4 - Our organisation has a caring ethos	○	○	○	○	○	○	○	○	
5 - Innovation is part of our culture	○	○	○	○	○	○	○	○	
6 - Our culture has a sense of purpose	○	○	○	○	○	○	○	○	
7 - Trial and error is part of our culture	○	○	○	○	○	○	○	○	
8 - An internal sense of community spirit is part of our culture	○	○	○	○	○	○	○	○	
9 - Environmental responsibility is part of our culture	○	○	○	○	○	○	○	○	
10 - Giving back to the community is part of our culture	○	○	○	○	○	○	○	○	

FIGURE A7.1 / The 6 Box Leadership data input example in the Culture box

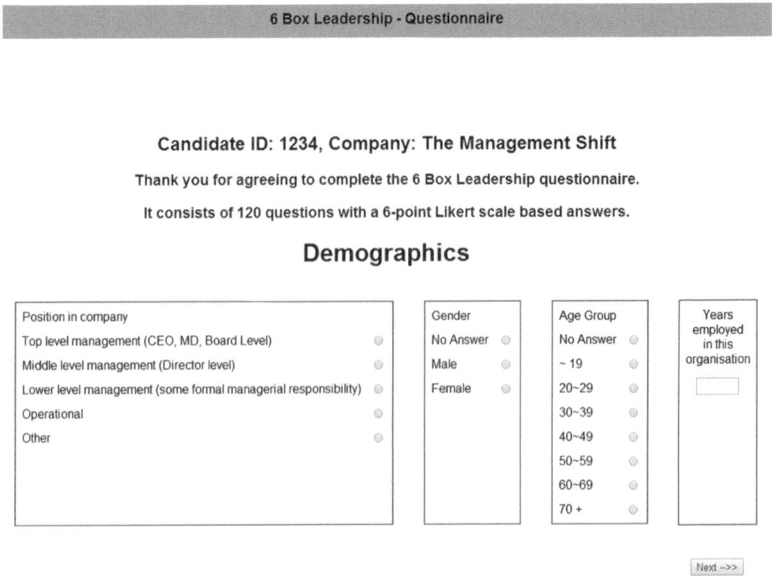

6 Box Leadership - Questionnaire

Candidate ID: 1234, Company: The Management Shift

Thank you for agreeing to complete the 6 Box Leadership questionnaire.

It consists of 120 questions with a 6-point Likert scale based answers.

Demographics

Position in company		Gender		Age Group		Years employed in this organisation
Top level management (CEO, MD, Board Level)	○	No Answer ○		No Answer ○		
Middle level management (Director level)	○	Male ○		~ 19 ○		
Lower level management (some formal managerial responsibility)	○	Female ○		20~29 ○		
Operational	○			30~39 ○		
Other	○			40~49 ○		
				50~59 ○		
				60~69 ○		
				70 + ○		

Next -->>

FIGURE A7.2 The 6 Box Leadership demographic data input example

Appendix 8

Examples of Statistical Tests Conducted

Normal distribution test

A normal distribution test was done on data in the sample using Cramer-von Mises coefficient with 95 percent confidence interval. As shown in Table A8.1, for all six groups of questions data is normally distributed.

TABLE A8.1   Normal distribution test for measuring distribution of data

Variable	Cramer-von Mises p Value
S1- Culture	>0.2500
S2 - Relationships	>0.2500
S3 - Individuals	0.0676
S4 - Strategy	0.0755
S5 - Systems	0.1058
S6 - Resources	0.0963

Correlation between groups of questions

Table A8.2 shows Pearson Correlation Coefficients measuring correlation between groups of questions. It is interesting to note that there is some correlation between all groups of questions. The highest correlation is between S4, Strategy, and S5, Systems (0.81098), and the lowest correlation is between S3, Individuals, and S6, Resources (0.32277).

TABLE A8.2   Pearson Correlation Coefficients

	S1	S2	S3	S4	S5	S6
		Pearson Correlation Coefficients **Prob > |r| under H0: Rho=0** **Number of Observations**				
S1	1.00000	0.60513	0.50891	0.76749	0.74916	0.63423
		<.0001	<.0001	<.0001	<.0001	<.0001
	456	422	440	393	423	405
S2	0.60513	1.00000	0.54813	0.55444	0.59498	0.44241
	<.0001		<.0001	<.0001	<.0001	<.0001
	422	423	420	378	407	389
S3	0.50891	0.54813	1.00000	0.41890	0.40096	0.32277
	<.0001	<.0001		<.0001	<.0001	<.0001
	440	420	441	393	423	406
S4	0.76749	0.55444	0.41890	1.00000	0.81098	0.69200
	<.0001	<.0001	<.0001		<.0001	<.0001
	393	378	393	394	385	371
S5	0.74916	0.59498	0.40096	0.81098	1.00000	0.76609
	<.0001	<.0001	<.0001	<.0001		<.0001
	423	407	423	385	424	404
S6	0.63423	0.44241	0.32277	0.69200	0.76609	1.00000
	<.0001	<.0001	<.0001	<.0001	<.0001	
	405	389	406	371	404	406

Regression analysis

Regression analysis was performed to determine the relationships between six groups of questions. Table A8.3 summarizes the results obtained for all six categories (variables).

TABLE A8.3   Regression analysis

Variable	Regression Model
S1- Culture	**S1**=2.76056+0.40834**S4**+0.11982**S2**+0.25876**S3**+0.21503**S5**
S2 - Relationships	**S2**=7.70747+0.13589**S1**+0.38247**S3**+0.16361**S5**
S3 - Individuals	S3=33.32189+0.24632**S1**+0.33190**S2**-0.05057**S5**
S4 - Strategy	S4=-1.70497+0.28403**S1**+0.24458**S5**+0.13857**S6**
S5 - Systems	**S5**=-3.38784+0.36565**S1**+0.28866**S2**+0.69618**S4**+0.75992**S6**
S6 - Resources	**S6**=4.90385+0.26383**S5**+0.15269**S4**

Appendix 9

An Example of the 6 Box Leadership Model's Aggregate Output

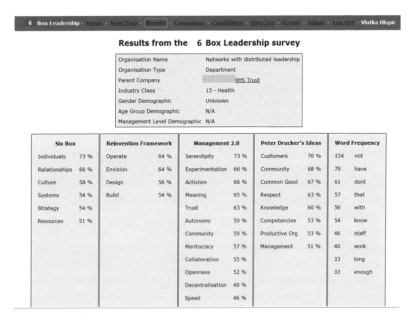

FIGURE A9.1 / The 6 Box Leadership diagnostic's aggregate output example for one company

Notes

Preface

1. P. Drucker (1954) *The Practice of Management* (New York: HarperCollins).
2. http://www.managers.org.uk/Insights/Management-2020.aspx
3. P. Boyle (1994) *Screaming Hawk: Flying Eagle's Training of a Mystic Warrior* (New York: Station Hill Press).

1. Why it is Time Now for The Management Shift

1. D. Hurst (2012) *The New Ecology of Leadership – Business Mastery in a Chaotic World* (New York: Columbia Business School Publishing).
2. G. Hamel (2007) *The Future of Management* (Boston: Harvard Business School Publishing).
3. J. Mackey and R. Sisodia (2013) *Conscious Capitalism: Liberating the Heroic Spirit of Business* (Boston: Harvard Business Review Press).
4. http://ow.ly/7TeUE
5. http://edgeperspectives.typepad.com/edge_perspectives/2010/11/2010-shift-index-passion-and-performance.html
6. G. Hamel (2012) *What Matters Now: How to Win in a World of Relentless Change, Ferocious Competition and Unstoppable Innovation* (San Francisco: Jossey-Bass).
7. http://www.managers.org.uk/Insights/Management-2020.aspx
8. P. Wilton, P. Woodman and K. Rudiger (2012) *Leadership & Management in the UK – The Key to Sustainable Growth* (London: BIS).
9. "International Comparisons of Productivity – Final Estimates", *Statistical Bulletin*, 20 February 2014 (London: ONS).
10. *Leadership & Management in the UK*.
11. dera.ioe.ac.uk/19271/1/evidence-report-81-ukces-employer-skills-survey-13-full report.pdf

12. The Commission on the Future of Management and Leadership (2014) "Management 2020: Leadership to Unlock Long-Term Growth" (London: CMI).

13. http://edgeperspectives.typepad.com/edge_perspectives/2010/11/2010-shift-index-passion-and-performance.html

14. http://www.forbes.com/sites/susanadams/2012/05/18/new-survey-majority-of-employees-dissatisfied/

15. http://careerchangechallenge.com/job-satisfaction-statistics/

16. http://www.towerswatson.com/Insights/IC-Types/Survey-Research-Results/2012/07/2012-Towers-Watson-Global-Workforce-Study

17. http://www.cipd.co.uk/pm/peoplemanagement/b/weblog/archive/2009/10/88/uk-job-satisfaction-has-plunged-says-cipd-report-2009-10.aspx

18. http://www.cipr.co.uk/sites/default/files/Trust%20Executive%20Summary_FINAL.pdf

19. http://www.scribd.com/doc/121501475/Executive-Summary-2013-Edelman-Trust-Barometer

20. http://www.nber.org/digest/dec08/w13982.html

21. http://corpgov.net/2011/01/ceo-ceo-pay-in-an-age-of-wikileaks-reporting-rationales-and-ratios/

22. http://www.huffingtonpost.com/2013/03/29/walmart-ceo-pay_n_2978180.html

23. M. Desai (2012) "The Incentive Bubble", *Harvard Business Review* (March 2012), http://hbr.org/2012/03/the-incentive-bubble/

24. http://www.ons.gov.uk/ons/rel/lms/labor-market-statistics/april-2013/sty-uk-unemployment-rizes.html

25. http://www.economist.com/news/business/21567885-skills-shortages-are-getting-worse-even-youth-unemployment-reaches-record-highs-great?fsrc=scn/tw/te/pe/thegreatmismatch

26. http://graphicsweb.wsj.com/documents/Failed-US-Banks.html

27. http://www.conference-board.org/data/consumerconfidence.cfm

28. http://www.guardian.co.uk/news/datablog/2012/nov/20/happiness-index-anxiety-satisfaction-uk

29. http://www.ism.ws/ISMReport/MfgROB.cfm?navItemNumber=12942

30. http://www.economicshelp.org/blog/5568/housing/uk-house-price-affordability/

31. http://www.economicshelp.org/blog/377/housing/factors-that-affect-the-housing-market/

32. http://www.djsresearch.co.uk/BusinessSupportMarketResearchInsightsAndFindings/article/Boardroom-Pay-Survey-Highlights-Gender-Gap-01017

33. http://www.djsresearch.co.uk/BusinessSupportMarketResearchInsightsAndFindings/article/Poll-Shows-Career-Stagnation-Puts-Business-Progression-at-Risk-00967

34. http://www.djsresearch.co.uk/CharityAndVoluntaryMarketResearch InsightsAndFindings/article/Market-Research-Highlights-Child-Poverty-Plight-00877

35. http://www.djsresearch.co.uk/FinancialServicesMarketResearchInsights AndFindings/article/Study-Highlights-Many-UK-Households-Struggling-with-Debt-01050

36. http://www.djsresearch.co.uk/FinancialServicesMarketResearchInsights AndFindings/article/Market-Research-Discovers-Worrying-Trend-of-Britons-Struggling-to-Pay-Bills-01014

37. http://www.djsresearch.co.uk/RetailMarketResearchInsightsAndFindings/ article/Market-Research-Suggests-High-Street-To-Continue-Suffering-As-Closures-Could-Reach-28-A-Day-01120

38. http://www.djsresearch.co.uk/TransportAndDistributionMarketResearch InsightsAndFindings/article/Market-Research-Uncovers-Public-Dissatisfaction-Over-Rail-Company-Services-01108

39. http://www.edgeperspectives.com/ShiftIndex2010.pdf

40. https://faculty.fuqua.duke.edu/~charvey/Research/Working_Papers/ W73_The_economic_implications.pdf

41. http://www.hbs.edu/faculty/Publication%20Files/12-035_a3c1f5d8-452d-4b48-9a49-812424424cc2.pdf

42. http://hbr.org/2012/07/what-good-are-shareholders/ar/1

43. http://www.telegraph.co.uk/finance/comment/8583476/Forget-shareholders-maximize-consumer-value-instead.html

44. http://www-935.ibm.com/services/uk/en/c-suite/ceostudy2012/

45. http://public.dhe.ibm.com/common/ssi/ecm/en/gbe03297usen/ GBE03297USEN.PDF

46. http://www.cipd.co.uk/pm/peoplemanagement/b/weblog/archive/ 2009/10/88/uk-job-satisfaction-has-plunged-says-cipd-report-2009-10.aspx

47. http://www.cipr.co.uk/sites/default/files/Trust%20Executive%20 Summary_FINAL.pdf

48. Hamel, *What Matters Now*.

49. F.W. Taylor (1911) *Principles of Scientific Management* (New York: Harper & Brothers).

50. G. Hamel (2009) "Moon Shots for Management", *Harvard Business Review* (February), http://hbr.org/2009/02/moon-shots-for-management/ar/1

51. http://www.managementexchange.com/m20-principles

52. A.D. Amar, C. Hentrich and V. Hlupic (2009) "To Be a Better Leader, Give up Authority", *Harvard Business Review*, 87:12, 22–4.

53. J. Holland (2006) "Studying Complex Adaptive Systems", *Journal of Systems Science and Complexity*, 19:1, 1–8.

54. P. Drucker (1954) *The Practice of Management* (New York: HarperCollins).

55. C. Handy (1989) *The Age of Unreason, New Thinking for a New World* (London: Random House Business Books).
56. H. Mintzberg (1998) "Covert Leadership: Notes on Managing Professionals. Knowledge Workers Respond to Inspiration, Not supervision", *Harvard Business Review*, 76, 140–7.
57. Hamel, *The Future of Management*.
58. A.D. Amar and V. Hlupic (2012) "Synthesizing Knowledge to Develop Leadership for Managing in Knowledge Organizations", presented at the Academy of Management Conference, Boston, August 2012, http://program.aomonline.org/2012/subMenu.asp?mode=setmenu&menuid=14
59. http://www.managementexchange.com/
60. http://www.managementexchange.com/m20-principles
61. K. Hopper and W. Hopper (2007) *The Puritan Gift: Reclaiming the American Dream Amidst Global Financial Chaos* (London: I.B Tauris & Co. Ltd).
62. J. Bergstrand (2009) *Reinvent Your Enterprise* (Charleston: Book Surge Publishing).
63. P.F. Drucker (1993) *Post-Capitalist Society* (1st edn) (New York: HarperBusiness).
64. Drucker, *The Practice of Management*.
65. P.F. Drucker (1999) *Management Challenges for the 21st Century* (Oxford: Butterworth-Heinemann).
66. P. Drucker (1959) *The Landmarks of Tomorrow* (New York: Harper & Row).
67. P. Drucker (1966) *The Effective Executive* (New York: HarperCollins).
68. P.F. Drucker (1992) *Managing for the Future* (Oxford: Butterworth-Heinemann).
69. Amar, Hentrich and Hlupic, "To Be a Better Leader, Give up Authority".
70. http://www.forbes.com/sites/stevedenning/2013/01/05/the-new-management-paradigm-john-mackeys-whole-foods/
71. http://www.hbs.edu/competitiveness/pdf/competitiveness-at-a-crossroads.pdf
72. http://www.forbes.com/sites/stevedenning/2013/03/10/the-surprising-reasons-why-america-lost-its-ability-to-compete/
73. http://www.forbes.com/sites/stevedenning/2011/11/18/clayton-christensen-how-pursuit-of-profits-kills-innovation-and-the-us-economy/
74. R. Martin (2011) *Fixing the Game: Bubbles, Crashes and What Capitalism Can Learn from the NFL* (Boston: Harvard Business Review Press).
75. Mackey and Sisodia, *Conscious Capitalism*.
76. *Ibid*, 21.
77. M. Jensen and W. Meckling (1976) "Theory of the Firm: Managerial Behavior, Agency Costs and Ownership Structure", *Journal of Financial Economics*, 3, 305–60.
78. O.E. Williamson (1975) *Markets and Hierarchies: Analysis and Antitrust Implications* (New York: Free Press).

79. M.E. Porter (1980) *Competitive Strategy: Techniques for Analyzing Industries and Firms* (New York: Free Press).
80. S. Ghoshal (2005) "Bad Management Theories Are Destroying Good Management Practice", *Academy of Management Learning & Education*, 4:1, 75–91.
81. M. Friedman (2002) *Capitalism and Freedom* (40th Anniversary edn) (Chicago: The University of Chicago Press).
82. E.L. Boyer (1997) *Scholarship Reconsidered* (New York: John Wiley & Sons).
83. L.W. Porter and L.E. McKibbin (1988) *Management Education and Development: Drift or Thrust into the 21st Century* (New York: McGraw-Hill).
84. H.J. Leavitt (1989) "Educating our MBAs: On Teaching What We Haven't Taught", *California Management Review*, 31:3, 38–50.
85. H. Mintzberg and J. Gosling (2002) "Educating Managers Beyond Borders", *Academy of Management Learning & Education*, 1:1, 64–76.
86. J. Pfeffer and C.T. Fong (2002) "The End of Business Schools? Less Success than Meets the Eye", *Academy of Management Learning & Education*, 1:1, 78–95.
87. Ghoshal, "Bad Management Theories".
88. R. Khurana (2007) *From Higher Aims to Hired Hands, The Social Transformation of American Business Schools and an Unfulfilled Promise of Management as a Profession* (Princeton: Princeton University Press).
89. *Ibid*, 364.
90. Mackey and Sisodia, *Conscious Capitalism*.
91. T.S. Khun (1962) *The Structure of Scientific Revolution* (Chicago: University of Chicago Press).
92. F.W. Taylor (1911) *Principles of Scientific Management* (New York: Harper & Brothers).
93. R. Lewin and B. Regine (1999) *The Soul at Work, Unleashing the Power of Complexity Science for Business Success* (London: Orion Business).
94. M.J. Wheatley (1999) *Leadership and the New Science, Discovering Order in a Chaotic World* (San Francisco: Berrett-Koehler).
95. Lewin and Regine, *The Soul at Work*.
96. J.H. Clippinger (1999) *The Biology of Business, Decoding the Natural Laws of Enterprise* (San Francisco: Jossey-Bass).
97. http://www.slideshare.net/HubSpot/the-hubspot-culture-code-creating-a-company-we-love?utm_source=slideshow&utm_medium=ssemail&utm_campaign=weekly_digest
98. R. Wartzman (2013) "Groupon's Andrew Mason's Biggest Regrets", *Forbes*, http://www.forbes.com/sites/drucker/2013/03/05/groupons-masons-regrets/
99. T. Peters (1999) *The Circle of Innovation: You Can't Shrink Your Way to Greatness* (New York: Random House).
100. Mackey and Sisodia, *Conscious Capitalism*.

101. R. Sisodia, D.B. Wolfe and J. Sheth (2007) *Firms of Endearment: How World-Class Companies Profit from Passion and Purpose* (New Jersey: Wharton School Publishing).
102. *Ibid*, 16.
103. J. Collins (2001) *Good to Great: Why Some Companies Make a Leap... and Others Don't* (New York: HarperCollins).
104. Mackey and Sisodia, *Conscious Capitalism*, 278.
105. http://money.cnn.com/magazines/fortune/best-companies/
106. http://m1.ethisphere.com/wme2013/index.html
107. Mackey and Sisodia, *Conscious Capitalism*, 280.
108. J. Kotter and J. Heskett (1992) *Corporate Culture and Performance* (New York: Free Press).
109. M.F. Sully de Luque, N. Washburn, D.A. Waldman and R.J. House (2008) "Unrequited Profits: The Relationship of Economic and Stakeholder Values to Leadership and Performance", *Administrative Science Quarterly*, 53: 626–54
110. Mackey and Sisodia, *Conscious Capitalism*, 284–9.
111. http://www.managementexchange.com/m20-principles
112. Sisodia, Wolfe and Sheth, *Firms of Endearment*.
113. http://www.betacodex.org/node/506
114. http://www.worldblu.com/awardee-profiles/2013.php

2. The Need for a New Type of Leadership

1. S. Covey (2004) *The 8th Habit* (New York: Free Press/Simon & Schuster).
2. http://govleaders.org/quotes6.htm
3. A.D. Amar and V. Hlupic (2012) "Synthesizing Knowledge to Develop Leadership for Managing in Knowledge Organizations", presented at the Academy of Management Conference, Boston, August 2012, http://program.aomonline.org/2012/subMenu.asp?mode=setmenu&menuid=14
4. R. Roberts (2012) "Did anyone learn anything from the Equitable Life? Lessons and Learning from Financial Crises", Institute of Contemporary British History, King's College London.
5. G. Hamel (2012) *What Matters Now: How to Win in a World of Relentless Change, Ferocious Competition, and Unstoppable Innovation* (San Francisco: Jossey-Bass).
6. http://www.goodreads.com/author/quotes/18541.Tim_O_Reilly
7. J. Lipman-Blumen (2011) "A Peace Plan: Make it Happen, A Connective Leadership Strategy for Global, Enduring and Sustainable Peace", presented at International Leadership Association (ILA) 12th Annual Meeting, London, October 2011.

8. C. Handy (2002) *The Hungry Spirit: New Thinking for a New World* (London: Arrow), 9.
9. http://www.consciouscapitalism.org/purpose
10. A. De Geus (1997) *The Living Company – Habits for the Survival in a Turbulent Business Environment* (Boston: Harvard Business School Press).
11. *Ibid.*
12. *Ibid.*
13. P. Drucker (2001) *The Essential Drucker* (New York: HarperBusiness).
14. P. Drucker (1954) *The Practice of Management* (New York: HarperCollins).
15. T. Sanders (2002) *Love is the Killer App: How to Win Business and Influence Friends* (New York: Three Rivers Press).
16. K. Roberts (2005) *Lovemarks: The Future Beyond Brands* (New York: Power House Books).
17. R. Sisodia, D.B. Wolfe, J. Sheth (2007) *Firms of Endearment: How World-Class Companies Profit from Passion and Purpose* (New Jersey: Wharton School Publishing).
18. http://brandvelocity.com/#/values/
19. V. Hlupic (2010) "Supporting Innovation Through Emergent Leadership", *Strategy Magazine,* October 2010, 25, 20–3.
20. Amar and Hlupic, "Synthesizing Knowledge".
21. A.D. Amar, C. Hentrich and V. Hlupic (2009) "To Be a Better Leader, Give up Authority", *Harvard Business Review*, 87:12, 22–4.
22. A.D. Amar, C. Hentrich, B. Bastani and V. Hlupic (2012) "How Managers Succeed by Letting Employees Lead", *Organizational Dynamics,* 47:1, 62–71.
23. http://humanresources.about.com/od/workrelationships/a/quotes_leaders.htm
24. http://www.forbes.com/sites/kevinkruse/2012/10/16/quotes-on-leadership/
25. D. Plowman, L.T. Baker, T. Beck, M. Kulkarni, S. Solansky and D. Travis (2007) "The Role of Leadership in Emergent, Self-organization", *Leadership Quarterly*, 18, 341–56.
26. P.E. Plsek and T. Wilson (2001) "Complexity, Leadership and Management in Healthcare Organizations", *British Medical Journal*, 323, 746–9.
27. M. Uhl-Bien, R. Marion and B. McKelvey (2004) "Emergent Leadership in Virtual Teams: What do Emergent Leaders Do?" *Information and Organization*, 14, 27–58.
28. J. Pfeffer (2005) "Producing Sustainable Competitive Advantage Through the Effective Management of People", *The Academy of Management Executive*, 19, 95–108.
29. S.D. Parks (2005) *Leadership Can be Taught: A Bold Approach for a Complex World* (Boston: Harvard Business Review Press).

30. M. Uhl-Bien, R. Marion and B. McKelvey (2007) "Complexity Leadership Theory: Shifting Leadership from the Industrial Age to the Knowledge Era", *Leadership Quarterly*, 18, 298–318.
31. R. Osborn and J. Hunt (2007) "Leadership and the Choice of Order: Complexity and Hierarchical Perspectives Near the Edge of Chaos", *Leadership Quarterly*, 18, 319–40.
32. R. Marion and M. Uhl-Bien (2001) "Leadership in Complex Organizations", *Leadership Quarterly*, 12, 389–418.
33. Uhl-Bien, Marion and McKelvey, "Complexity Leadership Theory", 18, 298–318.
34. C. Hooker and M. Csekszentmihalyi (2003) "Flow, Creativity and Shared Leadership" in C.L. Pearce and J.A. Conger (eds) *Shared Leadership: Reframing the Hows and Whys of Leadership* (London: Sage).
35. Osborn and Hunt, "Leadership and the Choice of Order", 18, 319–40.
36. A. Martin (2007) "The Future of Leadership: Where do we go from here?" *Industrial and Commercial Training*, 39, 3–8.
37. J. Appelo (2012) *Management 3.0: Leading Agile Developers, Developing Agile Leaders* (Boston: Pearson Education).
38. B. Joiner and S. Josephs (2007) "Developing Agile Leaders", *Industrial & Commercial Training*; 39:1, 35–42.
39. Amar and Hlupic, "Synthesizing Knowledge".
40. Amar, Hentrich and Hlupic, "To Be a Better Leader, Give up Authority".
41. Amar, Hentrich, Bastani and Hlupic, "How Managers Succeed by Letting Employees Lead".
42. P. Drucker (1959) *The Landmarks of Tomorrow* (New York: Harper & Row).
43. P. Drucker (1966) *The Effective Executive* (New York: HarperCollins).
44. P.F. Drucker (2001) *Management Challenges for the 21st Century* (Oxford: Elsevier Ltd).
45. *Ibid.*
46. P.F. Drucker (1992) *Managing for the Future* (Oxford: Butterworth-Heinemann).
47. A.D. Amar (2002) *Managing Knowledge Workers – Unleashing Innovation and Productivity* (Connecticut: Quorum Books).
48. http://www.forbes.com/sites/haydnshaughnessy/2011/10/08/what-is-the-creative-economy-really/
49. http://www.vanityfair.com/politics/2012/01/stiglitz-depression-201201
50. http://www.forbes.com/sites/stevedenning/2012/01/31/is-the-us-in-a-phase-change-to-the-creative-economy/
51. R. Florida (2003) *The Rise of Creative Class: And How It's Transforming Work, Leisure, Community, and Everyday Life* (Cambridge, MA: Basic Books).
52. http://www.billgeorge.org/page/gary-hamel-we-arent-in-the-knowledge-economy-were-in-the-creative-economy

53. http://www.mckinsey.com/Insights/Organization/Leaders_everywhere_A_ conversation_with_Gary_Hamel?cid=other-eml-alt-mip-mck-oth-1305

54. http://themamabee.wordpress.com/2009/03/27/management-friday-googles-8020-innovation-model/

55. http://www.billgeorge.org/page/gary-hamel-we-arent-in-the-knowledge-economy-were-in-the-creative-economy

56. R. Goffee and G. Jones (2007) "Leading Clever People", *Harvard Business Review*, March, 72–9.

57. D. Plowman, L.T. Baker, T. Beck, M. Kulkarni, S. Solansky and D. Travis (2007b) "The Role of Leadership in Emergent, Self-organization", *Leadership Quarterly*, 18, 341–56.

58. D. Pink (2009) *Drive: The Surprising About Truth What Motivates Us* (New York: Riverhead Books).

59. T. Davenport (2005) *Thinking for a Living, How to Get Better Performances and Results from Knowledge Workers* (Boston: Harvard Business Review Press).

60. K.E. Sveiby and T. Lloyd (1987): *Managing Knowhow* (London: Bloomsbury).

61. Drucker, *Management Challenges for the 21st Century*.

62. Amar and Hlupic, "Synthesizing Knowledge".

63. J. Rank, N.E. Nelson, T.D. Allen and X. Xu (2009) "Leadership Predictors of Innovation and Task Performance: Subordinates' Self-esteem and Self-presentation as Moderators", *Journal of Occupational and Organizational Psychology*, 82, 465–89.

64. H. Mintzberg (2008) *How Productivity Killed American Enterprise,* http://www.henrymintzberg.com/pdf/productivity2008.pdf

65. http://www.mckinsey.com/Insights/Organization/Leaders_everywhere_A_ conversation_with_Gary_Hamel?cid=other-eml-alt-mip-mck-oth-1305

66. http://www.forbes.com/sites/stevedenning/2013/05/01/leadership-in-the-three-speed-economy/

67. http://www.forbes.com/sites/stevedenning/2012/01/13/stoos-facilitating-a-tipping-point-for-organizations/

68. Amar and Hlupic, "Synthesizing Knowledge".

69. J.B. Rotter (1966) "Generalized Expectancies for Internal Versus External Control of Reinforcement", *Psychological Monographs*, 80, 1–28.

70. Amar and Hlupic, "Synthesizing Knowledge".

71. Amar, Hentrich and Hlupic, "To Be a Better Leader, Give up Authority".

72. Amar, Hentrich, Bastani and Hlupic, "How Managers Succeed by Letting Employees Lead".

73. http://online.wsj.com/article/SB10001424052702304811304577365782995320366.html

74. http://money.cnn.com/magazines/fortune/fortune_archive/2006/10/02/8387489/

75. Amar, Hentrich, Bastani and Hlupic, "How Managers Succeed by Letting Employees Lead".
76. Turnover increased from $4m in 1980 to $160m in 2003; S. Caulkin (2003) "Who's in Charge Here? No one" *Observer*, 27 April.
77. R. Semler (1993) *Maverick! The Success Story Behind the World's Most Unusual Workplace* (London: Random House).
78. R. Semler (2003) *The Seven-Day Weekend, A Better Way to Work in the 21st century* (London: Random House).
79. *Ibid.*
80. V. Nayar (2010) *Employees First, Customers Second* (Boston: Harvard Business School Publishing) 181–2.
81. P.F. Drucker (1993) *Post-Capitalist Society* (1st edn) (New York: HarperBusiness).
82. http://www.consultingmag.com/article/ART1078213?C=XW6913 PLPToyS1JO
83. http://ycharts.com/companies/WFM/revenues_ttm
84. J. Macker and R. Sisodia (2013) *Conscious Capitalism: Liberating the Heroic Spirit of Business* (Boston: Harvard Business Review Press).
85. http://www.gore.com/en_gb/aboutus/culture/index.html
86. Amar, Hentrich, Bastani and Hlupic, "How Managers Succeed by Letting Employees Lead".
87. http://www.businessinsider.com/zappos-ceo-tony-hsieh-on-leadership-2012-9

3. Insights from the Leading Management Thinkers – From the *Why* and *What* to the *How*

1. S. Sinek (2009) *Start with Why: How Great Leaders Inspire Everyone to Take Action* (New York: Penguin).
2. D. Seidman (2007) *How: Why HOW we Do Anything Means Everything* (New Jersey: Wiley).
3. http://www.thinkers50.com/
4. http://www.stevedenning.com/site/Default.aspx
5. A.D. Amar and V. Hlupic (2012) "Synthesizing Knowledge to Develop Leadership for Managing in Knowledge Organizations", presented at the Academy of Management Conference, Boston, August 2012, http://program.aomonline.org/2012/subMenu.asp?mode=setmenu&menuid=14
6. A.D. Amar and V. Hlupic (2011) "Leadership Function in Knowledge Based Organizations", Proceedings of the British Academy of Management Conference, Birmingham, UK, September 2011.
7. R. Gunter McGrath (2013) *The End of Competitive Advantage* (Boston: Harvard Business Press).
8. R.A. D'Aveni (2012) *Strategic Capitalism: The New Economic Strategy for Winning the Capitalist Cold War* (New York: McGraw-Hill).

9. S.L. Brown and K.M. Eisenhardt (1998) *Competing on the Edge: Strategy as Structured Chaos* (Boston: Harvard Business School Press).

10. Y. Doz and M. Kosonen (2007) *Fast Strategy: How Strategic Agility Will Help You Stay Ahead of the Game* (Harlow, UK: Pearson Education Limited).

11. O. Brafman and R.A. Beckstrom (2006) *The Starfish and the Spider: The Unstoppable Power of Leaderless Organizations* (New York: Penguin Group).

12. M. McKeown (2012) *Adaptability: The Art of Winning in an Age of Uncertainty* (London: Kogan Page).

13. D. Tapscott and D. Ticoll (2003) *The Naked Corporation: How the Age of Transparency will Revolutionize Business* (New York: Simon & Schuster).

14. C. Li (2010) *Open Leadership: How Social Technology Can Transform the Way You Lead* (San Francisco: Jossey-Bass).

15. D. Tapscott (1996) *The Digital Economy: Promise and Peril in the Age of Networked Intelligence* (New York: McGraw-Hill).

16. D. Tapscott and A.D. Williams (2006) *Wikinomics: How Mass Collaboration Changes Everything* (New York: Penguin Group).

17. P. Drucker (1954) *The Practice of Management* (New York: HarperCollins).

18. R. Martin (2011) *Fixing the Game* (Boston: Harvard Business School Review Press).

19. S. Denning (2010) *The Leader's Guide to Radical Management – Reinventing the Workplace for the 21st Century* (San Francisco: John Wiley & Sons).

20. R. Gulati (2009) *Reorganize for Resilience* (Boston: Harvard Business School Publishing Corporation).

21. F. Reichheld and R. Markey (2011) *The Ultimate Question 2.0: How Net Promoter Companies Thrive in a Customer-Driven World* (Boston: Harvard Business School Publishing).

22. Li, *Open Leadership.*

23. J. Mackey and R. Sisodia (2013) *Conscious Capitalism: Liberating the Heroic Spirit of Business* (Boston: Harvard Business Review Press).

24. G. Hamel (2007) *The Future of Management* (Boston: Harvard Business School Publishing).

25. R. Sisodia, D.B. Wolfe and J. Sheth (2007) *Firms of Endearment: How World-Class Companies Profit from Passion and Purpose* (New Jersey: Wharton School Publishing).

26. P. Kotler, D. Hessekiel and N.R. Lee (2012) *Good Works! Marketing and Corporate Initiatives that Build a Better World... and a Bottom Line* (New Jersey: John Wiley & Sons).

27. M. Porter and M. Kramer (2011) "Creating Shared Value", *Harvard Business Review*, http://hbr.org/2011/01/the-big-idea-creating-shared-value/ar/1

28. L. Stout (2012) *The Shareholder Value Myth: How Putting Shareholders First Harms Investors, Corporations, and the Public* (San Francisco: Berrett-Koehler).

29. P.F. Drucker (1993) *Post-Capitalist Society* (1st edn) (New York: HarperBusiness).

30. R. Moss Kanter (2009) *SuperCorp: How Vanguard Companies Create Innovation, Profits, Growth and Social Good* (New York: Crown Business).

31. N. Vitalari and H. Shaughnessy (2012) *Elastic Enterprise: The New Manifesto for Business Revolution* (Longboat Key, FL: Telemachus Press).

32. J. Hagel III, J. Seely Brown and L. Davison (2010) *The Power of Pull – How Small Moves, Smartly Made, Can Set Big Things in Motion* (New York: Basic Books).

33. http://www.brainyquote.com/quotes/keywords/innovation.html#Y2wY0it ZpMCdfXTO.99

34. T. Peters (1997) *Circle of Innovation: You Can't Shrink Your Way to Greatness* (California: Excel/A California Partnership).

35. http://blogs.hbr.org/2013/10/11-ways-big-companies-undermine-innovation/

36. http://www.brainyquote.com/quotes/keywords/innovation.html#rmi6 KL1QGzKLA5t5.99

37. http://www.brainyquote.com/quotes/keywords/innovation.html#Y2wY0it ZpMCdfXTO.99

38. C. Christensen (1997) *The Innovator's Dilemma: The Revolutionary Book That Will Change the Way You Do Business* (Boston: Harvard Business Press).

39. C. Christensen (2003) *The Innovator's Solution: Creating and Sustaining Successful Growth* (Boston: Harvard Business School Publishing Corporation).

40. J. Dyer, H. Gregersen and C. Christensen (2011) *The Innovator's DNA: Mastering the Five Skills of Disruptive Innovators* (Boston: Harvard Business Review Press).

41. S. Godin (2011) *Poke the Box: When Was the Last Time You Did Something for the First Time?* (New York: The Domino Project, Do You Zoom).

42. S.D. Anthony (2009) *The Silver Lining: An Innovation Playbook for Uncertain Times* (Boston: Harvard Business Press).

43. V. Govindarajan and C. Trimble (2010) *The Other Side of Innovation: Solving the Execution Challenge* (Boston: Harvard Business Press).

44. C.K. Prahalad and M.S. Krishnan (2008) *The New Age of Innovation: Driving Co-created Value through Global Networks* (New York: McGraw-Hill).

45. V.V. Vaitheeswaran (2012) *Need, Speed and Greed: How the New Rules of Innovation Can Transform Businesses, Propel Nations to Greatness, and Tame the World's Most Wicked Problems* (New York: HarperBusiness).

46. H. Chesbrough (2005) *Open Innovation, The New Imperative for Creating and Profiting from Technology* (Boston: Harvard Business Press).

47. S. Abrahamson, P. Ryder and B. Unterberg (2013) *Crowdstorm: The Future of Innovation, Ideas, and Problem Solving* (New York: John Wiley & Sons).

48. D. Tapscott and A.D. Williams (2012) *Macrowikinomics – Rebooting Business and the World* (New York: Portfolio).

49. D. Grey and T. Vander Wal (2012) *The Connected Company* (Sebastopol, CA: O'Reilly Media).
50. V. Govindarajan and C. Trimple (2012) *Reverse Innovation: Create Far From Home, Win Everywhere* (Boston: Harvard Business Review Press).
51. F. Hesselbein, M. Goldsmith and I. Somerville (eds) (2002) *Leading for Innovation and Organizing For Results* (San Francisco: Jossey-Bass).
52. N. Herman (1996) *The Whole Brain Business Book: Harnessing the Power of the Whole Brain Organization and the Whole Brain Individual* (New York: McGraw-Hill).
53. N. Radjou, J. Prabhu and S. Ahuja (2012*) Jugaad Innovation: Think Frugal, Be Flexible, Generate Breakthrough Growth* (San Francisco: Jossey-Bass).
54. G. Shapiro (2013) *Ninja Innovation: The Ten Killer Strategies of the World's Most Successful Businesses* (New York: William Morrow).
55. C.T. Foo (2007) "Steve Jobs, Ch'an Buddhism and Innovation", *Chinese Management Studies*, 6:1, http://www.emeraldinsight.com/journals.htm?articleid=17024799
56. http://journal.uwest.edu/index.php/hljhb/article/download/116/182
57. http://www.imagethink.net/imagethink-2/buddhist-geeks/
58. http://www.gallup.com/strategicconsulting/164735/state-global-workplace.aspx
59. http://www.haygroup.com/EngagementMatters/press/uk.aspx
60. D. Bowles and C. Cooper (2012) *The High Engagement Work Culture: Balancing Me and We* (Basingstoke, UK: Palgrave Macmillan).
61. J. Haudan (2008) *The Art of Engagement, Bridging the Gap Between People and Possibilities* (New York: McGraw-Hill).
62. G. Bains (2007) *Meaning, Inc., The Blueprint for Business Success in the 21st Century* (London: Profile Books).
63. J. Kourdi and J. Davies (2010) *The Truth about Talent: A Guide to Building a Dynamic Workforce, Realizing Potential, and Helping Leaders Succeed* (New York: John Wiley & Sons).
64. D. Ulrich and W. Ulrich (2010) *The Why of Work – How Great Leaders Build Abundant Organizations that Win* (New York: McGraw-Hill).
65. S. Ponterfact (2013) *Flat Army – Creating a Connected and Engaged Organization* (New York: John Wiley & Sons).
66. J.E. Glaser (2006) *The DNA of Leadership: Leverage Your Instincts to Communicate, Differentiate, Innovate* (Liverpool: Platinum Press).
67. S. Denning (2005) *The Leader's Guide to Storytelling – Mastering the Art and Discipline of Business Narrative* (San Francisco: Jossey-Bass).
68. M. Buckingham (2005) *The One Thing You Need to Know…About Great Managing, Great Leading, and Sustained Individual Success* (New York: Free Press).

69. G. Kawasaki (2011) *Enchantment – The Art of Changing Hearts, Minds, and Actions* (New York: Portfolio).
70. J.M. Kouzes and B.Z. Posner (2002) *The Leadership Challenge – How to Keep Getting Extraordinary Things Done in Organizations* (San Francisco: Jossey-Bass).
71. J. Adair (2003) *The Inspirational Leader – How to Motivate, Encourage and Achieve Success* (London: Kogan Page).
72. D. Goleman, R. Boyatzis and A. McKee (2002) *The New Leaders – Transforming the Art of Leadership into the Science of Results* (London: Little, Brown).
73. R. Goffee and G. Jones (2013) "Creating the Best Workplace on Earth", *Harvard Business Review*, May 2013, 99–106.
74. M. Buckingham (2007) *Go Put Your Strengths to Work, 6 Powerful Steps to Achieve Outstanding Performance* (New York: One Thing Productions).
75. M. Buckingham (2008) *The Truth About You – Your Secret to Success* (New York: Thomas Nelson).
76. M. Goldsmith and M. Reiter (2010) *Mojo – How to Get It, How to Keep It, and How to Get It Back If You Lose It* (New York: Hyperion).
77. T. Amabile and A. Kramer (2011) *The Progress Principle – Using Small Wins to Ignite Joy, Engagement, and Creativity at Work* (Boston: Harvard Business Review Press).
78. T. Schwartz, J. Gomes and C. McCarthy (2010) *The Way We're Working Isn't Working – The Four Forgotten Needs That Energize Great Performance* (New York: Free Press).
79. C. Conley (2007) *Peak – How Great Companies Get Their Mojo from Maslow* (San Francisco: Jossey-Bass).
80. L. Earle McLeod (2012) *Selling with Noble Purpose – How to Drive Revenue and Do Work that Makes You Proud* (New York: John Wiley & Sons).
81. Mackey and Sisodia, *Conscious Capitalism*.
82. Sisodia, Wolfe and Sheth, *Firms of Endearment*.
83. G. Hamel (2012) *What Matters Now – How to Win in a World of Relentless Change, Ferocious Competition, and Unstoppable Innovation* (San Francisco: Jossey-Bass).
84. http://www.druckerforum.org/2013/the-event/
85. http://www.forbes.com/sites/stevedenning/2013/11/18/a-new-center-of-gravity-for-management/?goback=%2Egde_3976256_member_58082589 60075038721#%21

4. The Emergent Leadership Model: From the Stagnating to the Unbounded Culture

1. K. Wilber (1997) "An Integral Theory of Consciousness", *Journal of Consciousness Studies*, 4:1, 71–92.

2. J. Loevinger (1976) *Ego Development* (Jossey-Bass: San Francisco).
3. A.H. Maslow (1943) "A Theory of Human Motivation", *Psychological Review*, 50:4, 370–96.
4. D. Beck and C. Cowan (1996) *Spiral Dynamics: Mastering Values, Leadership and Change* (Malden: Blackwell Business).
5. J. Loevinger (1970) *Measuring Ego Development* (San Fransciso: Jossey-Bass).
6. S.R. Cook-Greuter (2004) "Making the Case for a Developmental Perspective", *Industrial and Commercial Training*, 36:7, 275–81.
7. R. Barrett (2010) *The New Leadership Paradigm – Leading Self, Leading Others, Leading an Organization, Leading in Society* (London: Values Centre).
8. B. Schneider (2008) Energy *Leadership – Transforming Your Workplace and Your Life from the Core* (New Jersey: John Wiley & Sons).
9. L. Kohlberg (1973) "The Claim to Moral Adequacy of a Highest Stage of Moral Judgment", *Journal of Philosophy*, 70:18, 630–46.
10. D. Logan, J. King and H. Fischer-Wright (2008) D. Logan, King J., and Fischer-Wright H. (2008), *Tribal Leadership: How Successful Groups Form Organically: Leveraging Natural Groups to Build a Thriving Organization* (New York: HarperCollins).
11. A. Koestler (1967) *The Ghost in the Machine* (1990 reprint edn) (London: Penguin Group).
12. D. Goleman and R. Boyatzis (2008) "Social Intelligence and the Biology of Leadership", *Harvard Business Review*, September 2008, http://hbr. org/2008/09/social-intelligence-and-the-biology-of-leadership/ar/
13. A.D. Amar, C. Hentrich and V. Hlupic (2009) "To Be a Better Leader, Give up Authority", *Harvard Business Review*, 87:12, 22–4.
14. A.D. Amar, C. Hentrich, B. Bastani and V. Hlupic (2012) "How Managers Succeed by Letting Employees Lead", *Organizational Dynamics*, 47:1, 62–71.
15. A.D. Amar and V. Hlupic (2012) "Synthesizing Knowledge to Develop Leadership for Managing in Knowledge Organizations", presented at the Academy of Management Conference, Boston, August 2012, http://program. aomonline.org/2012/subMenu.asp?mode=setmenu&menuid=14
16. A.D. Amar and V. Hlupic (2011) "Leadership Function in Knowledge Based Organizations", Proceedings of the British Academy of Management Conference, Birmingham, UK, September 2011.
17. V. Hlupic, A. Braganza, B. Lewin and C. Hentrich (2011) "Emergent Capabilities: A Framework for Strategy in Practice", Proceedings of the British Academy of Management Conference, Birmingham, UK, September 2011.
18. A.D. Amar, B. Bastani, V. Hlupic and C. Hentrich (2008) "How to Manage Employees When We Cannot Use Authority: How the Theory Fits Practice Internationally", PDW presented at the Academy of Management Conference, Anaheim, USA, August 2008.

19. V. Hlupic (2006) "EXCELLENCE©: A Holistic Model for Executive Coaching and Leadership Development", Proceedings of the 5th International Conference on Studying Leadership: Knowledge Into Action, Cranfield Management School, UK, December.
20. Logan, King and Fischer-Wright, *Tribal Leadership*.
21. *Ibid.*
22. *Ibid.*
23. Goleman and Boyatzis, "Social Intelligence and the Biology of Leadership".
24. R. Roberts (2012) "Did Anyone Learn Anything from the Equitable Life? Lessons and Learning from Financial Crises", Institute of Contemporary British History, King's College London.
25. R. Connors and T. Smith (2011) *Change the Culture, Change the Game – The Breakthrough Strategy for Energizing Your Organization and Creating Accountability for Results* (New York: Portfolio).
26. J. Bergstrand (2009) *Reinvent Your Enterprise – Through Better Knowledge Work* (Atlanta: Brand Velocity).
27. L. Gratton (2007) *Hot Spots: Why Some Teams, Workplaces, and Organizations Buzz with Energy, and Other's Don't* (San Francisco: Berrett-Koehler Publishers).
28. D. Pink (2009) *Drive: The Surprising Truth about What Motivates Us* (New York: Riverhead Books).
29. S.M.R. Covey and R.R. Merrill (2006) *The Speed of Trust – The One Thing that Changes Everything* (San Francisco: Free Press).
30. W. Bennis, D. Goleman and J. O'Toole (2008) *Transparency – How Leaders Create a Culture of Candor* (San Francisco: Jossey-Bass).
31. Amar, Hentrich, Bastani and Hlupic, "How Managers Succeed by Letting Employees Lead".
32. Amar, Hentrich and Hlupic, "To Be a Better Leader, Give up Authority".
33. Amar, Hentrich, Bastani and Hlupic, "How Managers Succeed by Letting Employees Lead".
34. Amar and Hlupic, "Leadership Function in Knowledge Based Organizations".
35. G. Jampolski (1979) *Love is Letting Go of Fear* (California: Berkeley).

5. The 6 Box Leadership Model: An Organizational Body Scan

1. P. Drucker (1954) *The Practice of Management* (New York: HarperCollins).
2. C. Handy (1989) *The Age of Unreason, New Thinking for a New World* (London: Random House Business Books).
3. H. Mintzberg (1998) "Covert Leadership: Notes on Managing Professionals. Knowledge workers Respond to Inspiration, Not Supervision", *Harvard Business Review*, 76, 140–7.

4. G. Hamel (2007) *The Future of Management* (Boston: Harvard Business School Publishing).

5. A.D. Amar and V. Hlupic (2012) "Synthesizing Knowledge to Develop Leadership for Managing in Knowledge Organizations", presented at the Academy of Management Conference, Boston, August 2012, http://program. aomonline.org/2012/subMenu.asp?mode=setmenu&menuid=14

6. A.D. Amar, C. Hentrich and V. Hlupic (2009) "To Be a Better Leader, Give up Authority", *Harvard Business Review*, 87:12, 22–4.

7. P.F. Drucker (1973) *Management: Tasks, Responsibilities, Practices* (London: HarperCollins).

8. http://www.quoteswize.com/soichiro-honda-quotes-3.html

9. N. Herman (1996) *The Whole Brain Business Book: Harnessing the Power of the Whole Brain Organization and the Whole Brain Individual* (New York: McGraw-Hill).

10. K. Wilber (2000) *A Theory of Everything: An Integral Vision for Business, Politics, Science and Spirituality* (Boston: Shambhala Publications).

11. S. Esbjörn-Hargens (2010) "Introduction" in S. Esbjörn-Hargens (ed.) *Integral Theory in Action: Applied, Theoretical, and Constructive Perspectives on the AQAL Model* (Albany, NY: State University of New York Press).

12. http://integralleadershipreview.com/

13. A.D. Amar, C. Hentrich, B. Bastani and V. Hlupic (2012) "How Managers Succeed by Letting Employees Lead", *Organizational Dynamics,* 47:1, 62–71.

14. Amar, Hentrich and Hlupic, "To Be a Better Leader, Give up Authority".

15. A.D. Amar and V. Hlupic (2011) "Leadership Function in Knowledge Based Organizations", Proceedings of the British Academy of Management Conference, Birmingham, UK, September 2011.

16. J.L. Denis, A. Langley and V. Sergi (2012) "Leadership in the Plural", *The Academy of Management Annals*, 6:1, 211–83.

17. G. Von Krogh, I. Nonaka and L. Rechsteiner (2012) "Leadership in Organizational Knowledge Creation: A Review and Framework", *Journal of Management Studies*, 49:1, 240–77.

18. W. Currie and V. Hlupic (2003) "Simulation Modelling as the Link Between Change Management Approaches" in V. Hlupic (ed.) *Knowledge and Business Process Management* (Idea Group Publishing), 33–50.

19. W. Currie and V. Hlupic (2000) "Business Process Re-engineering and Simulation Modelling: The Missing Link" in D. Bustard, K. Kawalek and M. Norris (eds) *Systems Modelling for Business Process Improvement* (London: Artech House Books).

20. M. den Hengst, V. Hlupic and W. Currie (2004) "The Increasing Need for Integrating Simulation and Collaboration to Support Change Management Programs" in R.H. Sprague, Proceedings of the 37th Annual Hawaii International Conference on System Sciences (IEEE Computer Society).

21. M. Hammer (1990) "Re-engineering Work: Don't Automate, Obliterate", *Harvard Business Review*, November/December, 90:4, 104–12.
22. M. Hammer and J. Champy (1993) *Re-engineering the Corporation: A Manifesto for Business Revolution* (London: Nicholas Brearley Publishing).
23. H. Davenport (1993) *Process Innovation: Re-engineering Work Through Information Technology* (Boston: Harvard Business Press).
24. W.E. Deming (1982) "Improvement of Quality and Productivity Through Action by Management", *National Productivity Review*, Winter 1982, 12–22.
25. J.P. Gilbert (1989) "The State of JIT Implementation and Development in the USA", *International Journal of Production Research*, 28:6, 1099–109.
26. I. Nonaka and H. Takeuchi (1995) *The Knowledge-Creating Company: How Japanese Companies Create the Dynamics of Innovation* (Oxford: OUP).
27. E. Cameron and M. Green (2012) *Making Sense of Change Management – A Complete Guide to the Models, Tools and Techniques of Organizational Change* (3rd edn) (London: Kogan Page Limited).
28. J.W. Moran and B.K. Brightman (2001) "Leading Organizational Change", *Career Development International*, 6:2, 111–18.
29. R. Todnem (2005) "Organizational Change Management: A Critical Review", *Journal of Change Management*, 5:4, 369–80.
30. B. De Wit and R. Meyer (2005) *Strategy Synthesis: Resolving Strategy Paradoxes to Create Competitive Advantage* (2nd edn) (London: Thomson Learning).
31. R. Luecke (2003) *Managing Change and Transition* (Boston: Harvard Business School Press).
32. B. Burnes (2004) *Managing Change: A Strategic Approach to Organizational Dynamics* (4th edn) (London: Prentice Hall).
33. F. Graetz (2000) "Strategic Change Leadership", *Management Decision*, 38:8, 550–62.
34. J.P. Kotter (1996) *Leading Change* (Boston: Harvard Business School Press).
35. C.A. Carnall (2003) *Managing Change in Organizations* (4th edn) (London: Prentice Hall).
36. J. Balogun and V. Hope Hailey (2004) *Exploring Strategic Change* (2nd edn) (London: Prentice Hall).
37. R. Luecke (2003) *Managing Change and Transition* (Boston: Harvard Business School Press).
38. T. Guimaraes and C. Armstrong (1998) "Empirically Testing the Impact of Change Management Effectiveness on Company Performance", *European Journal of Innovation Management*, 1:2, 74–84
39. R.E. Boyatzis (1998) *Transforming Qualitative Information: Thematic Analysis and Code Development* (Thousand Oaks, CA: SAGE Publications).
40. G.R. Gibbs (2007) *Analyzing Qualitative Data* (London: SAGE Publications).

41. J. Saldana (2009) *The Coding Manual for Qualitative Researchers* (Thousand Oaks, CA: SAGE Publications).
42. C. Christensen (2003) *The Innovator's Solution: Creating and Sustaining Successful Growth* (Boston: Harvard Business School Publishing Corporation).
43. R. Likert (1932) "A Technique for the Measurement of Attitudes", *Archives of Psychology*, 140, 1–55.
44. http://www.goodreads.com/quotes/172730-what-s-measured-improves
45. J. Bergstrand (2009) *Reinvent Your Enterprise* (Charleston, SC: Book Surge Publishing).
46. P.F. Drucker (1993) *Post-Capitalist Society* (1st edn) (New York: HarperBusiness).
47. http://www.managementexchange.com/m20-principles
48. Drucker, *Post-Capitalist Society*.
49. Drucker, *The Practice of Management*.
50. P.F. Drucker (1999) *Management Challenges for the 21st Century* (Oxford: Butterworth-Heinemann).
51. P. Drucker (1959) *The Landmarks of Tomorrow* (New York: Harper & Row).
52. P. Drucker (1966) *The Effective Executive* (New York: HarperCollins).
53. P.F. Drucker (1992) *Managing for the Future* (Oxford: Butterworth-Heinemann).
54. Drucker, *Management: Tasks, Responsibilities, Practices*.
55. http://www.sas.com/en_us/home.html
56. Boyatzis, *Transforming Qualitative Information*.
57. J. Collins (2001) *Good to Great – Why Some Companies Make the Leap...and Others Don't* (New York: HarperCollins).

6. The 6 Box Leadership Model in Action: Practical Examples

1. http://www.goodreads.com/quotes/181571-the-knowledge-that-we-consider-knowledge-proves-itself-in-action
2. http://chiefexecutive.net/ideo-ceo-tim-brown-t-shaped-stars-the-backbone-of-ideoae%E2%84%A2s-collaborative-culture
3. https://www.valuescentre.com/
4. http://www.towerswatson.com/en-GB/Services/our-solutions/employee-surveys
5. http://www.ofactor.pro/
6. http://www.advancingyourorganization.com/?page_id=1106
7. R.S. Kaplan and D.P. Norton (1996) *The Balanced Scorecard: Translating Strategy into Action* (Boston: Harvard Business Press).
8. T. Peters and R.H. Waterman Jr (1982) *In Search of Excellence: Lessons from America's Best-Run Companies* (New York: Harper & Row).

9. C. Christensen (2003) *The Innovator's Solution: Creating and Sustaining Successful Growth* (Boston: Harvard Business School Publishing Corporation).
10. http://www.jimcollins.com/tools/diagnostic-tool.pdf

7. The Management Shift is Achievable Now: A Call for Action

1. R.A. Heifetz (1994) *Leadership without Easy Answers* (Cambridge, US: Belknap Press of Harvard University Press).
2. P.F. Drucker (1973) *Management: Tasks, Responsibilities, Practices* (New York: HarperCollins), 39.
3. *Ibid.*
4. P. Drucker (1959) *The Landmarks of Tomorrow* (New York: Harper & Row).
5. http://www.druckersocietylondon.com/
6. http://www.druckerinstitute.com/
7. L. Stout (2012) *The Shareholder Value Myth: How Putting Shareholders First Harms Investors, Corporations, and the Public* (San Francisco: Berrett-Koehler).
8. R. Martin (2011) *Fixing the Game* (Boston: Harvard Business School Review Press).
9. http://www.druckerinstitute.com/link/were-in-it-for-the-long-term/
10. http://www.managementexchange.com/
11. http://www.managementexchange.com/feature/hackathon
12. http://www.managementexchange.com/hack/using-traditionally-virtual-organizational-structure
13. http://www.managementexchange.com/hack/why-points-trump-hierarchy
14. http://www.managementexchange.com/hack/systemic-holistic-management
15. http://www.managementexchange.com/hack/leading-letting-go
16. http://www.youtube.com/watch?v=QdkLE2Gdrng
17. http://www.youtube.com/watch?v=vfH7fuw0L8w
18. http://www.collabworks.com/thought-leaders.html
19. http://www.sol-uk.org/
20. http://www.daedalustrust.org.uk/
21. http://www.ft.com/cms/s/2/cde6163c-7f4a-11e2-97f6-00144feabdc0.html#axzz2QepCX7KM
22. http://www.economist.com/news/business/21595929-business-schools-are-better-analysing-disruptive-innovation-dealing-it-those-who
23. http://www.forbes.com/sites/stevedenning/2014/02/07/why-arent-business-schools-more-business-like/
24. A. Brown and F. Roosli, "Can Business Schools Help us Cope with Complexity?", http://www.druckerforum.org/blog/?p=597

25. https://www/linkedin.com/groups?gid=8138844&trk=vsrp_groups_res_nam e&trkInfo=VSRPsearchId%3A33550611408782112777%2CVSRPtargetId%3 A8138844%2CVSRPcmpt%3Aprimary
26. http://hbr.org/2009/02/moon-shots-for-management/ar/1
27. http://www.forbes.com/sites/stevedenning/2013/07/07/don-tapscott-we-need-fundamental-change-in-all-our-institutions/
28. http://www.druckerforum.org/abstract-drucker-forum-2014/
29. http://online.wsj.com/news/articles/SB100014240527487044761045754397 23695579664
30. T. Paulus (1975) *Hope for the Flowers* (New Jersey: Paulist Press).
31. http://www.forbes.com/sites/kevinkruse/2012/10/16/quotes-on-leadership/
32. Brown and Roosli, "Can Business Schools Help Us Cope With Complexity?"
33. http://blogs.hbr.org/2013/09/it-takes-purpose-become-a-bill/
34. http://www.insidehighered.com/sites/default/server_files/files/FINAL%20 Embargoed%20Avalanche%20Paper%20130306%20%281%29.pdf
35. http://blogs.hbr.org/2010/02/what-will-you-do-differently-o/
36. S. Godin (2008) *Tribes – We Need You to Lead Us* (New York: Portfolio).
37. M. Gladwell (2000) *The Tipping Point: How Little Thinks Can Make a Big Difference* (London: Little, Brown).

Appendix 2. Mapping of Emergent Leadership Model's Five Levels to Other Relevant Models of Development

1. S.R. Cook-Greuter (2004) "Making the Case for a Developmental Perspective", *Industrial and Commercial Training*, 36:7, 275–81.
2. R. Barrett (2010) *The New Leadership Paradigm – Leading Self, Leading Others, Leading an Organization, Leading in Society* (London: Values Centre).
3. D. Beck and C. Cowan (1996) *Spiral Dynamics: Mastering Values, Leadership and Change* (Malden, UK: Blackwell Business).
4. D. Logan, J. King and H. Fischer-Wright (2008) D. Logan, King J., and Fischer-Wright H. (2008) *Tribal Leadership: How Successful Groups Form Organically: Leveraging Natural Groups to Build a Thriving Organization* (New York: HarperCollins).
5. B. Schneider (2008) *Energy Leadership – Transforming Your Workplace and Your Life from the Core* (New Jersey: John Wiley & Sons).
6. A.H. Maslow (1943) "A Theory of Human Motivation", *Psychological Review*, 50:4, 370–96.
7. J. Loevinger (1976) *Ego Development* (San Francisco: Jossey-Bass).
8. L. Kohlberg (1973) "The Claim to Moral Adequacy of a Highest Stage of Moral Judgment", *Journal of Philosophy*, 70:18, 630–46.

Appendix 3. Key Models and Tools for Organizational Change Compared to the 6 Box Leadership Model

1. R.S. Kaplan and D.P. Norton (1996) *The Balanced Scorecard: Translating Strategy into Action* (Boston: Harvard Business Press).
2. T. Peters and R.H. Waterman Jr (1982) *In Search of Excellence: Lessons from America's Best-Run Companies* (New York: Harper & Row).
3. C. Christensen (2003) *The Innovator's Solution: Creating and Sustaining Successful Growth* (Boston: Harvard Business School Publishing Corporation).
4. D. Logan, J. King and H. Fischer-Wright (2008) *D. Logan, King J., and Fischer-Wright H. (2008) Tribal Leadership: How Successful Groups Form Organically: Leveraging Natural Groups to Build a Thriving Organization* (New York: HarperCollins).
5. http://www.culturesync.net/toolbox/culturemeter-survey/
6. J. Collins (2001) *Good to Great – Why Some Companies Make the Leap...and Others Don't* (New York: HarperCollins).
7. http://www.jimcollins.com/tools/diagnostic-tool.pdf
8. R. Barrett (2010) *The New Leadership Paradigm* (Amazon: Marston Gate).

Appendix 4: Six Phases of Thematic Analysis Followed in this Research

1. R. Boyatzis (1998) *Transforming Qualitative Information: Thematic Analysis and Code Development* (Thousand Oaks, CA: SAGE Publications).
2. C. Christensen (2003) *The Innovator's Solution: Creating and Sustaining Successful Growth* (Boston: Harvard Business School Publishing Corporation).
3. *Ibid.*

Contact Details

Vlatka's quest to make a positive difference to as many individuals and organizations as possible is ongoing. In addition to writing about her knowledge and experience, she gives keynote presentations and lectures, provides consulting services and advisory work at Board levels. She also trains individuals, teams and organizations to use her models and tools and achieve The Management Shift.

Further information about these activities and links to free reports and a free trial for the 6 Box Leadership diagnostic are available on the website *www.themanagementshift.com*.

Vlatka can be contacted on *vlatka@themanagementshift.com*.

Free Trial of the 6 Box Leadership diagnostic

A free trial of the 6 Box Leadership diagnostic is offered to the first five qualifying executive teams from five different organizations that apply for the trial. A PDF report will be provided with information about the key strengths and developmental opportunities in the areas of Culture, Relationships, Individuals, Strategy, Systems and Resources.

For further details, please contact *info@themanagementshift.com*

Index

Bold entries refer to boxes, figures or tables.

Printed and bound by CPI Group (UK) Ltd, Croydon, CR0 4YY